THE

KIDFIXER

BABY

BOOK

THE KIDFIXER BABY BOOK

An Easy-to-Use Guide to Your Baby's First Year

STUART J. ALTMAN, M.D., F.A.A.P.

ILLUSTRATIONS BY ZACHARY JUDD SCHEER

BALLANTINE BOOKS

New York

A Ballantine Book

Published by The Random House Publishing Group

Copyright © 2004 by Stuart J. Altman, M.D., F.A.A.P.

All rights reserved under International and Pan-American
Copyright Conventions. Published in the United States
by Ballantine Books, an imprint of The Random House Publishing Group,
a division of Random House, Inc., New York, and simultaneously
in Canada by Random House of Canada Limited, Toronto.

BALLANTINE and colophon are registered trademarks
of Random House, Inc.

www.ballantinebooks.com

Library of Congress Cataloging-in-Publication Data
is available from the publisher upon request.

ISBN 0-8129-7017-9

Manufactured in the United States of America

2 4 6 8 9 7 5 3 1

First Edition: August 2004

Book design by Jo Anne Metsch

For my wife, Sherrill, who has always been there for our kids when they needed her and who is still here for me now, when I need her more than ever; and to my best friends, my sons, Sam and Josh, who encouraged me to keep working on this book and whose talent, intelligence, and humanity inspired it.

This book is also dedicated to four complete physicians and mentors: Philip Lanzkowsky, M.D., Michael Frogel, M.D., Lourdes Mendoza, M.D., and the late Arturo Aballi, M.D. Such physicians combine compassion and intellect in a way that most of us can only hope to emulate.

CONTENTS

INTRODUCTION

A USER'S GUIDE FOR YOUR BABY

Raising children is a spur-of-the-moment, seat-of-the-pants sort of deal, as any parent knows, particularly after an adult child says that his most searing memory consists of an offhand comment in the car on the way to second grade that the parent cannot even dimly recall.

— ANNA QUINDLEN

"Spur-of-the-moment" and "seat-of-the-pants" pretty much describes parenting. For all of our carefully laid plans, children never fail to take us by surprise and parenting itself becomes a feat of sheer improvisation. Yet even the best ad-libbers among us need a script sometimes. *The Kidfixer Baby Book* is designed to offer just that kind of help; it is a "user's guide" for your baby, covering everything from pregnancy right up to that first birthday party. Written by an experienced pediatrician and father of two—would you buy a manual about a TV from someone who only listens to the radio?—*Kidfixer* is an attempt to help brand-new moms and dads handle the surprising daily dilemmas and delights of raising a baby.

In twenty-five years as a Long Island pediatrician, I have spoken with enough moms and dads to know what they want: understandable answers to common questions. Have no fear, this is one manual that isn't written in "techno-speak." *The Kidfixer Baby Book* is your own easy-to-understand guide to preparing and caring for your new baby. After all, that DVD player comes with a reference guide and your laptop computer has an owner's manual, so why not have a user-friendly book for that brand-new stranger in your life who is about to change everything?

There are two ways to use this guide. First, pick it up during those seemingly endless days of your pregnancy and read it, cover to cover, to give you some idea of what's ahead. Second, and perhaps even more important, treat this book as a quick reference guide. Keep it at your fingertips, right there on the night table or kitchen countertop, to answer your specific questions as they arise.

The Kidfixer Baby Book is divided into six parts that will guide you step by step through the daily job of caring for your new baby. Here's a brief look at what you can expect:

PART I: BABY ON THE WAY

What kind of parent will I be? Is this question preying on your mind? You're not alone. Part I covers everything you need to know in order to prepare for Junior's arrival, including advice on diet, exercise, shopping, and the all-important task of finding the right pediatrician. You may be asking yourself, What should or shouldn't I eat? (Don't ask me to give up chocolate!) What medications am I allowed to take if I get sick? How much exercise is safe? How do I find the right pediatrician who won't think I'm crazy when I ask my crazy questions? And before I blow all of my savings, what should I buy to prepare for Junior's arrival? Here you'll find the answers.

PART II: FUEL—FEEDING YOUR BABY

Still debating between breast-feeding and bottle-feeding? In Part II, we'll discuss the advantages and disadvantages of each. Am I a failure as a mom if I decide to bottle-feed? How do you breast-feed, anyway? Can I nurse and supplement with formula? Can I nurse and still work full time? Which formula should I buy? And, since it won't be long before your hungry baby is off a strictly liquid diet, we'll take a look at some of the other tasty treats you'll soon be scraping off your ceiling.

PART III: LIVING WITH BABY

Let's take a closer look at your changing life with baby, as we become acquainted with his new little body, habits, and personality. What are all those lumps, bumps, and spots? Will I ever get some sleep? Are all those *vaccines really necessary? Will I ever be able to get out of the house? What kind of parent will I be? How do I know if I'll love my child?*

PART IV: GROWTH AND DEVELOPMENT

Here we'll put your mind at ease about the very wide range of what's considered normal growth and development. *How much should Inez grow each month? Is Jay too chubby and Ruthie too skinny? What new tricks can I expect Linda to do each month? Why isn't my Stuart talking yet? Does Kenny talk too much? Is baby Betty ready for Mensa? Exactly what's wrong with little Dougie?*

PART V: HEALTH AND SAFETY

Part V, the heart of our "user's manual," is full of useful information on all issues surrounding your baby's health and safety. *How can I make my home safe for my precious baby? What do I do when my baby runs a high temperature? Why is she always sick? And what do I do in an emergency? What is a colicky baby, anyway? And why is she always farting?*

PART VI: SPECIAL ISSUES FOR SPECIAL MOMS, DADS, AND KIDS

Finally, we'll look at some of the trials confronting today's busy parents and changing family units. *Is day care the best solution for working mothers? Can I work and still be a good mom? Can I be a good single mom or single dad? Can a gay parent raise a child? How do I find help and what exactly does an au pair do? What if my baby is born prematurely? What do you mean, I have more than one baby in there?*

Each chapter of *Kidfixer* will discuss some commonly held myths about child care. We've all heard them before: "Don't let your baby sleep on his back or he'll choke when he spits up," or "Starve a cold and feed a fever." We'll examine many such myths and then uncover the truths behind them.

And last but not least, we'll conclude each chapter of *The Kidfixer Baby Book* with frequently asked questions, just like the "FAQ" section in any technical manual. Drawing from specific questions that I've been asked numerous times in the office, on the phone, or through e-mail from anxious new parents just like you, I'll provide answers to the questions you have now, and even those you haven't yet thought to ask.

So read on if you're about to give birth to (or adopt) your first child, if you've recently brought home a newborn and feel you could use some help, or even if you've got a child or two at home already and need a refresher course for that new delivery you're expecting. Of course, this book in no way takes the place of your pediatrician. It certainly could never take the place of a loving grandma or a caring friend. But if you're pregnant or have recently brought home your new little alien, all wrapped up and shiny, and you think you might like a little written help, then read on.

PART I

BABY
ON THE WAY

I remember leaving the hospital — thinking, "Wait, are they going to let me just walk off with him? I don't know beans about babies! I don't have a license to do this." [We're] just amateurs.

— ANNE TYLER

1

BEFORE YOU GIVE BIRTH

SO, YOU'RE PREGNANT. CONGRATULATIONS! WHAT WILL YOU NAME THE BABY?

The inevitable question, after sharing the happy news with friends and family, is bound to be: do you have a name picked out? After twenty-five years as a pediatrician with a private practice on Long Island, I bet you can imagine the names I've heard. People find baby names in all kinds of places: movie credits, classical literature, baby-naming books, the Internet, and especially popular TV shows (we saw lots of Brandons, Kellys, Dylans, and Brendas when *Beverly Hills, 90210* first sprang into pop culture, and we still see the expected Rachels, Monicas, Rosses, and Phoebes). Some names are embedded in my memory: there was the classically inspired Isolde Shapiro, the whimsical Scylla Finkelstein, the very serious MacArthur Smith (a girl), and the unforgettable Princess Green (Princess was her first name, not a title). I have a bit of advice about naming your baby: before you subject your child to the burden of a life as Giuliani Schwartz, or Harry Potter Patel, just pause and think about how this growing child will feel about the name. Of course, if you've given it plenty of thought and are absolutely in love with a particular name, then trust your own opinion and don't be swayed too much by the opinion of family or friends. I remember attempting to pick a name as we waited for our first child, only to have each choice vetoed by a friend or relative who had known a kid in sixth grade with that name and hated him. It's amazing how, soon after he's born, little Goober will actually look like a Goober and act like a Goober. After a few short weeks, you'll wonder how you ever considered any other name for him.

WHAT KIND OF PARENT WILL I BE?

Is this question worrying you? I thought so. You're not alone. Here's my first serious bit of advice about waiting for your child to arrive: *relax*.

The thought of having a baby can be frightening, especially for first-time parents. Do you want to know what I tell prospective first-time moms every day in my practice? "Look around you. Go to a mall. Take a bus. Go to a matinee at the local mall movie theater. What do you see?" There are an awful lot of munchkins out there with a pretty interesting variety of moms. And guess what? Not all of those parents are rocket scientists. One or two didn't even attend an Ivy League University. A few, as you look further, may not even have advanced graduate degrees. The majority, in fact, are average, hardworking people of normal intelligence. In other words, as you've guessed, parenting takes all kinds.

I really can't predict who is going to be the next mother of the year when I meet pregnant moms, but I do know one thing: IQ doesn't have a heck of a lot to do with it. Nor does a hefty bank balance. Some of the best moms I know aren't exactly Einsteins or Rockefellers. In truth, there are only two important parental traits that can predict a relatively easy transition to parenthood. These are **common sense** and a **good heart,** and it's tough to measure either on an IQ test. Sound judgment and lots of love are the best credentials. Here are two examples.

Mrs. CEO is a mother in our practice. She's a thirty-something Princeton graduate who holds down a high-level job, as does her equally bright husband, Mr. CEO. The CEOs' cute little girl, Clio, is now ten years old and also quite gifted; Princeton, here she comes! Clio's busy parents send her to the best private school. She has the best music teacher and even her own personal trainer. Dance classes, voice coaches, acting lessons — she's had them all. Yet in spite of all these advantages, Clio is not a very happy child. Her parents, who certainly mean well, are just not so warm as they might be. Clio could use a walk to the ice cream stand with Mom and Dad, a few more play dates with friends her own age, and perhaps fewer appointments with coaches and tutors.

Ms. Clerk is another mom in my practice. When I first met her, several years ago, she was a nervous eighteen-year-old secretary who came for a prenatal interview with her mother, the future grandma. She had no plans to marry the baby's father, and had recruited Grandma to watch the baby while she worked. Ms. Clerk had just finished high school and wasn't sure what she wanted to do with her life, but she was certain that she wanted to do a good job as a parent. She seemed sincere, if a bit frightened, and I could see from the way she interacted with her own mother that she was a sweet person. Little Clark is now eight years old and a real buster. He's sharp as a tack, has a great personality, and is a dynamite soccer player. I don't know if Clark is on a direct track to Princeton, but he's a bright, well-adjusted kid, and he has a terrific mother whom he adores and who'll make sure he gets anything in life he needs to succeed.

Of course, these two scenarios aren't mentioned to suggest that wealthy parents can't be affectionate or that all poor parents are loving. The lesson to be learned, obviously, is that a good heart and a little common sense are more important predictors of success as a parent than a high IQ, tons of money, or an impressive family tree. So the next time you find yourself lying awake at night worrying about how you're going to do as a parent, just get out of bed, go to a mall or an all-night supermarket, and look around. It takes all kinds. And remember, a little common sense, along with a lot of love, can go a long way.

A HEALTHY PREGNANCY

Let's start with the day you discovered that you're pregnant. Perhaps your doctor has just told you the good news, or maybe your little home chemistry set has just turned blue. You've told the proud daddy—and helped him up off the floor. Or maybe you're a single parent who is celebrating alone or with a close friend. Perhaps you're about to adopt a baby. The legal arrangements have been made, and you're waiting out the birth of your child. Other than morning sickness, you've got plenty to think about, too. In our own case, as the doctor who received the test results first, I had the pleasure of telling my wife that she was pregnant.

I don't think she's ever forgiven me for depriving her of the chance to break the news that I was about to become a father.

Now that you know you're pregnant, it's time to pay special attention to your body, since what affects Mom will affect baby. If you're a health nut and already watch your diet, get plenty of exercise, and drink only one or two cups of coffee a day, this will be a breeze. If, however, you're like most of us and have a vice or two, then shape up! Remember you're eating for two now. You're drinking for two, also. You're puffing for two. And you're partying for two.

RULE #1: PUT OUT THAT CIGARETTE

Smoking is out. Every time a pregnant mother puts a cigarette to her lips, she is offering a drag to her unborn baby. Mothers who smoke increase their chances of miscarrying. Also, smoking during pregnancy makes babies susceptible to behavioral problems, short stature, asthma, bronchitis, pneumonia, and ear infections during early childhood, handicaps that may last right into adolescence. For that matter, stop smoking for good. Passive smoking (inhaling smoke from Mom or Dad's nearby cigarette) is just as bad. For every pack of cigarettes you smoke, the secondhand smoke your baby inhales is equivalent to one cigarette. In time your little one may develop a real smoker's cough, as well as more ear infections, and increased bouts of pneumonia, bronchitis, and asthma. He may even have learning and behavioral problems in school. To top it off, children of parents who smoke in the home have been found to have a greater risk of crib death.

If you try to stop and simply can't do it, at least cut down. If you can go from a pack a day to four or five cigarettes a day, it's a lot better than doing nothing. And when little Goober is born, if you must smoke, do it outside. Doing something to change your habits and improve your baby's health is always better than doing nothing.

RULE #2: LOSE THE BOOZE

How about alcohol? Can you still drink? Babies of heavy drinkers are often born with fetal alcohol syndrome, a condition characterized by small facial features (small heads, small chins, small jaws). More important, babies whose moms drink during pregnancy have lower birth weights and often never catch up. They end up being smaller kids and adults than they would have been expected to be based on their genetics. Fetal alcohol syndrome babies can also have smaller brains with slower-than-normal mental development and learning disorders. In fact, fetal alcohol syndrome is the leading cause of mental retardation in newborns. Finally, many of these babies have birth defects, such as a curved spine, finger and toe deformities, and organ defects. Like smoking, the more you drink, the more your baby will be harmed. Since nobody's sure just how much a safe amount of alcohol might be, it's best not to drink alcohol at all — not even an occasional drink. Your best bet: lose the booze.

RULE #3: DECAFFEINATE, BEFORE IT'S TOO LATE

How about coffee? Surely that's a vice that's permissible, no? Yes, but stick to a cup or two a day, or even better, switch to decaf. Moms who drink several cups of coffee each day during pregnancy tend to have smaller kids, and these little java-holic babes can go through caffeine withdrawal once they're born and their "supply" runs out. Such withdrawal babies are jittery, are restless, have rapid breathing, and vomit frequently.

RULE #4: NO DRUGS

Now that you've been turned off to smoking, drinking, and coffee, let's mention the *real* serious stuff — drugs. Make no mistake: although tobacco, alcohol, and caffeine are legal, they're still drugs. But as bad as they are, they pale in comparison to the effects of drugs such as cocaine and heroin. Nothing is as sad as the sight of a newborn addict going through withdrawal. Not only are these babies fighting addiction, they're fighting for their lives. Over 100,000 babies suffer from drug withdrawal in the United States each year. Those who make it may have birth defects, learning disorders, convulsions, growth retardation, even mental retardation. Marijuana, a "social" drug, can cause your baby to be inappropriately small and to have learning problems once he starts school. Remember, what you eat, drink, smoke, or snort is baby food.

A word about prescription drugs. Many medications taken during pregnancy can cause problems for your baby. For example, the sedatives Valium, Miltown, and barbiturates, as well as the antidepressants Elavil and Anafranil, can cause such newborn withdrawal symptoms as poor feeding, tremors (shaking), irritability, and high or low body temperature. Of course, some drugs may be not only beneficial but necessary, and taking Tylenol for a severe headache is allowable. I remember a mother-to-be telling me that she had a bad strep throat but was "toughing it out" without medication for the good of her baby. I had to remind her that the strep germ itself can pass through the placenta to the fetus, and this germ would be a lot more harmful than an antibiotic. In certain circumstances, taking medication during pregnancy is necessary. Just one suggestion: before taking *any* medication other than Tylenol or pre-natal vitamins while pregnant, speak to your obstetrician or your future pediatrician and ask if that medication is safe for the baby. This will prevent a lot of worry later on.

Your baby's health is a question not just of what *not* to do, but what *to do* during pregnancy as well. To keep your baby comfortable and safe inside his little "trailer home," keep yourself healthy, too. As you see your profile changing from statuesque to Santa-esque, there's a tendency to panic. Don't. Also, don't let friends or family scare you. Even though that little critter inside may weigh only 7 or 8 pounds when he makes his debut, there's a lot going on in there that adds tonnage. Your breasts are getting bigger, your uterus is getting thicker, and the placenta, which is the organ that actually passes all that cheesecake on to little Goober, is no lightweight, either. It's not unusual for a woman to gain 20 to 30 pounds during pregnancy. More important to you and Goober than how much you gain is what types of food you eat.

GENERAL PRINCIPLES FOR A HEALTHY DIET

Carbs, Fats, and Protein
Most of your diet should consist of complex carbohydrates, such foods as breads, pasta, vegetables, and grains. Ideally, complex carbs should

make up 40 to 50 percent of your diet. Fats, such as oils, butter, margarine and mayonnaise, account for about 30 percent of the calories you take in each day. The remaining 20–30 percent of your calories should come from protein, found in meats, fish, dairy, and legumes. This means the old-fashioned dinner of a nice big 8-ounce sirloin steak garnished with a spoonful of peas and a large dollop of buttery mashed potatoes is not the best meal, on a regular basis. In the course of a whole day, most adults need no more than 6 to 10 ounces of meat, poultry, or fish. You'll find that if you keep your intake of meats down, your fat intake will stay down as well, since there's a heck of a lot more fat in any meat than in a serving of veggies of the same size.

This doesn't mean that your pregnancy is the time to become obsessed with your diet. An occasional ice cream sundae is fine for baby, and probably a good way to treat yourself, too. My wife always indulged in a weekly Carvel shake during her pregnancies (*after* her weigh-in at the obstetrician). Just keep moderation in mind, and an occasional thought about the 40–50 percent carbs, 30 percent fat, and 20–30 percent protein ideal can be a good general guide.

Milk and Fluids

Sometimes people get funny ideas about health, and these myths are passed on from generation to generation with little if any scientific basis. For example, who hasn't heard the old adages "An apple a day keeps the doctor away" and "Starve a cold and feed a fever"? From time to time in this book we'll try to correct such misconceptions. Our first myth deals with milk intake during pregnancy, and it's a real pip.

 **MYTH:** You have to drink milk to make milk.
TRUTH: Cow's milk does not equal breast milk.

The milk you drink is cow's milk. The milk that you want to produce for Goober is human milk. Big difference. To make breast milk you need a well-balanced diet. If you're a good weight for your age and size now, add about 500 more calories to your daily total. Also, drink plenty of liquids. Six to eight glasses of fluids a day is a good minimum, more if you're very active. However, those six to eight glasses don't have to be filled with milk. Usually, one to two glasses of low-fat milk will do the trick.

Prenatal Vitamin

As a final general principle, I recommend that all women take a good prenatal multiple vitamin. Your obstetrician will prescribe one for you. Actually, it's a good idea to start the vitamin several months before you become pregnant, if possible. We know that moms who have supplemented their diets with extra folic acid for a year before conception have much lower rates of delivering a baby with abnormalities of the spinal cord such as spina bifida. So make sure the vitamin your obstetrician chooses contains all the vitamin groups, including folic acid. Also, if you plan to nurse your baby, it's a good idea to continue the vitamin after you give birth.

FOODS TO AVOID DURING PREGNANCY

Fish

During pregnancy, watch out for big scary fish. No, I don't mean when you swim. I mean when you eat. Fish is a great low-fat source of protein, and most people don't get enough of it in their diets. Of course, like most things in life, too much of a good thing can be a problem, especially if you're eating the *wrong* fish.

Mercury, a pollutant in the air, settles into our water. Bacteria gobble up the mercury, and little fish gobble up the bacteria. Bigger fish eat smaller fish, and the amount of mercury contamination increases. At the end of this chain, a big predator fish will have a higher mercury level and will pose a greater risk to us than a little fish would.

The problem with mercury is that it's toxic to our nervous systems (the Mad Hatter in *Alice in Wonderland* was driven mad from the mercury used in hat making). Insomnia, forgetfulness, visual deficits, hearing loss, tremors, and other neurologic problems can result when we ingest too much of this element. Pregnant moms should be particularly careful about mercury intake, since the mercury they ingest is passed on to their little passengers, and is even more dangerous to the developing mind of the fetus and infant. For this reason, nursing moms and young children have to be careful about their fish intake.

So how do we eat nice, fresh, healthy, low-fat, high-protein fish without risking mercury exposure? The best advice is to eat less of those fish that tend to have the highest mercury levels. The four worst mercury-gobblers are:

- tilefish
- swordfish
- king mackerel
- shark

The FDA suggests that pregnant moms stay away from these four altogether, and that children and nursing women limit their intake of these fish to only 7 ounces a week. Fish that are less serious mercury-gobblers but which also contain a significant amount of mercury, are tuna, North American lobster, sablefish, and pollock. It's probably best to avoid these during pregnancy as well. As far as other fish, they all have *some* mercury, so try to limit your total fish consumption to no more than 12 ounces a week during your pregnancy.

Peanut Butter
Yes, I know, you *love* peanut butter. Unfortunately, we now know that pregnant moms who eat peanut butter are more likely to have kids with peanut allergies, and peanut allergy is the very worst food allergy a child can have, with such symptoms as severe hives, facial swelling and even respiratory distress. So give up peanuts, peanut butter, and even peanut oil (it's in most stir-fried Chinese food) throughout your pregnancy.

WHAT ELSE TO AVOID: SICKIES

A word about avoiding sick people. Common sense will be your best guide. If you're invited to a friend's house and she has a 5-year-old with a high fever, a cough that shakes the walls, and a runny nose, skip the visit. Not that catching a cold is the end of the world, but who needs it?

Pamper yourself a little and stay home. On the other hand, don't avoid a trip to the supermarket because there *might* be someone there with a cold. Unless you seal yourself in a plastic bag, you're going to be exposed to germs. If you're in good general health, your immune system will fight off most of these anyway. Keep in mind also that most infections are contagious *before* they even become apparent. So that healthy-looking guy on the bus could be passing more germs to you than the lady with that funny-looking rash. I mention this not to make you paranoid, but to let you know that there's a lot of luck involved in avoiding infections. Again, use common sense, and avoid the obvious sicky.

One thing I would avoid, if possible, is a germ called **toxoplasmosis.** You've probably never heard of it, but fetuses just hate it. Toxo, as it's known to doctors, is a common parasite carried by millions of people. Most people have enough immunity so that they don't actually become sick from it. Pigs, sheep, and other animals become infected with toxo by eating feed contaminated with toxo spores. People acquire this parasite either by eating undercooked meat, by working in the garden without gloves, or by handling cat litter. At its worst this bug can cause your baby to be born with a life-threatening infection. In its sneakier form, it can cause learning problems and visual problems that may not show up until much later in life. The best way to avoid toxo is to cook all meat thoroughly (until the juices are no longer pink), wash all fruits and vegetables well before eating them, wash all cutting boards and knives well, use gloves when working in the garden, and let someone else change the kitty litter for you. Tell them to change it daily, since the parasite needs several days once excreted in a cat's feces to become infectious.

LET'S GET PHYSICAL: EXERCISE

As part of keeping yourself and your little passenger in good shape, **exercise,** in moderation, is a good idea. If you're a walker, keep it up. If you're a swimmer, keep paddling. If tennis is your game, keep swinging. If you're into a gym workout, that's okay, too. Just a few words of caution: first, don't overdo it. Strenuous exercise can cause you to miscarry. The best expert regarding your exercise during pregnancy is your obstetrician. Ask your doc, at your first visit, for a good exercise regimen that suits both your needs and your baby's.

Second, pregnancy is probably not the best time to *begin* a strenuous exercise regimen. If you're not a runner, don't start to run now. Walking, which is just as valuable, would be a good way to begin exercising if you're currently a couch potato. Whatever you decide to do, start slowly, and remember to check with your obstetrician if you're not sure about what *you* can do safely.

KIDFIXER FREQUENTLY ASKED QUESTIONS

As I mentioned in the introduction, each chapter will conclude with a section for "frequently asked questions." These are real questions that I am asked in my practice, during office visits, on the phone, or as e-mail questions in our "e-consult" service. Here are the first of the "FAQs," which deal with our subject of a healthy pregnancy.

Q: *I'm a vegetarian and I want to be healthy for my baby. Is there anything I'm lacking? Do I need any supplements?*

A: Actually, you probably don't need any additional supplement. Vegetarians get plenty of protein from dairy, eggs, and even beans, so your baby is not at risk. Vegans (these are people who eat no animal products at all, including dairy and eggs) can still get enough protein from tofu, TVP (textured vegetable protein), and beans. The only issue for vegans is that they can be deficient in certain vitamins that are found naturally in animal sources. Taking a prenatal vitamin is good insurance for both vegetarians and vegans.

Q: *I've heard that taking a vitamin called folic acid during my pregnancy can prevent spina bifida in my baby. How much do I need?*

A: This is true, to some extent. Spina bifida is a condition in which a baby is born with an opening in the bones protecting the spinal cord. It occurs, in some form, in about 1 in 1,000 births. Taking 400 micrograms of folic acid each day will prevent over half of the cases of spina bifida. Unfortunately, to be most effective this supplementation has to be started *before* conception. Since many pregnancies are unplanned, it's a good idea for all women of childbearing age to take this amount of folic acid every day and, of course, to continue it throughout pregnancy. This is one reason why your obstetrician will ask you to take a prenatal vitamin, since most prenatal vitamins contain folic acid.

Q: *My obstetrician has recommended that I have amniocentesis during my pregnancy, since I'm over 35 years of age. Is this safe for my baby? Is it necessary?*

A: Amniocentesis, the quick and practically painless insertion of a needle through a pregnant mom's belly into the amniotic fluid to perform certain tests, is not without risks, but these risks are usually offset by some very important information. Women over 35 are at an increased risk of having chromosomal abnormalities, with the result that their babies may have such problems as Down syndrome (mongolism). An amnio is also done when there is a family history of a chromosomal problem, when a sonogram has shown that there is a possible chromosomal disorder, or when blood tests on a pregnant woman and her husband show that there is a risk of the fetus having some health problem. For example, if your obstetrician finds that your AFP (alpha-fetoprotein) blood level is elevated, you may be at risk for having a child with a spinal cord abnormality. Amniocentesis can make certain that the baby is fine. Another indication for amniocentesis would be if you and your husband are carriers of Tay-Sachs disease, a rare inherited condition seen mostly in Jews of European descent. Testing of the amniotic fluid can determine if the baby has inherited this serious illness.

Q: *I've read that I should save my umbilical cord blood, when I give birth, in case my child develops a serious illness later on and needs a transfusion with these blood cells. Is this a good idea?*

A: Umbilical cord blood is made up of lots of immature blood cells, which have the potential to develop into many different types of mature cells. This versatility is a very handy trait in case a condition necessitates a transfusion with a particular type of cell. For example, children who develop certain rare types of cancer may benefit from a transplant with immature cells taken from the bone marrow of a close relative. An alternative to this type of transplantation is to use a child's own saved cells—the "supercells" banked from umbilical cord blood. Of course, the chance that a child will actually need such a transplant is very unlikely (estimates are anywhere from 1 in 1,000 to 1 in 200,000). Also, there are few studies that show such transplants to be safe, and even fewer that show them to be curative. Certainly if a family member, such as a sibling, has been diagnosed with an illness that may require a transplant of such cells, then banking a newborn's cord blood makes a lot of sense. Without this indication, however, such a procedure is still probably too new to be recommended routinely.

2

CHOOSING YOUR BABY'S DOCTOR

THE PRENATAL INTERVIEW

I really enjoy this meeting between parents-to-be and myself. I love it because I get to see the cute little round lady and her proud hubby before their life has been changed by the little alien. They're so bright and shiny, innocent and unsuspecting. Of course we know all that will soon change.

Seriously, the prenatal interview is a good time to meet your new best friend—your pediatrician. I say this because parents and pediatricians spend a lot of time together, both in the office and on the phone. If she's a good pediatrician, your doctor won't mind scheduling an interview with you. After all, if she can't make time for you now, will she have time for you once the baby is born? Here's a helpful rule of thumb: if you call to schedule an interview and you're told that the doctor doesn't do interviews, don't "do" her.

To help you organize your thoughts for the meeting, make a list of questions before you meet the pediatrician. Here are three you should ask.

1. Is the doctor on staff at a hospital, and if so, where?

In the event of an emergency, you would want to bring little Missy to the nearest hospital and consult with her pediatrician then and there. What many people don't realize, however, is that doctors can't treat patients at any hospital they please. To examine your baby at the hospital and to discuss her findings with you, a doctor must be on staff at that particular hospital. This usually means that the hospital feels she is medically competent, is adequately trained, and poses no risk to the hospital or its patients.

Often, though not always, more prestigious hospitals have more stringent criteria for their attending physicians. It may be easier, for example, to get on staff at Main Street County Hospital than to be approved by Major University Hospital. Therefore, if there is a major university-affiliated medical center nearby and your doctor is on staff there, that's usually a good sign. Of course, this is an oversimplification. Your doctor may have elected not to apply to Major University Hospital because it requires attendings to donate too much time to the hospital, in the form of clinic or teaching duty. If she's not on staff there, just ask why.

Here's another reason why hospital affiliation is so important: some babies actually do get very sick. Thank God most childhood illnesses are minor ones. There are, however, exceptions. If Missy does become ill, you will want her to be treated in a hospital with a pediatric unit. Let's face it, anyone can treat a common cold or a stomach virus, but if your child is *really* sick, she should be treated in a good hospital with specialists trained in childhood illnesses.

Sometimes, especially in rural areas, the nearest major hospital might be far away. In that case your newborn might be cared for in a local community hospital. The community hospital may have an arrangement whereby your baby can be transferred to a larger hospital if some specialized need arises. Now is the time to ask your prospective pediatrician about such a transfer and what part she would play in it.

2. When you call the doctor's office with a question, who will answer that question for you? When you bring your child to the office, who will see you?

I remember one interview with a mother who moved to our town and was shortly due to deliver her second baby. She told me that she loved her old solo practitioner because, when she called him with a question at any time of the day or night, she always got an answer, and it always came from him. He never took a day off and was always on call at night. When I asked her if this saint was in a great mood being on call every night by himself, she replied that she didn't actually speak to him directly, but rather she spoke to his assistant, who then called Dr. Midnight for advice. Armed with information from the doctor, the assistant then called back the mother and told her what to do. A little checking revealed that the assistant was a nurse who never even called the doctor. Instead the nurse would decide what to do herself and then call the mother back, attributing the advice to the omniscient and insomniac sainted doc. This probably wouldn't be so terrible, assuming that the nurse was well trained, but don't you think the mother deserved to know from whom the advice was coming?

Sure, there are times when a nurse or a receptionist can answer a quick question. Most pediatricians will allow their receptionists or assistants to remind a parent about a dosage of Tylenol. Similarly, a simple question such as "When is my child due for her next checkup?" can be answered without the doctor's participation. And nurses and nurse-practitioners are certainly well trained to answer many questions that arise. Some doctors no longer take after-hours calls and instead have phone calls answered by an on-call pediatric resident or intern. This might be fine for simple advice about treatment of a cold, a diaper rash, or a mild case of diarrhea. Yet you, as the baby's parent, are entitled to know who is making decisions about your child. If these decisions are coming from someone other than your pediatrician, then you have a right to know this. You, as the parent, *must* have the option to speak to your doctor when *you* feel it is necessary. If you feel that it is an emergency, your doctor must be available to you.

This brings up the issue of covering doctors. Let's face it, the days of the wise old solo practitioner are over. Any pediatrician will take a day off now and then. She'll also probably not be on call each night and weekend. Do you really want to see a tired, annoyed, overworked doctor with your fresh new baby?

When I was an intern, I learned to spot "night crawlers"—doctors who never took time off and who never allowed other doctors to cover for them. They were easy to identify late at night, their eyes ringed with bags, their bottoms dragging on the ground. In the office from 7 a.m. until 9 p.m., they would make hospital rounds at 10. I remember thinking, "They look so tired and wrinkled." And with no partners or covering physicians to consult for reassurance or a second opinion, they put practically every sick kid in the hospital. When night crawlers wanted to take a rare break and get out of the office for a day, all their sick kids would be directed to the emergency room for the intern or medical student to evaluate.

You don't want a night crawler. They're tired, burned out, and bitter, and they resent their patients. Believe me, you want your precious little bundle to be cared for by a well-rested and enthusiastic doctor; this means you want a doctor who takes some time off. Doctors can arrange to take time off and have vacations in one of several ways.

• *Group practice.* In a group practice, two or more pediatricians share an office. If your doctor is away and you have a question, you will usually speak to one of her partners. If your child must be seen for an illness, he will see one of the partners in the office.

• *Cross-covering.* A solo practitioner can arrange, on her days or weeks off, to have her practice cared for by another pediatrician (or group of pediatricians). Not infrequently, several solo doctors in a neighborhood will cross-cover one another's practices, thus allowing for ample time off. If you call your regular doctor at night, and it's a night when she's at the movies, your call will be answered by a covering doctor. Keep in mind that, with a covering doctor, as opposed to a partner in a group practice, the physician will probably not have access to

Missy's records. If Missy has an allergy to a medication or hates green-colored medicine, the covering doc won't know this. You will have to tell her. Also, if Dr. Jones is covering for Dr. Smith and you want him to see your child, you will probably have to go to Dr. Jones's office, a place that will be new to you and to Missy.

• *Cross-covering groups.* Just to make things confusing, some group practices cross-cover with other groups. Sunnyvale pediatrics, with their five pediatricians, might decide to share coverage with the five pediatricians from nearby Cloudyvale Pediatrics.

This may all seem confusing to you, but just remember this. As much as you may like your primary doctor, and no matter how much she assures you that she's "always available," your child will, from time to time, be treated by someone else. Your phone calls, even those middle-of-the-night emergency calls, will often be answered by someone else. Make sure you know *who* is covering for your doctor. Ask her. If she says nobody ever covers for her, she's probably less than honest. Or else she's a night crawler. In either case, you don't want that doctor.

3. *What is all this going to cost?*

Make no mistake, baby care is expensive. Of course, some medical insurance plans take a good deal of the sting out of the costs of care for your child. Make sure you know just what your insurance will cover and what it won't. If your doctor participates in your health care plan, your visits may cost very little. If she is a nonparticipating doctor, you may have to pay more. Just one word: if you feel that one pediatrician is much better for your child than another, cost, while always important, should not be the *only* factor in making your decision.

MYTH: All doctors are fine. Just pick one who's on your plan. After all, your insurance company will only allow a doctor into its plan if she's capable.
TRUTH: Don't let your insurance company pick your doctor for you. That's your job.

Unlike most university hospitals, many insurance companies do not screen their physicians very carefully. There may be doctors in your insurance company's book who shouldn't be there and, conversely, some excellent doctors who aren't listed there. The reason a doctor chooses to join a particular health care plan will usually have a lot to do with how the company pays her as well as how free she is to order the tests and procedures she feels are appropriate.

Consider this. If one doctor costs you $20 more each visit, because she's not fully on your plan, and you see that doctor twenty times during the first year, you'll be paying $400 extra that year. If you really feel this doctor is better for your child and you can afford the $400 difference, consider it a worthwhile expense. After all, you were willing to go for the more expensive TV—the one with the picture-in-picture—that cost $400 more. Similarly, the laptop you chose wasn't the cheapest model either, was it? There were some options you wanted, and you were willing to pay extra for these. Well, your baby's doctor is a pretty important "purchase," too. If you want the best care and you feel that it may cost a little more, go for it. Of course, if you're deciding between two doctors, both of whom are on staff at excellent hospitals, and both of whom have great reputations, and one doctor will be free for you while the other will cause you to go bankrupt, go for the cheapie.

4. There is no question number four.

Only these three. Magazines often prepare lists of questions to ask a prospective pediatrician. All other questions are unnecessary, and I'll show you why. Here are some of these unnecessary questions:

MYTH: Ask the doctor if she has a call-in hour.

TRUTH: Your doctor will probably be available to you any time she's in her office.

Call-in hour is a system whereby your doctor allows one hour each day to answer parents' routine phone questions. What if call-in time is from 8 to 9 a.m. and you have a question at 9:15 a.m.? Are you supposed to wait twenty-three hours and forty-five minutes to ask your question? Forget that. As long as your doctor is in her office and not at home, she should be able to return your routine phone call within a reasonable amount of time. And she will, too. So whether or not you call within that strict period of time, your call should be (and probably will be) answered.

MYTH: Ask the doctor if she has a separate waiting room for sick kids.
TRUTH: It's hard to separate kids into "sick" and "well."

If your child has a high fever, is vomiting yesterday's Happy Meal, and has a rash that looks like a topographic map of the moon, then she's a sick kid. She should, of course, be isolated from other waiting patients. If you have a one-week-old newborn, fresh out of the hospital, then that's a healthy child, and she should be kept only with other healthy, pristine kids. But what if Missy is your average 5-year-old, with the usual bubbly nose and chocolate stains on her jeans, in the office for her yearly checkup? Where does Missy sit? Surely Missy's mom would prefer she stay away from the vomiter. On the other hand, our new mommy wants no part of Missy's runny nose. What's a mother to do? What's a doctor to do? Where does little Missy sit? The answer is this: use common sense. There are too many in-between cases to simply divide a waiting room in half. Most waiting rooms have enough nooks and crannies, corners and alcoves, so that you can maintain some reasonable amount of separation. Besides, most receptionists will want to get the vomiter out of the waiting room and into an examining room as quickly as possible. Who do you think cleans up the mess? Don't get too uptight about catching germs in the doctor's office. It's a lot easier to pick up a bug in a classroom or at the local baby "gym," where thirty kids are all drooling over the same blocks for two hours at a time, than in a waiting room.

MYTH: Ask the doctor if she believes in breast-feeding.
TRUTH: Now, who's going to answer no to that question?

No doctor would say she's against breast-feeding. Why? Well, first of all, who is *against* breast-feeding? Even if she's ambivalent about nursing, why impose that opinion on you? All pediatricians will help you if you decide to nurse your baby. They will also assist you in bottle-feeding, if that's your choice.

So what else should you do during your interview after you've asked the three smart questions? After all, that may take all of two minutes. This is what you do: talk.

Talk about yourself. Unless she's an egomaniac, the doctor will ask you about yourself, your family health history, your background, and so on. Don't be afraid to chat about other things as well. Ask her what she thinks about a particular health-related article you read in a magazine or a health issue discussed on TV. Talk about the weather. Talk about your trip to the office and how you got lost three times. Talk about your husband, if he was unable to make the visit with you. Comment on the pictures on her desk of her funny-looking kids and husband. And observe. This will give you a window into the personality and disposition of the doctor. Does she listen to you? Is she rushing you out of her office after five minutes? Does she seem tense? Does she act as though she's God and you're a peasant? Do you feel comfortable talking to her? Much of the advice your pediatrician gives you will not be engraved on stone tablets. Remember, she may have *trained* at Mount Sinai, but she didn't *descend* from there.

Many of the decisions you make as a parent are made in partnership with your pediatrician. I remember one mother telling me that her former pediatrician insisted that her baby start solid foods at five months; no earlier, no later. This was a problem for her because she was scheduled to go on vacation at that time, and she preferred waiting until six months to start solids. Dr. Lord refused. This is so silly when you consider that the Academy of Pediatrics, which makes recommendations to pediatricians about such matters as feeding, is flexible about schedules. It makes suggestions to the pediatrician. And that's what your doctor should do for you: make suggestions, not commandments.

So chat with your new friend. Get a feel for her manner. Make sure she seems comfortable with you and you feel comfortable with her. She should be personable and flexible, not abrupt and rigid. And while you're at it, ask friends with children what the doctor is like when they bring their kids to her. Any doctor can have a bad day, but if a friend tells you that she dreads seeing her doctor or fears being ridiculed about a question she asks, her doctor is not for you.

What if you don't know whom to interview in the first place? Ask a friend for a recommendation. Ask her how she gets along with her pediatrician. Ask her the three "smart" questions, about hospital affiliation, about whom she speaks to when she calls and sees when her doctor is away, and about costs. Ask her what kind of personality her doctor has. Is she easy to talk to and flexible? If your friend is a lot like you, you'll probably agree about the doctor. Better still, ask your friend if you can come along with her at her next visit.

MYTH: Consider only the pediatrician suggested by your obstetrician.
TRUTH: Consider his recommendation, but consider others as well.

In all honesty, your friend's opinion is probably worth almost as much as your obstetrician's. After all, the obstetrician doesn't have to deal with the pediatrician in the same way as a new parent. He may golf with the pediatrician or play tennis with her. He may even have trained with her. But he doesn't have to ask her about feeding or diaper rashes or a high fever in the middle of the night. You will. I know one obstetrician who sends his own children to a particular pediatrician, because he knows he's the best doc around. When his expectant mommies ask for a recommendation, however, he refers them to a different doctor, who just happens to be his golf buddy and his partner in a business venture. A good tip: **when your obstetrician gives you the name of a pediatrician, ask him whom he uses to care for his own kids.**

I've spent a lot of time discussing how to choose your pediatrician because it's a very important consideration. You will probably spend more time in just the next year with this person than you have with all other doctors so far in your life. You'll speak to her more on the phone than you will to many of your good friends. Also, although this book will guide you through the next year, it is only a guide. Most of your questions will be answered by the pediatrician. If your child is sick, you will want to speak to someone you trust. If your child is *very* sick, you will need to see someone you trust. Every day another mother says to me, "I speak to you more than I do to my husband." This is close to the truth. There is a gradual bonding process that takes place between a pediatrician and a parent. It will take a while for you and your pediatrician to feel completely comfortable with each other, but eventually, and ideally, the relationship becomes a friendship. Most of the parents in our practice become our friends. We get to share in their good news and to help comfort them when the news is not so good. As their kids grow to teens and even adults, these kids become our friends too. Good friends are hard to find, but once a friendship is established, it's a very valuable commodity. So take your time and find a good pediatrician who, hopefully, will become a new good friend.

KIDFIXER FREQUENTLY ASKED QUESTIONS

Q: *There is no pediatrician where I live, but only a family practice doctor. Help!*

A: Terrific! Over the years I've met some amazing family physicians. I don't know how they do it. They have to keep up to date on all fields of medicine: pediatrics, internal medicine, obstetrics and gynecology, even general surgery. It takes me hours each week just to read through all of my pediatric journals. Somehow, many family physicians do just fine, and they usually know when to ask for the help of a specialist. Again, try to find a family physician who's on staff at a good hospital, so that she can get all the help she needs.

Q: *I'm new in town, and I don't know any doctors. I haven't yet made any good friends and I don't even know my new obstetrician too well either. How can I find a pediatrician?*

A: Call up the nearest university-affiliated hospital and ask to speak to someone in the Department of Pediatrics. A doctor in the department, or even a secretary, will have a list of hospital-affiliated pediatricians in your area. As we said earlier, if a doctor has been approved by the hospital, you're probably getting someone who is competent and morally sound. From that list you can fine-tune your choice during a prenatal interview.

Q: *I'm a working mom, and I will probably need to make appointments either early in the morning or in the evening. What can I do?*

A: You're not the only working mom out there, and your pediatrician will not be serving your needs (along with the needs of all the other working moms) if she has hours only from 9 to 5. Sure, Grandma or your nanny or au pair will make some visits for you, but you or your hubby really will want to be there for most of your baby's well-care visits and will certainly want to be around if you're particularly concerned about an illness. The good news is that most doctors will either have hours early in the morning, say 7:30 or 8:00, or else will have evening hours, often until 6:00 or 6:30.

Q: *Does it matter if my child's pediatrician is a man or a woman?*

A: For a newborn, no. Later on, when little Missy has decided that she's embarrassed by a "boy doctor," she may prefer a woman pediatrician. Conversely, little Jay may be embarrassed sitting in his boxers with a "girl" in the room. Most of the time a sensitive pediatrician can get around this by allowing a child to remain dressed during the exam, exposing one little arm or leg at a time. Of course, this is one area where having a group practice comes in handy. We're blessed with two "boy doctors" and two "girl doctors," and our moms eventually allow their kids to determine whom they'd like to see.

3

SUPPLIES:

BATTERIES NOT INCLUDED

It can be extremely expensive, not to mention confusing, when you set out to assemble all the clothing, supplies, and gizmos for your new baby. There are new products added continuously to the shelves of baby specialty stores, some of them handy, some frivolous. This chapter is an attempt to help you pick out some of the basics. I'll try not to make this too expensive.

THE CAR SEAT

Buy this first—before you get the layette, before you buy the special funny-looking outfit for the baby's trip home from the hospital, before you buy bottles or nipples or diapers, even before you buy the pink or blue bubble gum cigars. This is the first thing. Why?

More kids are killed each year in the United States from car accidents than from any other cause. That's right, it's the leading cause of death. Don't even think about bringing little Kenny home in the car nestled comfortably in your arms or in grandma's lap. It just doesn't work. The force generated by any kind of impact, or even a sudden stop, after going 30 miles per hour in a car, is so great that not even Superman could hold on to the baby. Every trip in the car, beginning with the first, no matter how short, *must* be made in a car seat.

The basic types of car seats include:

• The *infant-only car seat* is a rear-facing seat for babies up to 20–22 pounds and 1 year old. These seats allow a baby to be comfortably reclined, but at just the correct angle for easy breathing. Many are now stroller-compatible—the car seat actually fits into a stroller frame.

• *Forward-facing* car seats are for children one year or older who weigh at least 20 pounds.

• The *convertible car seat* is used as a rear-facing seat until a baby reaches 20 pounds and 1 year of age. Then it can be can be turned around to face forward and used until a child reaches 40 pounds, usually at about 4 or 5 years of age. Most convertible seats are not stroller-compatible, but they save you the expense of buying a new seat when your baby outgrows an infant seat.

• *Booster car seats* are usually for children between 40 and 80 pounds. The booster raises your child so that the lap/shoulder seat belt fits properly. Booster seats are used until your child can correctly fit in a seat belt.

• *Toddler-booster car seats* are also convertible; they will take your child from 20 or 22 pounds up to 40 pounds, and then will convert into a booster seat that will last until your child is about 80 pounds and ready for a seat belt.

A few general rules to consider in choosing a car seat for your child:

• Make sure that your infant fits into his seat; it should be neither too big nor too small.
• Make sure that all buckles and catches are easily released, and easy to use.
• Make sure your seat belt can fit into the car seat when needed.
• The rear seat is the safest place to put your baby, and the middle of the rear seat is the best, if possible.

- If you have a passenger-side air bag in front, the car seat *must* be placed in the rear of the car to prevent the baby being crushed by the exploding bag.

MYTH: A more expensive infant seat will be safer.
TRUTH: As with many choices in life, more expensive does not always mean better.

Paying more for looks, a fancy designer brand name, or for the other unnecessary bells and whistles is money thrown away.

MYTH: Once a baby is a year old, it's safe to turn the convertible car seat around.
TRUTH: Nope. He must be 20 pounds *and* 1 year.

A 1-year-old baby may weigh 23 or 24 pounds, in which case turning the seat around is fine. On the other hand, what if Kenny was a 5-pound premie? He may only weigh 18 or 19 pounds at a year. In that case, turning the seat around is *not* ideal for him. In order to ensure that Kenny is safe, he needs to be at least 1 year old *and* at least 20 pounds.

Car seat recommendations and "rules" do change quite frequently. For the latest on choices, a good source is a publication called *Family Shopping Guide to Car Seats,* which is published by the American Academy of Pediatrics Safe Ride Program, at 141 Northwest Point Blvd., P.O. Box 927, Elk Grove Village, Illinois, 60009-0927. You can find the same information on the Internet at www.aap.org/family/carseatguide. htm. Also, *Consumer Reports* does a nice job of reviewing car seats. Look for their latest review.

STROLLERS

For any lifestyle and any budget there is a stroller, and the latest strollers are also reviewed periodically in *Consumer Reports*. Most mobile parents prefer the car seat–stroller combos, where the infant seat fits into the stroller. These handy vehicles come with many of the same options as your family car, right down to the cushy air-filled tires—some even have cup holders!

The basic stroller types include:

• *Traditional strollers.* Many of these are lightweight and convenient to use. The superlight umbrella stroller is as easy as you can get.

• *Car seat–stroller combos.* The car seat fits neatly into the stroller. Once the child outgrows the infant car seat, at 1 year and 20 pounds, most combos allow you to use the stroller alone.

• *Jogger strollers.* These allow moms in training for the marathon to jog along with their babies, with room for Mom's churning legs. Many are even off-road-capable, like that sport-ute in your garage. Hold off, however, on jogging with your baby until your future runner is at least 6 months old and can better support his head.

• *Double strollers.* For twins or for two close-in-age children, double strollers come as side-by-side or one-behind-the-other models. Some double strollers are car-seat-ready.

A stroller is one purchase that you should make yourself (if someone wants to buy you one as a gift, suggest a gift certificate). Try opening, closing, and lifting the stroller with one hand—the other hand will be holding Kenny. Make sure your feet don't hit the wheels when you walk. Also, since Kenny won't be able to sit up for several months, he will need either a stroller that allows him to lie down or one that accepts an infant car seat. Finally, if you'll be hopping on buses and trains, a lightweight, portable stroller will work best for you.

When using your stroller, keep in mind these general **stroller safety tips:**

- Don't leave your child unattended in a stroller.
- Keep to the stroller's weight limit.
- Don't use your stroller to carry heavy packages on the handles. It can tip over.
- Make sure the frame is fully locked.
- Watch out for your baby's fingers when you're folding and unfolding your stroller.
- Always use the seat belt or harness.

PLAYPENS

A must-have for many moms, a playpen also can be dangerous. Babies are injured when the collapsible sides of playpens aren't locked properly or when they become trapped under the loose mesh sides of a playpen that was not properly opened.

Some rules for buying a playpen, supplied by the U.S. Consumer Product Safety Commission:

- For playpens with a hinge in the center of the top rails, make sure the rails automatically lock when opened up.
- If you buy a playpen with mesh netting, make sure the netting has a small weave—less than ¼ inch—so that little fingers and toes aren't trapped.
- If the playpen is wooden, make sure slats are no more than 2⅜ inches in width.

CLOTHING

This is, of course, an area where you'll need very little help from me. Seasons determine what clothing you'll buy right away, but consider these commonsense suggestions.

- Don't buy a lot in any one size. Babies grow faster than that pile of credit card bills on your desk. If you buy twenty kimonos, all size 6 months, you'll probably never get to use half of them.

• Always buy a bigger size than the baby's chronological age, unless Kenny is a premie. These outfits will shrink—Kenny will not. Some sales people encourage you to buy "perfect-fit" outfits, so that after one washing you'll be back for another round of buying. Get Kenny's clothes a little big, so they will fit for a few months as he grows and as his clothes shrink.

• Before you buy that great-looking ballerina outfit with the lace and ruffles, just ask yourself, "Will my baby be comfortable in this, or am I buying it for me?"

• If you're not sure whether to buy the lightweight outfit or the heavier one, always go with the lighter one. Underdress; don't overdress.

• Hand-me-downs are fine. No one will know, and they're bound to be comfy.

With these generalities in mind, and with the understanding that needs and finances vary, here is a sample layette:

- Cotton T-shirts or "onesies": 12
- Cotton nightgowns, kimonos, or sacks: 6 to 8
- Cotton receiving blankets: 6 to 8
- Bibs: 3 to 4
- Cotton stretchies or PJs: 4 to 6
- Lightweight sweaters: 2 or 3
- Blanket sleepers (if you live in areas with cold nights): 1 or 2
- Socks or booties: 4 to 6
- Hats: 3 to 4
- Snowsuit: 1 (again, not for you Floridians)
- A really cute outfit for the trip home from the hospital and for pictures

THE DIAPER BAG AND THE BABY BLUES

You *must* get out of the house. That's an order. Shortly after giving birth many new mothers get the **baby blues.** Peaking around the fourth day after birth, and lasting for ten days to two weeks, many moms will be weepy, irritable, anxious, and even confused. More serious and not uncommon is true **postpartum depression.** Occurring in about one out of every eight births (especially if there is a history of depression in the family), postpartum depression is largely the result of a sharp drop in the reproductive hormones of pregnancy. All those nice hormones that were helping you to nurture Kenny while he was inside are now gone. When hormone levels suddenly drop, the chemical "shock" to your system often results in a true clinical depression, which can last for months. Moms who suffer from postpartum depression have trouble sleeping (even when their babies sleep), eating, and making decisions. They feel anxious and edgy all the time. Sometimes postpartum depression requires medication to help a mom make it through this rocky time. Getting out of the house and resuming, as much as possible, normal activities is a good way to fight postpartum depression. Let's face it, spending a whole day trapped in your apartment or house, wondering what surprise Kenny has in store for you today, is a good recipe for depression. Get out, see your friends, show off Kenny to your fellow workers, visit your mom for support. In short, try to get on with life.

To this end, a large, well-stocked diaper bag is a must. Make the bag light but big. Your diaper bag should have everything you'll definitely need, everything you *may* need, and everything you'll probably never need. Make sure you're carrying:

- Diapers: 2 for every hour you're out—you'll see!
- Baby wipes in travel case
- Diaper ointment
- Baby bottle (unless you only nurse)
- Formula: either ready-to-pour or powdered (again, if you aren't strictly nursing)
- Bibs: 3 to 4
- Cloth diapers for spills: 2
- Changing pad
- One extra outfit for baby
- An extra T-shirt for you—you'll see!
- Cookies (for you and for Kenny, when he's older)
- A large bottle of water (for you and to mix with powdered formula)

- Baby's favorite small toy
- Your favorite small toy: a cell phone (if you have one)
- Zipper-lock bags for a variety of messes

OTHER SUPPLIES

We're not done yet. That little bundle of joy is costing you a bundle of cash already. Consider this a list of some miscellaneous bare essentials you may need in the first few months:

- Crib sheets: 3 or 4
- Quilted crib pads: 2 or 3
- Mattress covers: 2 or 3
- Cloth diapers, for spills, wet burps, and general cleanups: 2 dozen
- Disposable diapers, any brand: 5 to 6 dozen
- Washcloths: 5 to 6
- Towels: 3 to 4 (some with hoods would be great)
- Baby bathtub
- Baby scissors or nail clippers
- Baby rectal thermometer
- Baby hairbrush
- Vaseline or other bland ointment such as A&D, zinc oxide, or Triple Paste
- Disposable wipes

- Cotton balls
- Baby soap, castile soap, Cetaphil, Dove, or any other mild soap
- Rubbing alcohol
- Infant acetaminophen (Tylenol, etc.); of course, if your newborn has a fever (which is anything over 100 degrees), let your doctor know.

THE CRIB

What is it about putting together a crib? No matter how handy you may be and no matter how well you read the instructions, it seems that there are always extra parts left over. It may be an extra screw or a washer. Sometimes it's something major, like a large slat of wood. This can be scary, because we all want our babies to be safe. I remember moving and having to dismantle my son's crib. When it came time to reassemble it at our new apartment, we ended up with three extra screws, an important-looking bolt, and an assortment of washers. There is no scientific reason for this. After years of hearing the same story from other parents, I've just decided that crib building defies the laws of science. In any case, even a supernatural crib should be a safe one.

When you make your choice of crib, keep a few facts in mind:

- Make sure that the crib is safe. This is usually no problem, since virtually all cribs built in the last twenty years meet safety standards. If, however, you are using an antique crib, passed down from your grandmother, make sure that the slats on the crib are no more than 2⅜ inches apart, that there are no cut-outs for the baby's head to get stuck in, and that there is no lead-based paint used on the crib.

- Make sure the mattress is kept at a level low enough so that little Kenny can't climb out. This will necessitate lowering the level as he grows. By the time they are about 3 feet tall, most babies can climb out of a crib and need to be moved to a bed.

- Keep the side rails up when you leave your child unattended. It only takes a few seconds for a child to roll out of a crib.

• Once little Kenny can stand up, remove all toys from the crib that he might be able to stand on. Similarly, remove the crib bumpers at this time.

• Make sure that there are no loose strings or threads in the crib. These can come from toys, from frayed mattresses, or from shredded blankets. Babies can get what's known as tourniquet injuries from loose threads that become wrapped around fingers, toes, or even necks.

• *Always put your baby to sleep on the* back, *not on the belly.* Yes, this is different from the way your mom put you to bed, but we now know that crib death is much more common when babies are put to sleep on their bellies. Even the side position is less safe than on the back. There are exceptions to this rule. For example, some babies who have very severe gastroesophageal reflux, a condition where they vomit force-fully many times each day, may do better on their stomachs. Let your pediatrician tell you if your baby is such an exception. Otherwise, put little Kenny to sleep on his back. Remember, back is best!

KIDFIXER FREQUENTLY ASKED QUESTIONS

Q: *What type of cradle do I need? Should I buy a bassinet?*

A: Unless you're pressed for space, don't bother with either. Some parents like cradles and bassinets because they feel that a crib is too large for a newborn baby. Believe me, your baby couldn't care less how big his bed is. After nine months in "lockup," Kenny is either delighted to have a place to stretch out or else he's so overwhelmed by having *any* room that the difference between a crib and a bassinet is incomprehensible to him.

Many moms and dads use bassinets or cradles because they are small enough to allow parents to keep their babies in their bedroom. To them I say, go ahead, if you must, but I think you and Kenny will be spending enough time together over the next year without having to be roommates at night as well. If you have the separate room, by all means use it. If you're forced into being roommates by a lack of space, as we were in our first apartment, then a cradle or bassinet may be your only choice. Unfortunately, you'll awaken with every little peep your baby makes. You don't need this. If you get up with each little sniffle or sigh, neither of you will ever learn to sleep through the night. Put Kenny in his own room (if you have a room for him) and in a crib—from day one. We'll discuss sleep problems later on, but the first step in promoting good sleep habits is putting your baby to sleep in a crib.

Q: *My baby was premature. What do I do about a car seat?*

A: Make sure your premie has a seat without a shield (the traylike device that swings down in front of some infant seats). A small baby's face could hit a shield in a crash. Some very small premies require a car bed for travel.

Q: *What if my car safety seat was in a crash?*

A: Don't use it! Get rid of it and buy a new one.

Q: *Can I use a car safety seat on an airplane?*

A: Sure. The Federal Aviation Administration (FAA) recommends that children be seated in child safety seats until 4 years of age. Most infant and convertible seats are certified for use in planes.

Q: *Which is the best car safety seat?*

A: No one seat is safest or best. The best car safety seat is one that fits your child and can be installed correctly in your car.

Q: *What if my car has airbags?*

A: Airbags are great, but they can be dangerous when used with rear-facing car safety seats. If your car has a passenger airbag, infants in rear-facing seats *must* ride in the backseat. Even in a low-speed crash, the airbag can inflate, strike the car safety seat, and cause serious injury.

Q: What is LATCH?

A: LATCH (this stands for "lower anchors and tethers for children") is a relatively new car safety seat attachment system, developed to make car safety seats safer and easier to use. With LATCH you no longer need to use seat belts to secure the car safety seat. Most new cars and new safety seats are now equipped with lower anchors and tethers. Of course, unless both the vehicle and the car safety seat have the LATCH system, you will still need seat belts to secure your car seat.

Q: Can I use my infant car seat to keep my baby safe when I'm shopping in the supermarket?

A: No! When an infant seat is placed high in a shopping cart, it makes the cart top-heavy and more likely to tip over. Even shopping carts with built-in infant seats are unsafe. Thousands of children are injured each year falling from shopping carts or from carts tipping over. If you must shop with your baby, use a stroller with a large basket or a baby backpack or sling.

PART II

FUEL—
FEEDING YOUR BABY

Even when freshly washed and relieved of all obvious confections, children tend to be sticky.

— FRAN LEBOWITZ

4

BREAST VS. BOTTLE

We have hundreds of babies in our practice. I would estimate that half of them have been nursed and half have been strictly bottle-fed. Of those who have been nursed, half have tried supplemental bottles. They're all great kids and most of their parents are wonderful as well. And yet every time you pick up a magazine, you read that nursing is the *only* way to feed a baby. Are a full half of our mothers bad moms? The answer: moms are allowed to be different, just as babies are.

MYTH: The *only* way to feed a baby is to nurse.
TRUTH: It may be the best way for many, but it's *not* the only way.

Then why all this pressure to nurse? In underdeveloped countries, hygiene is poor and bottle-feeding can be an adventure. Formulas in these countries are largely of the homemade variety: a pinch of sugar, a dash of salt, 8 ounces of dirty water, and a lot of luck. Under these circumstances, the *safest* way to feed a baby is to nurse.

In the United States there are also many areas where clean water and pre-made formula are not always available. If you live in such an area, by all means make every attempt to nurse. On the other hand, if cost and cleanliness are not major issues for you, the choice is yours. Don't let anyone force you into a decision as important as how you feed your baby.

One thing is for sure: whichever way you decide to feed your infant, you will not succeed if you are doing something that makes you uncomfortable or unhappy. Also, keep in mind that if you decide to nurse and don't enjoy it, you can always stop. On the other hand, if you bottle-feed exclusively for the first several days of your baby's life, it then may be impossible to start nursing. So if you have any inclination at all that you might like to try nursing, go ahead. It's not a lifetime commitment. In either case, however, make sure that your decision is an informed decision. To that end, here are a few advantages and some common myths about nursing, which will be followed by a few advantages of bottle-feeding.

ADVANTAGES OF NURSING

Why nurse?

- *Breast-feeding helps your baby fight infection.* Breast milk contains antibodies (chemicals that fight infection), phagocytes (cells that gobble up germs), and other exotic substances (called glycoconjugates) to help your baby resist infection. Such infections as otitis (middle ear infections), pneumonia, meningitis, gastroenteritis (stomach virus), and even botulism are less common in nursed babies than in those who are bottle-fed.

- *Nursing saves money.* Even figuring in the extra nutrition you'll need to "eat for two," it's a heck of a lot cheaper than formula.

- *Breast-feeding is uncomplicated and convenient.* You can nurse anywhere, with no equipment. You don't have bottles to wash and you don't have to mix breast milk with anything before "serving."

- *It reduces the incidence of several medical conditions.* Inflammatory bowel diseases (Crohn's disease and ulcerative colitis), diabetes, allergic diseases, and certain malignancies appear to be less common in kids who were breast-fed.

• *Nursing may reduce your baby's risk for sudden infant death syndrome (crib death).*

• *Breast-feeding makes for healthier moms.* Nursing reduces the uterine bleeding after a baby is born. Also, lactating women have an earlier return to their pre-pregnant weights and tend to have stronger bones. Many recent studies even indicate that nursing reduces a mom's risk of developing breast or ovarian cancer in later years.

• *It's a great way to "introduce" yourself to little Ralphie.* The physical contact helps begin the very long ongoing process of "bonding."

Some breast-feeding myths:

MYTH: Breast-feeding is painful.
TRUTH: Only if you're doing it wrong.

MYTH: Breast-feeding makes you fat.
TRUTH: No truth to this at all. Breast-feeding actually helps you burn up calories.

MYTH: Breast-feeding mothers are not allowed to have sex as often.
TRUTH: Wrong; they can have sex as often as they like.

MYTH: Breast-fed babies don't get enough nutrition.
TRUTH: Breast milk has 20 calories per ounce. So does formula.

Breast-fed babies actually do often gain just a bit more slowly, but we don't think that's necessarily a bad thing. In baby growth, bigger is not always better.

MYTH: You can't take any prescription medication while nursing.

TRUTH: There are lots of medications you can't take while nursing and lots you can take. Also, if you're on a particular medication that's a nursing no-no, there's a good chance your doctor can find a substitute that works just as well and is safe for your baby.

Some of the **medications that you cannot take while nursing** include:

- Antineoplastic agents (cancer drugs)
- Radiopharmaceuticals
- Ergot alkaloids
- Iodides
- Mercurials
- Atropine
- Lithium carbonate
- Chloramphenicol
- Cyclosporine
- Bromocriptine

Keep in mind that this is only a partial list. **Take no medication while nursing, other than acetaminophen (Tylenol) and vitamins, without discussing it with your doctor.**

MYTH: If you get sick, you'll just have to stop breast-feeding anyway.

TRUTH: Quite to the contrary. You *can* and *should* nurse when you're sick.

When you're sick, your body makes antibodies, little chemicals that help fight off your infection. Let's say you've got a cold and you've been hugging, kissing, and otherwise contaminating little Ralphie. Do you stop nursing? No way. Nursing passes these nice protective antibodies, which your body has made for you, on to Ralphie. This "free" dose of antibodies will protect Ralphie from your germs or help him fight the germs if he already has caught your cold.

So should you try nursing? If you think you want to nurse, great. If you're not sure, please give it a try. It is the healthiest way to feed a baby, and remember, you can always stop. Just recently, in talking to a new-mommies group, I chatted with one first-time mother who was still breast-feeding her adorable redheaded year-old daughter. I asked this mom if she had intended to nurse for a year. She explained that she had told herself she would try nursing for three months and then would take it from there. After three months she was still enjoying it, so she stuck with nursing for another three-month trial. Now on her fourth such "trial period," she was happy (and a bit surprised) that she still enjoyed nursing so much. The message to be learned? Try it and take it from there.

ADVANTAGES OF BOTTLE-FEEDING

How about bottle-feeding? What does that have to offer?

• *Daddies can't nurse their babies, so bottle-feeding, even as a supplement, allows a new daddy to start getting involved.* The value of this involvement should not be underestimated. If you start a new pop off early, he'll become a great helper. If you keep him in the den, watching TV, while you struggle with feedings, baths, and changing, then he'll be of no use when you need him. Remember this when diapers need changing, too. Don't worry, Dad, you'll love it!

• *Some women with full-time jobs find formula-feeding, at least as a part-time method, easier.* This is variable, however. Some of the hardest-working women I know nurse their babies.

• *Sometimes a physical condition precludes breast-feeding.* HIV-positive moms should bottle-feed. Similarly, the rare woman with active tuberculosis should not breast-feed. Adoptive parents, of course, will usually bottle-feed.

• *Some women are not emotionally comfortable nursing.* Many women tell me that they just do not feel comfortable with the act of nursing. This is understandable and does not make these women bad moms. They nourish their children with love, support, and formula. They just do not nurse.

In conclusion, if you'd like to nurse exclusively, wonderful. Breast-feeding and supplementing with formula or pumped breast milk at times is great, too. If, however, you're sure that you have no interest in nursing and you don't want to try, that's absolutely fine as well. You have my "blessing." Your baby will do great. The key is to make an informed decision, and one with which you are comfortable.

KIDFIXER FREQUENTLY ASKED QUESTIONS

Q: *I've read that if babies aren't nursed right at the time of delivery, then there will be no bonding. Is this true?*

A: Bonding is not a one-time event or some mystical process that occurs suddenly at a critical time, like a nuclear reaction or a touchdown. Your feelings toward Ralphie will grow each day, gradually, as will his love for you. Sure, it's nice to be able to hold and nurse your baby in the delivery room, and even to pass him over to Daddy, but it's not essential. And holding your baby for a few seconds at birth will not compensate for the next fifteen years of less-than-ideal care. Again, use common sense. As Pamela Novotny says in *The Joy of Twins*, "Many people have an oversimplified picture of bonding that could be called the 'epoxy' theory of relationships . . . if you don't get prop-

erly 'glued' to your babies at exactly the right time, which only occurs very soon after birth, then you will have missed your chance."

Bonding, then, is a gradual process that you build with your baby,
regardless of whether you nurse or bottle-feed.

Q: *Will I be able to work at my full-time job and still nurse?*
A: Sure. First of all, if you'd like to supplement with formula, nurse in
the morning, before work, have your caregiver formula-feed your
baby while you're away, and then nurse again when you come home.
You can also pump your breasts, on weekends and even at work,
store your breast milk in the fridge (or freezer), and have your caregiver feed this pumped milk to your baby. Defrosted breast milk is
perfectly nutritious.

Q: *Is it foolish to nurse for only a few months? Should I even bother?*
A: There's nothing foolish about it at all. If nursing is a good thing, and
by now we've established that it is, then isn't a little of a good thing
better than none at all? Isn't giving $5 to charity better than not giv-
ing anything? If you decide that, for whatever reason, you want to
nurse only for three months, why not nurse for three months? It *must*
be better than not nursing at all. Also, you might just decide, like that
nice mom with the redheaded baby, that you enjoy nursing more
than you thought you would, and that you want to keep it up longer
than you expected. Go for it!

Q: *Can I nurse with inverted nipples?*
A: Sure. First of all, many women with inverted nipples find that during pregnancy the natural enlargement of their breasts makes their
inverted nipples stand out. Also, as we will see in the next chapter,
with the proper technique inverted nipples are not an obstacle to
nursing.

5

NURSING

So, you've decided to give nursing a try. Great idea! Let's go through this step by step. If you've already nursed six or seven babies, you can skip this chapter. Also, if you've decided to exclusively bottle-feed, you *could* skip ahead to the next chapter, but don't. Skim it quickly, since there's some advice on burping and other things that will come in handy for bottle-feeders. Let me preface this section by saying that with nursing, as with many other topics in this book, there's more than one right way to do things. I will present some basics to give you a start, but you might want to ask your pediatrician to refer you to a trained lactation consultant for one-on-one help. There's more on lactation consultants later in this chapter. Another good source of information is the American Academy of Pediatrics Web site, www.aap.org/family/brstguid.htm.

BEFORE THE BABY IS BORN: GETTING READY TO NURSE

Before little Nina arrives, toughen your nipples by exposing them to air whenever possible. The exposure will actually make the skin of your breasts more resistant to irritation. Next, wear a well-fitting support bra to help you with your new, temporarily voluptuous body. Later in pregnancy get a nursing bra with flaps that open to allow your breasts to be exposed to air. When you bathe, avoid using any strong or scented soaps, lotions, or creams, which can be drying and irritating. Warm water is all you'll need to clean your breasts.

The Nursing Diet

You'll need about an extra 500 calories daily to help support your new dairy business. The diet that was healthiest during pregnancy—40 to 50 percent carbohydrate, 30 percent fat, and 20 to 30 percent protein—will serve you well again while you're nursing. If you're a high-protein, low-carb type, this is fine as well, but try not to go cold turkey on the carbs. Your baby needs a well-balanced diet from her mom. At the very least, a third of your calories should be from carbohydrates. Also, as a kind of insurance policy, continue your prenatal vitamin while nursing, even though your baby will be getting her own vitamins soon.

- *"Forbidden" foods for nursers.* There really are very few besides peanuts and peanut butter. A balanced healthy diet is your main goal. Occasionally, though not too often, your baby may have a mild digestive problem. This can take the form of excessive spitting up or abnormally frequent stools. Or else she may have a bad rash. In either case, your doctor may suggest altering your diet. For example, he might tell you to cut out the following foods for a while:
  - **Dairy.** Milk, cheese, butter, and other milk products are the most notorious culprits for a distressed nursing baby.
  - **Allergenic foods.** Chocolate, nuts, berries, and shellfish can cause rashes and upset tummies.
  - **Gassy veggies.** Watch out for broccoli, cauliflower, onions, and leafy vegetables.

This is the kind of decision you should make either over the phone with your pediatrician or in his office.

As we mentioned in the section regarding diet during pregnancy, remember to keep your intake of high-mercury fish—**swordfish, tilefish, king mackerel, and shark**—down to 7 ounces or less a week while you're nursing, and your total fish intake to 12 ounces or less each week.

- *Dieting.* This is not the time to starve yourself (or your new little pal).

MYTH: If you diet while nursing, your baby will still get enough nutrition. You'll just lose weight faster.

TRUTH: If you diet strenuously, your baby will not get enough nutrition.

Once Nina is born, your breast milk supply will be inadequate if you diet too strenuously. Of course, the "stay-out-of-McDonald's" diet is fine. The Slim-Fast diet is not; Nina will be forced to slim down while her mom is slimming. So eat enough, drink plenty, and eat the right stuff.

• ***Lose the booze; no drugs.*** As we mentioned in the section on drugs in the first chapter, what you ingest, your baby ingests. Although an occasional glass of wine or a beer with dinner is now "legal," a drunken mom makes a drunken baby. Also, take *no drugs*, even legal ones, other than acetaminophen (Tylenol) and vitamins, without consulting your pediatrician.

HOW YOUR BREASTS MAKE MILK: WHAT'S HAPPENING IN THERE?

During pregnancy, the pituitary gland at the base of your brain makes increased amounts of **prolactin,** a hormone that stimulates breast milk production. When nursing, your prolactin level goes up still more. **Oxytocin,** another pituitary hormone that increases during pregnancy and nursing, actually "squeezes" milk out of the milk ducts in your breast, pushing it out through the nipple. Each time you nurse your baby, this squeezing (called "letdown") occurs. Your baby's sucking actually makes your pituitary gland produce more oxytocin. That's why nursing frequently in the first few weeks is so important; the more you nurse, the more your body will make oxytocin, and the easier it will be for Nina to get her breakfast.

MYTH: Small-breasted women make less milk.

TRUTH: Petite moms, fear not. This is one time when bigger is not better. Large breasts don't make any more milk than small breasts.

A NURSING SCHEDULE

Feed Nina when she's hungry. Sound simple? You feed yourself when you're hungry, so why not do the same for her? Of course, it's doubtful that she's going to tell you she's hungry, since all she can say is "Whaaa, whaaa, whaaa," which can mean "hi" or "I'm wet" or even "I want out of this crib already." It can also mean "Feed me!"

You'll be surprised how soon you'll be able to discern the different meanings of little Nina's cries, but here's one bit of advice. If she cries for a few seconds and quickly stops on her own, she's probably not too hungry. If she cries but stops when you change her, she probably wasn't too hungry either, just wet. If she cries but stops with a hug and a few gentle rocks, she probably wasn't starving, but just wanted a minute of mom time. On the other hand, if she cries and doesn't stop with a diaper change or a hug, she's saying, *"Feed me, Seymour!"*

Notice that the amount of time between feedings hasn't come into play. Babies are notoriously bad at telling time. Some babies, especially in the first few weeks, will want to be fed every hour or two. Others may hold out for two or three hours. Still others wait almost four full hours before turning on their sirens. Don't get too hung up on the clock, especially in the first few weeks. Just accept the fact that Nina will be hungry a lot, and remember, not every little peep will be the lunch whistle. So if you've just nursed for a while and you're called back to service, take your time getting there, check for a wet diaper or a "load," give a hug and a rock or two, and you may put Nina back to sleep without another feeding.

Oh, one little exception about the clock. If Nina is one of those sleepyheads who would rather snooze than do anything else (you lucky parent), don't let her go more than four hours between daytime feedings. If you do, she might reverse her days and nights. That is, she'll think that daytime is sleep time and nighttime is stay-up-and-party time. If you'd eventually like to sleep at night, consider waking Nina after four hours of daytime sleep.

NURSING POSITIONS

Roll up your sleeves, wash your hands, and jump right in. You'll be surprised how quickly you'll get the hang of nursing. Don't expect Nina to feed like a vulture right away, however. She's going to be a real sleepyhead for a few days. Actually, babies, most of whom prefer sleep to food, usually lose weight in the first week of life, and that's fine. In fact, a 7-pound baby may lose 8 to 12 ounces before she starts to bulk up.

As far as the nursing position to use, here are some of the more popular (and comfortable) positions, courtesy of the National Women's Health Information Center (www.4woman.gov).

The cradle position. Many moms choose this very common position, most comfortable in an old easy chair or rocker. Put a pillow under the baby's butt to raise her to the level of your breast, and cradle her in the crook of your arm.

The football position. Other moms prefer the football position, where you put the baby under your arm, like a football player running for a touchdown. The football position is a comfortable and effective placement for moms with large breasts or inverted nipples.

The cross cradle position. Many moms prefer the cross cradle position, right arm holding baby to left breast and vice versa. This position gives baby extra head support. It's great for premies and babies with a weak suck or with trouble latching on.

The side lying position. In this position, you and baby lie on your sides, facing each other, with a pillow supporting both your backs. This is a good way to let Mom rest while baby nurses. It's also great if you've had a cesarean section, since baby is not putting pressure on your belly.

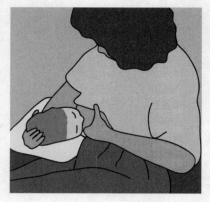

The slide-over position. In this position, a good one to encourage a baby to nurse on the less preferred breast, the baby lies behind you, usually on a pillow, and extends forward to your breast.

As long as you are comfortable and the baby is close enough so that she doesn't pull your breast away from you while she nurses, then you should be fine. If you're nursing in a sitting position, try to keep your back fairly straight. This way you won't get back pain or neck pain, and your nipples will be pointing straight out, making it easier for Nina to latch on. The straight-backed chair usually works well, but if you prefer a couch or easy chair, then prop your back up with a pillow or two to make you more erect. Try to put Nina in a position so that her head and body are both facing the same way. You don't want her twisted like a pretzel to get her milk. After the first few days you and your baby will become really "portable," nursing in a variety of positions and places. This portability will help you adapt nursing to your own lifestyle.

BRINGING BABY TO THE BREAST: HOW TO BREAST-FEED

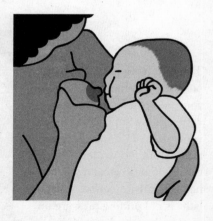

Now that you've settled into a comfortable position, offer the baby your nipple. Do this by gently touching your nipple, as well as some of the surrounding areola (the colored area around the nipple), to her lower lip. It's important to give the baby some areola as well as nipple, since the areola contains ducts that store the milk. Place your thumb above the areola, and your index finger under it.

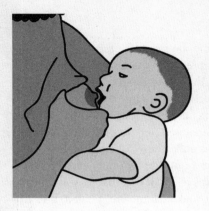

You don't have to force your nipple into the baby's mouth. Magically, babies root for the nipple. Rooting is a reflex that allows babies to find their milk suppliers despite really poor vision. Just gently touch the baby's lip or even the corner of her mouth with your nipple, and she will turn her mouth toward the nipple to feed.

When she opens her mouth, gently place your nipple and some areola into her mouth. Her face should line up with your face, and her belly should line up with your belly. Once she's opened her mouth and turned toward the nipple, move her face onto your breast so that your nipple and some of your areola enter her mouth.

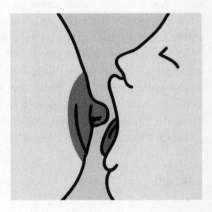

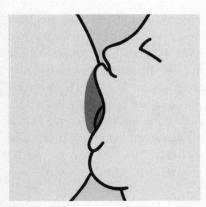

You will quickly feel the soon-to-be-familiar sensation of your baby's jaws working away. See how *both* the nipple and some areola go in the baby's mouth. The baby's lips will be turned out, not tucked in.

HOW LONG TO NURSE

As far as how long to nurse at a time, be flexible. Start in the hospital with three or four minutes on each breast. By the time you come home from the hospital, you can feed for five to ten minutes a side, and up to ten to fifteen minutes on each breast by the end of the first week. In some cases you may notice that Nina only feeds for a few minutes on the second breast. That's because she's pooped out. To give each breast an equal workout and to ensure a good milk supply, alternate the side you start on. That is, if you start on your right side for one feeding, start on the left side for the next. Some moms feel that their babies want to feed forever. Sorry, Nina. This will just make Mom sore, chafed, and irritated. Most of what babies drink comes in the first fifteen to twenty minutes. After that, you're just being used as a human pacifier. So don't feel guilty about setting limits on feedings.

When you switch from one breast to the other midway through your feeding, you may find that little Nina isn't ready to take a time-out and is still clutching you. To break the seal of her mouth on your breast, simply put your index finger in the corner of her mouth. That will relieve the pressure and give you a chance to switch sides. Before you move on to side two, take a quick break for a burp.

BURPING

Burping is pretty easy. As with nursing, there are several different positions that you can use. Turn Nina toward you, with her head over your shoulder, in an upright position. If you prefer, lay her facedown across your lap. Or else sit her up on your lap, with one hand supporting her back and your other hand under her jaw supporting her chin. Once you've chosen a comfortable position, gently pat her lower back several times. Eventually, you will hear the unmistakable sound of a burp. This sound may be accompanied by a little milk, but don't worry. This is quite normal. Don't wear that nice silk blouse while nursing. In fact, put it in storage until your baby's second birthday.

MYTH: If your baby doesn't burp, she'll spit up everything you gave her.
TRUTH: How long are you supposed to wait?!?

Don't become a burp-a-holic. If your baby doesn't burp after five minutes, try another position. If there's still no luck, forget it. The worst that will happen is that she'll be a little gassy until she finally burps on her own later on. Or else she'll spit up a bit after her feeding. It may seem as though a gallon of milk is pouring out, and you've wasted a whole feeding, but relax. A lot of that spit-up consists of stomach juices. Miraculously, even babies who are lousy burpers and great spitters manage to gain weight beautifully. After you've finished your second side, attempt to burp again. Even though you'll soon be putting Nina back to bed, don't be a marathon burper. Give it a few minutes, try another position, and then forget it.

WHEN TO STOP NURSING

The choice is yours. As long as you're enjoying it, keep it up. If you no longer enjoy it, stop. Some mothers nurse past the first year. Others nurse for a few months. Either is fine. Remember, the early milk, called colostrum, is great at fighting serious newborn illnesses. So even if you try nursing in the hospital, keep it up for a few weeks, and then decide that it's not for you, that's okay. The only thing that will *guarantee* an unsuccessful nursing experience is a new mom who feels coerced into nursing. Feel guilty about weaning? Depressed? Afraid you and Nina will miss that special relationship you've developed? Give Nina a little extra cuddling and a few extra kisses. Remember that weaning is a natural step in the separation process. Separation is tough, but it's a necessary part of your child's maturation.

BREAST-FEEDING STYLES

Nina may be a real gung-ho nurser who can't wait to get at that breast and chow down. On the other hand, her best friend, Sandy, might be more of a dainty eater, satisfied with five minutes on one side and barely a sip on the other. Just as every baby is different, each will develop her own style of nursing. Miraculously, both babies will eventually get more than enough milk to grow.

Years ago researchers at Yale University developed names for five common breast-feeding patterns. As related in the American Academy of Pediatrics' excellent publication *A Woman's Guide to Breastfeeding*, these patterns can be summarized as follows:

• *Barracudas* get right down to business. As soon as they're put to the breast, they grasp the areola and suck energetically for ten to twenty minutes.

• *Excited ineffectives* become frantic at the sight of the breast. In a frenzied cycle they grasp it, lose it, and start screaming in frustration. They must be calmed down several times during each feeding. The key to nourishing this type of baby is to feed her as soon as she wakes up, before she gets desperately hungry.

• *Procrastinators* are newborns who can't be bothered with nursing for the first few days until the milk comes in. As long as the reward is just colostrum, they're not interested. Continue to put them to the breast regularly, whenever they appear alert or make mouthing movements. Also, you can use a pump between feedings to stimulate milk production. Just don't give up.

• *Gourmets or mouthers* insist on playing with the nipple, tasting the milk first and smacking their lips before digging in. If hurried or prodded they become furious and scream in protest. The best solution is tolerance. After a few minutes of playing, they settle down and nurse well.

• *Resters* prefer to nurse for a few minutes, rest a few minutes, and resume nursing. Some fall asleep on the breast, nap for half an hour or so, and then wake ready for dessert. This pattern can be confusing, but resters cannot be hurried. The solution? Schedule extra time for feedings and remain flexible.

BACK TO WORK

If it's time to go back to work, you can still nurse your baby. Here are some ways working moms continue their breast-feeding:

- Ask for an extension on your maternity leave (Got a nice boss?).
- If you have child care facilities at work, nurse on your lunch break.
- Of course, if working at home is an option, even for part of the week, this is a great alternative.
- Can you work part time for a while, before returning full time?
- Nurse when you are with your baby. When you are at work, have the baby bottle-fed (expressed milk or formula). Then nurse when you're back home. This will work best if your breasts get stimulation by pumping while you're at work. All you need for this is a small fridge to store the pumped breast milk.

THE LACTATION CONSULTANT

A good lactation consultant is often worth her weight in gold. We refer mothers to some wonderful women who are well trained and who have helped many moms continue to nurse when they would otherwise have been discouraged. The lactation consultant is a trained expert in nursing, but not all consultants are equally trained. To find a qualified nursing expert, make sure that she is credentialed from the International Board of Lactation Consultant Examiners (IBLCE). Lactation consultants provide:

- Preparation for breast-feeding while you are pregnant
- Advice about nursing positions and techniques
- Suggestions to relieve engorgement and lessen nursing pain
- Dietary advice

- Pumping techniques
- Advice for special nursing issues, such as nursing twins and premies

PUMPING YOUR BREASTS TO EXPRESS BREAST MILK

Pumping milk, to feed later in a bottle, is a handy option for nursing mothers. It comes in particularly handy if Dad wants to feed (give him the 2 a.m. shift). Also, working mothers find this is a great way to continue to supply their babies with breast milk after they've gone back to work. Even as a break, to prevent that feeling of being tied down, a bottle of breast milk can be a welcome relief.

Before you begin, wash your hands and then try to fool your breasts into thinking that the baby is there. Gently massage all around the areola and nipple from the outside toward the nipple. The idea is to start that letdown reflex working. Do this for several seconds, all around the circumference of the areola.

Some women prefer to pump by hand. It's a quiet, inexpensive way to pump and doesn't require any special equipment. If you're using only your hand, without a pump, place your thumb above your nipple and your index and middle fingers below. As you press in toward your ribs, gently roll your thumb and fingers together toward the nipple. After a while, little drops, squirts, or even a stream will be produced.

Other moms prefer breast pumps, which can be hand-operated or electric.

- Most **hand pumps** have a funnel that attaches directly to the breast. The other end of the funnel is attached to two concentric cylinders. When you slide the outside cylinder up and down over the inside one, a suction develops, much like that of a nursing infant. This suction causes milk to be released from your nipple and flow into the collecting end of the pump. Other hand pumps have a handle that you squeeze to make suction. In either case, once the milk has been collected, either attach a special nipple and feed directly from the pump, transfer the milk to a regular bottle for feeding, or else store the milk in a collecting container. The pump can then be cleaned in a dishwasher or with hot soapy water and a good rinse.

• **Electric pumps** cost more but are more effective in pumping milk. A mom who does most of her feeding with pumped breast milk, rather than nursing directly, will often choose the electric pump.

Once you've pumped, put your expressed milk in a plastic container or bottle that has been cleaned in the dishwasher (if you don't have a dishwasher, you will need to sterilize the container by boiling) and re- frigerate it. If you don't use the milk within the next forty-eight hours, then freeze it and it will stay good for at least one month (three to six months if kept at 0 degrees). When you're ready to feed, defrost the milk in the fridge (note that milk thawed in the fridge must be used within twenty-four hours), take the chill off by placing it in a pot of warm water, and you're ready to go. As with formula feeding (discussed later), you're better off discarding any leftover milk rather than reusing it. This keeps the bacterial count down and ensures that Nina is getting fresh milk.

WEANING

You can wean first to a bottle and then later to a cup, or, if your baby is old enough (usually at least 7 to 8 months), you can wean directly to a cup.

Either way, try to wean gradually. If you're nursing six times daily, cut down to five times for a few days, substituting a bottle or cup for a nurs- ing. Then cut down to four nursings a day for a few days, with the other two feedings as bottles (cups). After a few more days, you can cut down to three and three. Keep up this process until, after a couple of weeks, you're down to one nursing, which you can give at any time during the day. If you'd like, keep up a once-daily nursing, assuming you still have some milk supply.

NURSING WHILE YOU'RE SICK

It's okay to nurse with diarrhea, a sore throat, a headache, bronchitis, or almost any illness. The infections that your baby will catch from you are caught by breathing on the baby, not by nursing. Furthermore, most infections are transmitted at the beginning of an illness, before you've even figured out that you're really sick! Notice that I said you can nurse with *almost* any infection. If you have HIV, nursing is not a good idea as it appears that this virus is transmitted through breast milk. If you're not sure if your illness warrants holding off on nursing, ask your pediatrician for help. Again, very few illnesses will preclude nursing.

In fact, for most bacteria and viruses, nursing will actually help protect your baby by passing on antibodies. Remember, helping your baby fight infections is one of the reasons you chose to nurse. This advantage is especially important in the first few months of life, when little Nina has not yet figured out how to make her own antibodies. So nurse away and feel good about it, too.

WHEN TO STOP NURSING

There's really only one reason to stop nursing: you have decided that you no longer want to breast-feed. As long as you are enjoying nursing, keep it up. Many moms nurse for a few months, supplement a bit for another month or two, then switch to bottle-feeding. Other moms nurse exclusively for eight or nine months and wean directly to a cup. A few moms nurse for over a year. The choice of when to stop nursing, like the choice of whether or not to nurse at all, is yours.

KIDFIXER FREQUENTLY ASKED QUESTIONS

Q: I just began nursing. Why doesn't my breast milk look like milk?
A: That yellow sticky stuff is called **colostrum,** and it's completely normal. Colostrum has loads of chemicals, called antibodies, that help

fight infection. Don't worry when you see this "witches' milk." It's normal, as are you, and it will soon be replaced by good old grade A breast milk.

Q: *What do I do about leaky breasts?*

A: This is quite common and in no way a defect. Your new breasts have what's called a letdown reflex. When your baby sucks at the breast, the letdown reflex makes your breasts pump out more milk. Obviously this is a pretty handy thing. Unfortunately, letdown is not too specific and can react to stimuli other than your baby's sucking. For instance, you can leak milk just from hearing your baby cry, from accidentally touching your breasts, or even for no apparent reason at all. If you're uncomfortable or embarrassed by leaking, consider wearing a breast pad.

Q: *Can you suggest something to relieve my sore nipples?*

A: Relief is on the way! First, make sure you are offering Nina the areola and not just the nipple. Next, when socially possible, try to expose your nipples to air, which will prevent them from becoming chafed. Next, try changing position, and see if that doesn't relieve some discomfort. Try nursing on the less sore nipple first. That way Nina may be a little gentler by the time she gets around to the sore nipple. Avoid plastic breast shields or plastic-lined nursing pads, which can hold in moisture and breed bacteria. After you nurse, gently pat your nipples dry and dab on some of your own breast milk as a natural "lotion." Finally, use only warm water, not soap, when washing your breasts.

If your breast looks very inflamed and feels hot, you may have a breast inflammation called **mastitis.** This does not mean that you have to stop nursing, but a trip to your obstetrician is a good idea. If there is an infection, then you may even need an antibiotic. Mastitis is a common condition in nursing moms and is easily treated and quickly resolved.

Q: *The act of nursing itself hurts. Help!*

A: Change your position. Your breast may be getting "stretched" because the baby is too far away. Or else she may have her nose pressed up against your breast because she is too close. If nursing is painful, stop for a minute or two, rearrange yourself and your baby, and start again.

Q: *How can I know that my baby, Inez, is getting enough milk?*

A: If you're not producing enough milk, you'll be seeing lots of dry diapers. No kidding. Babies who aren't fed enough fluids will hoard their own body fluids to prevent dehydration. So if you see four or five wet diapers a day, relax. Also, most pediatricians see newborns for an office visit in the baby's first week. At this time you two can weigh Inez and put your heads together to make absolutely certain that she's getting plenty of breast milk.

Q: *My breasts are very swollen and feel too full. Am I doing something wrong?*

A: This is breast engorgement, and a little engorgement is normal, as long as you're not feeling pain. After all, you've got two very efficient milk factories working overtime. If your breasts are *painfully* engorged:

- Express a little milk before you put the baby on the breast.
- Try changing your position. If you are sitting, lie down. If you're in a rocker, try a more erect position in a straight chair.
- More frequent feeding may help, even every one to two hours for a while.
- If the swelling is mild, try a warm compress. For *severe* engorgement, you might find relief by using ice packs between feedings.
- Make sure you're using a support bra.
- Don't make the mistake of feeding less often if your breasts are engorged. This will only make the swelling worse.
- Don't stop nursing just because you're engorged. This is not a sign that you're doing something wrong. On the contrary, it means you're a super milk maker. Engorgement is a temporary condition that most moms will have, especially in the first few weeks. It will pass. Again, this is something you can expect and shouldn't be alarmed about.
- If you develop a fever, or if one breast looks very angry and red, you may have mastitis, as discussed above, and you should give your obstetrician a call.

Q: Can I nurse my premie?

A: Sure. Breast milk is especially valuable to premies. Unfortunately, if your baby is very premature, you may not have access to her as often as you'd like. In that case you may want to pump your breasts. The pumped breast milk can then be fed to her by the nurses, or else it can be frozen for later use at home. At the very least, pumping will stimulate further milk production.

Q: What about twins? Can I nurse them?

A: Yes and yes. If you've got twins, or even triplets, you will still be able to nurse. Some mothers use a double football hold and feed both babies at the same time. Others nurse one at a time. Whichever way you decide to do it, you should be fine as long as you get plenty of calories and plenty of water into your diet. Nursing twins or triplets may very well require some supplementation. Again, if you need to supplement with formula, do so without guilt. Your little multiples are better off getting some of their nutrition from breast milk than they would be getting none.

Q: I'm nursing and my baby looks yellow. What's going on?

A: This is jaundice, and it's expected. Some babies will appear yellow or jaundiced in the first few weeks of life. Jaundice is much more common with nursed babies, since breast milk contains a substance that slows the breakdown of bilirubin. If your baby seems particularly yellow to you, let your pediatrician have a look. Some jaundiced newborns have too high a level of bilirubin and require treatment.

Q: I'm nursing and want to supplement, but my daughter won't take a bottle. Help!

A: Sometimes babies grow to love the breast so much that they want absolutely nothing to do with a bottle. **To encourage a nursed baby to take a supplemental bottle, try the following:**
- Have someone else feed the baby (Dad, a friend, Grandma).
- Wrap your daughter in a piece of your nightgown (with your smell) while feeding.
- Offer the bottle before she is very hungry.

- Try laying the bottle nipple near her mouth and allow the rooting reflex to take over.
- Warm the bottle and nipple to body temperature.
- Experiment with different feeding positions.
- Offer the bottle while moving (rocking, walking, or swaying).
- Try experimenting with other nipples, such as a juice nipple, or with other bottles.

Despite all these attempts, some nursed babies simply like to nurse and want no part of a bottle. Such babies will eventually learn to take a supplemental bottle, but usually will only do this when they are very hungry. It may take skipping a feeding or two to get such a baby desperate enough to accept a bottle. If it seems a bit cruel, don't fret. She will not be in any danger if she misses a feeding or two. The great majority of the time, this is all it will take for a baby to accept a bottle.

Q: What do I do about my inverted nipples?

A: Don't worry, you can still nurse. Remember, your baby takes not only the nipple but some of the breast in her mouth as well, so inverted nipples are not necessarily a problem. If you express a bit of milk onto your breast before beginning your nursing, your baby should get the idea that sucking will get results. Also, if only one nipple is inverted (or even if you have had a mastectomy and only have one breast available for nursing), you can do just fine using only one breast to nurse. If all else fails, you can express your milk and feed that in a bottle. Expressing your milk may only be necessary for the first week. When your baby becomes more expert at sucking, try again to nurse and you may find that the results are better. Finally, keep in mind that many moms who have had inverted nipples no longer have this minor problem when their breasts get larger during pregnancy and nursing.

Q: I have a lot of breast milk frozen for future use. Would it be more beneficial for me to give it all to my son over a few days until it is all used up, or would he benefit more by getting only one bottle of breast milk a day over a period of a few weeks so that he gets some of the antibodies over an extended period of time?

A: The sooner you use it, the better it is. Although frozen breast milk is safe to use for even a few months, it does lose some of its infection-fighting capability with time. Also, as a baby gets older, his own immune defenses build up and breast milk, although always a good choice, is less vital. The most important time to supply breast milk to a newborn is the first few months. So use it now, rather than meting it out over a period of time.

Q: *My 11-week-old son, Chuck, has recently started to reject breast-feeding. When I put him to my breast he will suck for maybe five minutes and then pull off and cry every time I try to get him back on. I've had to then give him a bottle. He does take the bottle but he doesn't seem aggressively hungry. Why is this happening?*

A: There are lots of reasons why Chuck may be feeding for a shorter period of time. Some babies just become more efficient at nursing after a couple of months of practice. They can drink in five minutes as much as they used to take in fifteen or twenty. Certainly, if Chuck is lasting three hours between feedings, he's getting enough to be satisfied. If you find that he's still urinating at least four or five times a day, then that's further evidence that he's getting enough.

Two other reasons for shorter feeding should also be considered. Some babies resist nursing when they have what is called gastroesophageal reflux. In reflux, acid backs up into the esophagus and causes heartburn. In this case, Chuck would be fussing with feeds. He may also spit up more. Finally, babies with thrush, a mild fungal condition of the tongue and mouth, also fuss when being nursed. For peace of mind, bring Chuck into the office for a visit.

Q: *How long is breast milk safe to use if left outside the fridge? How long will it stay fresh in the fridge?*

A: Assuming that it's not a very hot day (a room temperature of 77 degrees or less), you can still use the milk if it's been out for less than four hours. If it's warmer than this, keep it to no more than two hours. Breast milk stays fresh in the fridge for three days, unless it's been frozen previously, in which case it's good for one day after being defrosted.

Q: What's the best way to defrost frozen breast milk?

A: Simply put the frozen milk in the fridge. It will defrost in about twelve hours. Remember to swirl the breast milk before using it, since the fat will tend to separate.

Q: I am returning to work, but only for a few hours a day. I'd like to pump my breasts but will probably only be doing this a few times a week. What would be the best breast pump for me?

A: Either a hand-operated or a small battery-operated pump would be ideal. Medela makes some good hand-powered breast pumps, as does Hollister. Medela also makes an excellent battery-operated pump.

Q: Is it safe to have an occasional alcoholic drink when I'm nursing?

A: One glass of wine, one beer, or one mixed drink would be fine, especially if you nurse right before you drink. In this way there will be more time for the alcohol to leave your system before you nurse again. If you plan to do any more drinking than that, use pumped breast milk for the next few feedings.

6

BOTTLE-FEEDING

Whether you've decided to exclusively bottle-feed your baby or you're using a bottle to supplement breast-feeding, you'll need some guidance. First, a few words about sterilizing.

STERILIZING THE BOTTLES

MYTH: You must sterilize your baby's bottles.
TRUTH: Your baby's mouth isn't sterile, so there's no need to sterilize what you put into it.

Even breasts aren't sterile. Of course it's not as simple as that. After all, breast milk is served up fresh at every meal, with no storage and no re-frigeration. Nevertheless, I'm always amused to see a mother sterilize a bottle, but when the baby's pacifier falls out of his mouth onto the floor, Mom will pick it up, "wash" it by putting it in her *own* mouth, and then pop it back in baby's unsuspecting mouth. Now, what's the thinking behind this? I hate to disillusion a parent who obviously feels she's risking her own health for her baby, but there are an awful lot more germs in Mom's mouth than on the floor.

In any case, cleaning bottles and nipples in the dishwasher will do just fine, and no, you don't have to use a separate load for the bottles. It's perfectly okay to wash the baby's bottle along with that crusty lasagna pan. If you don't have a dishwasher, and you live in an area where the water is clean, you'll do just fine with good clean hot water, plenty of dish-washing liquid, and a very thorough rinse.

PREPARING A BOTTLE

If you're preparing your daily supply of formula in the morning, pour the ready-to-pour formula into enough clean bottles for the day and put them in the fridge. If you're using concentrated formula, which has to be mixed with water, it's a good idea to use water that has been boiled, although bottled water is also fine. Mix this water with the concentrated formula, as the directions indicate, and, if you boiled the water, then let the mixed formula cool slightly before putting on the nipple and putting it in the fridge.

When you hear Felipe cry, take out a bottle, loosen the nipple, and warm the bottle back to room temperature in a small pot with a few inches of water. If you decide to warm the bottle in a microwave oven, heat it thirty seconds for 4 ounces, forty-five seconds for 8 ounces, and thoroughly swirl or shake the formula. In either case, always test the temperature carefully by dropping a bit of formula onto the sensitive inner part of your forearm. The bottle may be cool on the outside while the formula is scalding hot on the inside. Each year hundreds of babies get bad burns in their mouths and throats from feeding with scalding for-mula.

HOW MUCH DO I FEED?

MYTH: You must give a specified num-ber of ounces at each feeding.
TRUTH: Put away that calculator; let your baby's appetite determine how much he'll take.

New parents really get into counting things—number of ounces the baby drinks, number of poops the baby makes, number of spoonfuls of baby bananas he eats. My wife and I counted all these things, too. Only we were even sillier. We would seek out other parents so that we could *brag* about our son's formula totals. And, unless my memory fails me, I could swear that we bragged about poops, too! How competitive can you get?

Counting ounces is silly because babies are just like real people— they have hungry days and not-so-hungry days. The infant who downs 20 ounces one day may very well drink only 15 ounces the next. Also, some babies will have bigger appetites than others and will gain weight at different rates. Finally, as your baby gets older, his appetite may change. The sipper at two months may become the guzzler at four months. We count these things because measuring and counting give us a sense of security. It's only natural. But if you must quantify these amounts, keep it to yourself. I'm sure nobody cared how many poops my kids had or how many ounces of formula they drank. Nevertheless, here's a *rough* guide. Start off in the hospital with only ½ ounce. After a day, increase to an ounce or two. Don't worry if Felipe seems to be dieting. Don't forget that this drinking business is new to him, and he may take a few days to catch on.

By the time you come home from the hospital, the best way to determine how much formula to give is to make sure there's a little left at the end of the bottle. When your baby is regularly downing three ounces, go up to four. When he's drinking all four, go up to five. Unless he's having watery diarrhea or is vomiting everything you give him, this "keeping a little ahead" method will serve you well and will ensure that Felipe is not hungry and still looking to drink more. His own hunger will determine how much he drinks. Another way to ensure that he's getting enough is to make sure you see several wet diapers each day. Most babies who are taking in enough formula will urinate at least four to five times daily. Of course, when you visit your pediatrician, you'll have a weight to guide you further.

HOW OFTEN DO I FEED?

MYTH: Feed every four hours.
TRUTH: Babies can't tell time. Listen to your baby; he'll tell you when he's hungry.

As with breast-feeding, don't stare at the clock to determine when it's time to feed. For details about scheduling, read "a nursing schedule" in Chapter five.

HOW TO BOTTLE-FEED

It's 8:00 in the morning, and little Felipe has just gotten up for the day (you should be so lucky). You've got your nice bottle of formula in one hand and a hungry baby in your lap. First, make sure that the nipple hole is big enough to allow the formula to flow freely. Turn the bottle upside down and make sure the formula runs out at a rate of about a drop a second. As silly as you may feel timing this, it's actually important. A slow bottle will make Felipe work too hard to drink. He'll suck and suck and most of what he'll get will be air instead of formula. Then, when he burps or passes gas, he'll quickly be hungry again. You'll find that you're feeding every hour and that he's only taking an ounce or two at a time. So make sure the formula runs out fast enough. It's *much* better to have a sloppy guzzler who chugs his bottle than a neat sipper who works like crazy to get an ounce and then is exhausted from the effort.

If the formula is coming too slowly, try loosening the plastic collar around the neck of the bottle. If that doesn't speed things up, try **enlarging the nipple hole.** Take a large sewing needle and sterilize it in a flame (don't burn your fingers the way I always did; hold the needle in a cork to save yourself from blisters). While the needle is still red hot, poke it into the nipple right next to the nipple hole. This will either widen the existing hole or else create a second hole right next to the first. In either case, more formula will come out. Keep in mind that some babies are better suckers than others. Your child may be slow even with two or three new nipple holes. If this is the case, experiment with different-sized nipples, such as a premie nipple or a juice nipple, and see how they work for you. Whatever it takes to get Felipe to drink easily is fine.

Another way to determine if the formula is flowing easily enough is to time how long a feeding takes. Even with burping, your baby should be able to down 4 or 5 ounces in about twenty to twenty-five minutes. By the time he gets up to an 8-ounce bottle, he'll be older and more skilled at feeding, so even this much formula should go down in about the same time. If you find yourself taking forty-five minutes to an hour to feed a bottle, speed things up.

Now that we've made sure the formula is flowing quickly enough, tilt the baby back at about a 45-degree slant, put the nipple into his mouth and watch him do the rest. It's important to avoid feeding your baby while he's flat, since this can predispose him to ear infections. At first, he may have no idea what he's supposed to do. Soon, however, he'll get the hang of it. Remember, babies suck as a reflex. They do it even while they're inside the uterus, sometimes sucking on their fingers and toes (you may notice a sucking callus on your newborn's top lip). So don't worry, he'll soon remember what he's supposed to do.

Sometimes, when you're really going great with a feeding, there's a temptation not to stop to burp. Stop anyway, or you'll end up losing some of that formula as your baby spits up all over you (for details about burping, see Chapter 5). Most bottle-fed babies need to be burped every ounce for the first few days. After that, try to burp after every 2 ounces. Soon—and this will vary—most babies will get by with one burp in the middle of a bottle and one at the end.

Let's say you've fed Felipe his bottle and he's conked out after 3 ounces, leaving an ounce or two at the bottom of the bottle. You think, "Hey, this stuff is pretty expensive. Maybe I can use it again for the next feeding." As

tempting as this is, unless you're really strapped financially, you're better off discarding the rest of that feeding and starting with a fresh bottle next time. Felipe's germs will contaminate the rest of the bottle, and these germs will multiply, even in the fridge, as you wait for the next feeding. For similar reasons of hygiene, it's not a great idea to leave formula out of the fridge too long before feeding (of course, this doesn't apply to twist-and-feed bottles or to powdered formula that hasn't been reconstituted). In cool weather, you're probably safe for four hours; in hot weather, try not to keep the formula out of the fridge for more than two hours.

THE BOTTLE

Thanks to some very good marketers, there are enough baby bottles out there to make your baby's head spin and to deplete your finances if you try them all. Here are the different types:

• *Standard straight bottles.* These good old glass reusable bottles are dishwasher-safe and have straight necks and bodies.

• *Angled-neck bottles.* Feeding upright helps prevent gas, reduces vomiting, and may even reduce a baby's chances of getting ear infections. Angled-neck bottles claim to allow you to feed your baby upright while still keeping the nipple full of formula and relatively free of air. At least that's the theory. You can, of course, just tilt a standard bottle to achieve the same result.

• *Disposable bottles.* Inside these hard plastic bottles are disposable sterile plastic bags. After you use these, you toss out the bags. Although they claim to reduce gas, I've never known them to be any better than traditional bottles.

THE NIPPLE

Like bottles, there are enough choices to keep a new parent busy. Also, as is the case with bottles, the differences are very slight.

• *Traditional, bell-shaped nipples.* The gold standard for nipples, these come in all sizes and in one-hole, multiple-hole, and cross-cut-hole types. The ideal nipple is big enough so that your baby won't have to suck too hard.

• *Orthodontic nipples.* Orthodontic nipples are shaped a bit more like an actual mother's nipple and are marketed as the best nipple for supplementing a breast-fed infant. If you are trying to supplement and your baby refuses a bottle, try an orthodontic nipple.

• *Latex nipples.* These are longer so that milk can be dropped right on the back of baby's tongue. Pediatricians aren't too crazy about latex, however, since early exposure to latex can cause a baby to develop latex allergy.

• *Silicone nipples.* These are made of tough silicone, so they last longer when washed in a dishwasher. Of course, they tend to cost more, so the dishwasher advantage is a . . . wash?

• *Specialty bottle-nipple systems.* Such popular bottle-nipple systems as the Dr. Brown bottle and the Avent bottle claim to reduce gas, and thus colic. To date, no good controlled studies have shown these products to be significantly better than any other bottle and nipple. Is it worth a shot, in the very fussy infant, to try one of these special bottles? Sure.

THE PACKAGING

Regardless of which formula you use, there are a number of ways in which formula is sold.

• You can buy *ready-to-pour formula,* where the formula needs only to be poured into a clean bottle and "served." With these, you first clean bottles and nipples, open a quart can of formula, and divide the formula into the number of bottles you'll need for the day. Keep the bottles in the fridge until your baby starts hollering; then take the chill off the formula in a pot of hot water and feed.

• There is also **concentrated formula,** which must be mixed with boiled or bottled water, usually in equal parts of formula to water.

• **Powdered formula,** where the formula is packaged in a powdered form, and must be dissolved in water, is a convenient choice for people on the go; carry some powder and bottled water and you've got an instant meal.

• Finally, there is **twist-and-feed formula.** With this packaging the formula is already in a sterile bottle, topped by a sterile nipple covered with plastic. Twist off the plastic and *voilà*—dinner is served. Obviously, twist-and-feeds are the easiest bottles to use, but as you might guess, they're expensive.

Which type of packaging you choose is up to you and your bank balance, but if someone really wants to get you a great present, tell him to forget the Britney Spears leotard and buy a few cases of twist-and-feed formula. Even if you only use them for those middle-of-the-night half-asleep-eyes-not-focused-gotta-get-up-in-two-hours feedings, they can be a real luxury.

THE FORMULA

This is great stuff!

Infant formula tastes like the sweet milk left in the bottom of the cereal bowl after you finished your frosted flakes. However, don't let that sweetness fool you; most formulas have the same number of calories as cow's milk (20 calories per ounce). Breast milk, by the way, also has the same number of calories and is just as sweet as formula. Your pediatrician will suggest which formula to use to start. One word of advice: Whether you start with Enfamil, Similac, Carnation, Isomil, Prosobee, or any of the numerous formulas on the market, **don't buy too much.** You may have to change formulas, either because the baby develops an intolerance to the formula, or because some illness necessitates a temporary switch. In either case, you can get stuck with a lot of expensive formula if you buy more than a few cases to start.

There are several different types of infant formula:

• *Cow's milk formulas.* Since the 1920s most infant formulas have been made from cow's milk. Such formulas as Similac and Enfamil are a first choice for most doctors because they have stood the test of time and they are close to breast milk in composition, with approximately 43 percent of calories as carbohydrate, 50 percent as fat, and 7 percent as protein. The carbohydrate used, as in breast milk, is lactose (milk sugar), the fat is vegetable oil, and the protein source is mostly casein (breast milk protein is a mixture of a little casein and a lot of whey). Although cow's milk formulas are available with and without iron supplementation, most pediatricians recommend iron-fortified formulas.

MYTH: The iron in iron-fortified formulas will make a baby gassy and constipated.
TRUTH: Gas and constipation are not usually caused by the iron in formulas.

The iron in infant formulas is in such small quantities and of such a nature that it seldom causes any upset tummies. Leaving the iron out of Felipe's formula will predispose him to iron deficiency anemia, and that's not a good thing for his developing brain.

• *Special cow's milk formulas.* With the goal of making cow's milk formula more like breast milk, formula makers have come up with specialized formulas that are a bit closer in composition to mother's own milk. For example, some formulas (Enfamil Lipil and Similac Advance are two brands) now supplement their products with **arachidonic acid** (ARA) and **docosahexaenoic acid** (DHA), two fatty acids that are believed, in a small way, to contribute to the health and neurologic development of babies.

ARA can be found in lean meat, egg yolks, and some fish oils. DHA occurs in oily fish, such as herring, salmon, and mackerel, and to a lesser extent in lean meat. Moms who nurse pass their own DHA and ARA along to their babies, but most infant formulas have little or no ARA or DHA. Some research studies seem to show that extra ARA and DHA help premies gain weight more quickly and perhaps help babies' neurologic development. Whether the short-term benefits seen in such studies will be permanent is still open to debate.

• *Soy formulas* such as Prosobee, Nursoy, and Isomil substitute soy protein for cow's milk protein. Although soy protein is almost as allergenic as cow's milk protein, it's a good first choice for babies who cannot tolerate cow's milk, since it's relatively inexpensive. Soy formulas are also lactose-free.

• *Lactose-free cow's-milk-based formulas,* such as Lactofree, treat feeding difficulties caused by lactose intolerance—rarely seen in babies. These formulas are similar to the usual cow's milk formulas, such as Enfamil and Similac but substitute corn syrup for lactose.

• *Hydrolysate formulas* break down (hydrolyze) formula protein into smaller, easier-to-digest and less allergenic proteins. Such **casein hydrolysate formulas** as Alimentum, Nutramigen, and Pregestamil, such **whey hydrolysate formulas** as Good Start, and such **amino acid formulas** as Neocate are good choices for babies with definite cow's milk intolerance. Unfortunately, they're expensive. Also, Good Start contains lactose and can't be used to treat lactose intolerance.

• *Premature formulas* such as Neosure have more calories, more protein, and more calcium and phosphorus than regular formulas, all of which help premies catch up in size more quickly.

FORMULA INTOLERANCE: DON'T PLAY FORMULA ROULETTE

Babies, especially very young ones, can often be fussy. Because babies spend much of their time feeding, it is not surprising that parents believe that formula intolerance is a source of the fussiness. The baby who has the typical fussy period or "witching hours" every night from 7 to 10 but who is happy and peppy all day probably does not have a formula intolerance. The infant who gulps down a 6-ounce bottle in no time flat and who is growing beautifully but who occasionally spits up or has a few loose stools similarly needs no change in formula. On the other hand, a baby who is gaining poorly and who has frequent loose bloody stools or vomits every feeding may be, after a visit to the pediatrician, a good candidate for a formula change.

All of the abovementioned special formulas exist because a small percentage of babies are intolerant of cow's milk formula. Most babies will do just fine on the formulas they start. They gain weight well, don't spit up too much, make soft bowel movements a few times a day, and aren't terribly gassy. That's about all a baby can ask of a formula. It's not too exciting, but it's all a baby needs. Remember, however, that I said not to buy too much formula in case you have to change. Obviously there must be some times when things don't work out so smoothly. There must be times when it *is* necessary to change from one type of formula to another.

There are all kinds of myths about switching formulas:

MYTH: Change formula if your baby spits up.
TRUTH: Don't do it. Spitting up can be normal.

MYTH: Change formula if your baby has loose stools.
TRUTH: Don't do it. Some babies have looser stools than others.

MYTH: Change formula if your baby has frequent stools.
TRUTH: Don't do it. Many babies have seven or eight bowel movements each day.

MYTH: Change formula if your baby is passing a lot of gas.
TRUTH: Don't do it. Passing gas is a *good* sign.

MYTH: Change formula if your baby cries like crazy from 5 to 7 p.m. every night.
TRUTH: Don't do it. This is fussy period, not formula intolerance.

MYTH: Change formula if your baby has a rash.
TRUTH: Don't do it. There are all kinds of reasons for rashes.

Some spitting up is normal. Even if Felipe spits up more than you think he should, there can be other reasons besides formula intolerance for his spitting. Don't switch for this reason. If he has four or five loose movements a day and they're not really watery, such a pattern can be fine. Babies have what's known as a **gastro-colic reflex.** When you stretch their stomachs by feeding them, they often move their bowels. If you feed your baby six or seven times a day, then he may have six or seven bowel movements. As long as they're not completely watery, such a bowel pattern is fine.

As far as passing gas, good for him! If he *can't* pass the gas, then you have a problem. As long as he's farting, he's happy. Just don't let him accompany you to a black-tie cocktail party.

Crying from 5 to 7, or from 3 to 5, or from 9 to midnight is a normal fussy time or witching hour. It's annoying as can be, and you may feel like putting him up for adoption, but don't change his formula. It won't help.

As far as rashes, all babies get rashes. They get eczema and seborrhea, contact rashes from things that irritate them, diaper rashes, even little pimples on their cheeks called baby acne. If a rash is the only sign of a possible formula problem, it will have to be a bad generalized rash, not just a few spots around the mouth, and not just a diaper rash. Rashes from formula intolerance are, for the most part, *extensive* and *severe*. So if your baby has a little eczema on the legs, this is probably not due to his formula. If he has eczema all over the body and it's red and angry-looking, it may be. If Felipe has one small, pale hive on one cheek, don't change formulas for that. If he has bright red hives all over, then consider that the formula may be the culprit. Again, we're looking for *extensive* and *severe*.

Changing formulas too quickly—doctors call this "formula roulette"— is a common problem for new parents. If you change formulas with each spit-up, each loose movement, or each rash, you'll quickly run out of formulas, and little Felipe will soon be drinking nothing but water.

Okay, so we know not to overreact to common problems by quickly changing formulas every time something comes up. How about some reasons to consider a formula change? Notice first that I use the term *consider*. Even if you strongly suspect a problem with formula, the wisest course is to speak to your pediatrician first, before you change. If the two of you put your heads together over the phone, you may decide that other steps, less drastic than a formula change, should be tried first. He may ask you to come in to the office so he can look at a rash and examine the baby. Even if no visit is deemed necessary and his advice is given over the phone, you will still benefit from his experience. He may suggest a larger nipple, for example, if your baby is too gassy. Or your description of the baby's stools may not seem quite so bad to him as it does to you. Even if you both decide to make a change, you'll need his help in deciding what special formula to choose. There are plenty of choices.

So when we talk about possible reasons to change formula, what we really mean is reasons to consult your pediatrician about possibly changing formula. **Consider changing formulas if your baby:**

• *Is vomiting practically every feeding.* Not only may this be a sign of formula intolerance, as we will discuss in the section on vomiting, but it can be a sign of other, more serious problems.

• *Has frequent,* **watery stools.** Poops vary, not only from baby to baby but from week to week. Nevertheless, persistent, frequent watery stools deserve at least a phone call, if not a visit. As with vomiting, diarrhea can be a sign of formula intolerance or other, more serious problems.

• *Has blood in his stools.* Although a slight streak of blood in a baby's stool can be normal, just from straining or from the irritation of all those moist stools, if there is more than just a slight streak of blood, or if the blood occurs frequently, call the doctor.

• *Seems gassy or fussy all day, every day.* Remember, a fussy period is normal. A fussy *life* is not. Some babies are kvetchier than others, but a baby who seems truly uncomfortable *all day* deserves a visit to the doctor. Again, there are many reasons why a baby may cry all day.

• *Is covered in rashes.* Remember, we're looking for a rash that is severe and extensive.

One last word about formula intolerance. There are lots of different types of formula intolerance, some short-lived and mild, others chronic and severe. A baby may have:

• *Cow's milk protein allergy.* Remember, most formulas are based on cow's milk. This is a long-lasting protein allergy, though not always a lifelong one. Some babies do outgrow protein allergies, but not quickly. If your doctor determines that Felipe has a true protein allergy, he may have to avoid *all* dairy products for months or even years. Fortunately, true milk protein allergy is not very common.

• *Temporary lactose intolerance.* After a severe stomach virus, some babies become intolerant to lactose. Such babies will have a more protracted course of vomiting and diarrhea than others with the same bug. In this case, your doctor may suggest a temporary switch to a lactose-free formula. In a week or two, Felipe will be right back on his old formula.

• *Familial lactose intolerance.* People with this condition can usually tolerate some dairy, splashing a little milk on cereal or a bit of cheese on pizza, but when they try to drink a whole glass of milk, they become gassy and crampy. Although familial lactose intolerance can show up at any time, from childhood to adulthood, it is rarely a major problem in babies.

As you can see, the decision to change formulas is not always an easy one. The most important things to remember, however, are these:

• *Don't overreact* to normal baby problems by quickly changing formulas every time your baby burps, or else you'll be playing formula roulette and quickly run out of choices.

• *Ask your pediatrician for help.* Yes Grandma and your best friend are helpful, but some particularly dramatic "life experience" that they may have had with formula may not apply to you and your baby. They may have been "born again" by a switch to soy formula, but that doesn't mean soy will be your baby's "holy water." Every baby is different.

KIDFIXER FREQUENTLY ASKED QUESTIONS

Q: My baby spits up a little, one or two feedings a day. What can I do?

A: Do nothing. Just stay away from fancy shirts. As we've said, there are all kinds of reasons why a baby will spit up, most of them minor. As long as it's only once or twice, he's relatively comfortable most of the day, and he's gaining well, ignore mild vomiting.

Q: I had a problem with cow's milk formula as a baby. Should I start my baby off with soy?

A: No. Although you had that problem, your milk intolerance may not be passed down to your baby. Also, soy formulas are just about as allergenic as cow's milk formulas, so starting with soy is no guarantee that your baby will have smooth sailing.

Q: What's in soy formula besides soy?

A: Instead of cow's milk protein, soy formulas use soybeans as a protein source. Instead of lactose, they use cornstarch, tapioca starch, or sucrose as a source of carbohydrate. The fat is mostly vegetable oil.

Q: When can we stop burping our bottle-fed 5-month-old twins? It often seems that we're spending an eternity coaxing a burp that only annoys them when it finally wakes them up as they're dropping off to sleep.

A: You now have my official dispensation to stop burping the twins. The worst-case scenario is that they may spit up a bit more, but by 5 months, let them burp on their own.

Q: *At what point should I be trying to phase out the bottle and give my 10-month-old daughter formula in a cup?*

A: As far as the bottle is concerned, as long as she is not refusing all of her solids, then it's fine to allow her to enjoy her bottle until 15 to 18 months of age. If she regularly refuses all solids, then you might want to get rid of the bottle earlier.

7

A CHANGING DIET

We pediatricians are just as excited as parents when it comes to starting solid foods. We know that it's fun (if a bit messy) to see an infant react to that first teaspoon of cereal with a mixture of wonder and enjoyment. Just one question: What's the rush?

WHEN TO FEED SOLIDS

Two common myths regarding feeding solids to infants that should be addressed and dispelled stat are:

MYTH: Babies need to start cereal to help them sleep through the night.
TRUTH: Sleep patterns are usually unaffected by the introduction of solids.

MYTH: Earlier feeding prevents iron deficiency.
TRUTH: Iron deficiency is not a major concern until 5 or 6 months of age.

These two myths were largely responsible for the old practice of starting babies on solids at 2 to 3 months of age. We now know that most babies do quite well when fed nothing but breast milk or formula for the first 5 or even 6 months of life. Many parents assume that a 3-month-old baby awakening from sleep is doing so because he's hungry. This is rarely the case. Most of the time you can get that 3-month-old back to sleep with a brief pat on the back and a soothing tone. If you offer him the breast or bottle, he may only take an ounce before he's back in dreamland—hardly an indication that he awoke because he was hungry. If eating cereal really did make us sleepy, we adults wouldn't need sleeping pills, just Cheerios. If you're starting cereal to help little Sammy sleep through the night, forget it. It just doesn't work. Sammy will sleep through the night when he's ready, and that additional cereal won't make a difference.

Developing iron deficiency anemia in the first 6 months is rare in full-term infants, and certainly not so big an issue that supplemental iron, in the form of solid food, is required. Premies frequently do require extra iron in the first few months of life, but their sensitive digestive systems do better with iron drops than with cereal.

Thus it was that the American Academy of Pediatrics, the group of pediatricians who help us set general guidelines on child care, decided, appropriately, to recommend starting solids later on. If you have a baby who is doing fine on only breast or bottle, they suggested, hang in there until age 5 or 6 months, a recommendation with which I heartily agree. Finally, delaying solids may help prevent food allergy.

On the other hand, consider this myth:

MYTH: You should *never* start solids until at least 5 months.
TRUTH: The correct time to begin feeding solids is not written in stone.

If a mother tells me that her 4½-month-old is drinking 40 ounces of formula a day and can't wait even three hours to eat, I have no problem starting solids a bit earlier. Guidelines are just that, not commandments. A little flexibility goes a long way toward making your baby's life, and yours, a lot easier.

I remember one older mother who was in the office with her fourth child, a vigorous, hungry 4-month-old. When I told her she shouldn't feed her child solids for another month, she asked me why. I told her that we now know that late feeding is better for kids.

"Dr. Altman," she said, "when I had my first child, you told me to start solids at 2 months. When I gave birth to my second, you said we now know that 3 months is the perfect time to start solids. When my third child was born, you insisted that I hold off until 4 months. Now you tell me that 5 months is the time to start. Are you getting smarter with each child, or could it be that this is not such an exact science after all?"

I looked at her kids, ages three through seven, each one as robust and healthy as can be, and knew that recommendations not only change with the times but should be flexible as well.

Only a stodgy, conservative doctor will blindly follow every suggestion from an advisory board in every case. A good pediatrician will incorporate such guidelines into his decisions. There's as much to learn from patients and parents as there is from academies.

All that aside, most babies will do fine on a "liquid diet" for the first 5 or 6 months of life. Speak to your pediatrician about when to start introducing solids to your child.

WHAT TO FEED

Just as with the decision about when to feed, the choice of what to feed is not chiseled in stone. There are many good regimens for the introduction of solid foods; as always, discuss your baby's schedule with your doctor. The following guide is only a sample. Remember, though, very few babies adhere to schedules of any kind. First of all, they can't read. Second, they are all different, with different needs. Third, your scheduling needs are different as well. With that in mind, here's a sample schedule for starting solid food:

5 months: cereal
6 months: fruit
7 months: veggies

8 months: meats, combination ("junior") dinners
9–12 months: *slowly* start soft table foods

Cereal

Most babies begin their solids with cereal because it's a good source of iron, and by 5 or 6 months many babies will need a little extra iron, even if they've been breast-fed or given a formula with added iron. Another reason to start with cereal is that for the first few days little Sammy will have absolutely *no idea* what he's supposed to do with that strange food you keep shoveling into his mouth. When he spits it back at you, at least you'll be wearing a neutral shade of cereal on your clothes all day rather than a loud pea green or berry red.

To start, mix a teaspoon or two of dry infant rice cereal (if your baby tends to be constipated, start with baby oatmeal) with enough formula or breast milk to make a thin paste. Then, using a baby spoon, ladle a little of the mixture into his mouth. Scrape it off the spoon against Sammy's palate, so that he's less likely to spit it right back at you. At first, this will still come out as fast as it went in. Eventually, even the most finicky eater will get the idea and keep some in. Gradually thicken the mixture until it's the consistency of regular oatmeal and, if he actually seems to like it, begin to slowly increase the amount. As with all baby foods, there is no set amount to feed. When little Sammy slows down, and no longer seems interested, stop. This may happen after two teaspoons or five tablespoons. Don't get too hung up on amounts. He may eat like a pig one day and like a bird the next. Allow him to have his hungry days and his not-interested days. Miraculously, he'll gain just the right amount so that he'll look cute in his baby pictures.

After you've given rice cereal for a few days, move on to oatmeal, barley, and even the "exotic" mixed cereals. Don't move too fast, however.

If you try more than one new food at a time, and Sammy gets hives or diarrhea or he vomits, you'll have a hard time pinpointing the cause of the reaction. To be on the safe side, **wait at least three or four days between each new food tried.**

As far as what time of the day to feed, most parents find it convenient to feed once in the morning, around a normal breakfast time, and again in the evening, before bed. Don't be a slave to this type of schedule, however. If you're a working mom or dad and you'd like to feed solids at lunch and dinner, or just once a day before you go to work, such a schedule is fine, too.

It also makes no difference whether you feed cereal before or after the bottle or breast. Most people will try solids beforehand, since babies are more likely to be hungry, and therefore more receptive, before they've guzzled their 6 to 8 ounces. On the other hand, if your baby is so hungry that he seems intent on having nothing but his bottle, it's also fine to give a few ounces of bottle (or one breast) first, then the solids, and then finish up his bottle (or give the second breast). Any way that seems convenient to you is fine.

Fruits

MYTH: Feed veggies before fruit or your baby will develop a sweet tooth.
TRUTH: Everyone has a sweet tooth. There's no avoiding it.

Everybody likes fruits better than veggies, and it doesn't matter which one we started first. So, forget about having your baby grow up as a vegeholic. He may or may not like vegetables when he's older, but starting vegetables a month before versus a month after fruits will have nothing to do with it.

Psychologists have developed a cool little experiment that you and your child can try when he's a bit older. Put a plate down in front of him with, let's say, a few peas, a potato, a mashed cheeseburger and some chocolate mousse. Then walk away. When you come back later, if you haven't annoyed him by begging him to eat his veggies or meat, he'll actually have eaten a little of everything. Maybe not each day, but hypothetically, at the end of the week, or month, he will have eaten equal amounts of burger, peas, potato, and mousse. The lesson here is that, left to their own appetites and developing tastes, babies will usually sample all types of foods.

In any case, back to fruits. Most babies do well starting with applesauce or pears, or even a mashed, slightly overripe banana. Start slowly, with only a spoonful or two at a time. Gradually, your baby may work his way up to a full small jar at a feeding. As with the cereal, offer fruits at breakfast and dinner, although feel free to adjust your baby's schedule to meet your own needs. It also makes no difference whether you feed all the cereal, then the fruit, move back and forth, or mix it all together into a stew. It all looks the same on the inside.

Make your way through all the fruits, sampling each for a few days before trying another. Some babies will get slightly looser bowel movements with fruit, especially fruits with pits such as peaches, apricots, and cherries. If your baby's stools become watery, cut down on the amount or avoid such fruits. Here's a sample schedule that may help you organize your day:

8 a.m.:	cereal and fruit
	bottle or breast
12 noon:	bottle or breast
4 p.m.:	bottle or breast
6 to 8 p.m.:	cereal and fruit
	bottle or breast
12 midnight:	bottle or breast
4 a.m.:*	bottle or breast

*Many babies will have given up this feeding by now.

Vegetables

When starting veggies, most pediatricians begin with the yellow varieties (carrots, squash, and sweet potatoes), because they're more easily digested. Try a new veggie every three to four days. Once again, amounts are not important, but many babies will go through a small jar of vegetables at a meal.

MYTH: If your baby looks yellow when he eats veggies, stop giving yellow veggies.

TRUTH: There's no need to stop. This yellow coloring is not harmful.

After a few weeks of eating veggies, you may notice that Sammy looks a little yellow, especially around his nose, ears, and the palms of his hands. Don't worry; this is not jaundice but simply an accumulation of natural vegetable color in the baby's skin. This temporary bronzing, called **carotenemia,** will eventually fade. Giving yellow vegetables less often and green ones more often will hasten its disappearance, but really there's no need to do this, as the coloring is harmless.

A sample schedule at about 7 months may now look something like this:

8 a.m.:	cereal and fruit bottle or breast
12 noon:	vegetable and fruit bottle or breast
3 to 4 p.m.:	bottle or breast
6 to 8 p.m.:	cereal and fruit bottle or breast
10 p.m. to 12 midnight:*	bottle or breast

*Many babies will have given up this feeding by now.

Meats

When I think back to feeding strained meats to my kids, I could almost become a vegetarian. The smell of infant meats is absolutely repellent. I remember my wife and I throwing out about a half dozen jars of baby meats before we realized that they weren't rotten — that's just the way infant meats smell. We also tried to "dress up" infant meats with a little creative seasoning, such as a dash of oregano or a smidgen of garlic. Of course, after getting this astronaut paste spit at us a few hundred times, we just spooned it right out of the jar. Despite all attempts at disguise, few babies love infant meats. Just tell yourself, as we did, that it's cold pâté from Sunday brunch at the Plaza, and maybe you'll be able to stomach it.

When you do finally get up the nerve to serve this glop to Sammy, start with chicken or turkey. Eventually move on to lamb and beef. Give a little to begin, and gradually work your way up to a half jar or so at a meal.

By the time you're up to meats, many babies will tolerate so-called stage two or junior foods, which, although a bit thicker, are basically the same foods you've tried all along. Junior dinners are combinations of meats, vegetables and sometimes fruits, all in the same jar. Thus, you can now offer the delicious-sounding "turkey-rice dinner" or "beef and pasta supreme." Some babies find these mixed dinners at least marginally more palatable than the single foods, but often the only "supreme" quality about them is their price.

Of course, there is an alternative to the strained meats and mixed dinners: make your own baby food. Although most parents stick to jarred foods, for convenience, the unpleasant meat experience compels many to try their hands at **homemade baby food.** Here's how to do it.

Cook up your special gourmet chicken or turkey or the family secret pot roast. Some spice is fine, but try to do without salt. Purée the meat, along with some cooked veggies, through a food mill or processor. Divide the puree into the sections of an ice cube tray and freeze. When you're ready to serve this homemade feast, just defrost, warm, and serve one, two, or three "cubes" of food.

If your homemade delicacies fail to win Sammy over, don't be disappointed. In a couple of months your little connoisseur will be sharing little pieces of your very own hamburger or turkey dinner. So if he's declared himself a temporary vegetarian, that's perfectly all right. Remember, he'll get plenty of protein and enough iron from his breast milk or formula and from his cereal.

Here's another sample schedule that incorporates the foods your baby may be eating at about 8 months of age:

8 a.m.:	cereal and fruit
	bottle or breast
Noon:	meat, vegetable, and fruit
	bottle or breast
3 p.m.:	bottle or breast
6 p.m.:	cereal and fruit
	bottle or breast

Table Food

By the eighth or ninth month many babies will have tried a bit of table food. This usually begins rather informally. While eating your favorite frozen yogurt, you touch the tip of the spoon to Sammy's lips. Before you know it, he's eaten half the cup. Or maybe you're at a diner and Sam seems to be eyeing Dad's burger and fries with a look of profound jealousy. You break off a piece of french fry and, miraculously, he gobbles it down.

In most cases, such a casual introduction to table foods is fine; common sense will probably prevent you from stuffing Sammy with a whole cheeseburger. However, here are a few general rules to consider as you start the gradual **transition to table foods** and away from strained foods:

• *Go slowly.* While most babies can handle some table food by 8 or 9 months of age, keep in mind one important point: **baby food is health food,** with rarely any preservatives, much salt, or any unnecessary chemicals. Also, you don't have to worry about Sammy choking on his jarred peaches or mushy banana. Finally, don't think your boredom with the same strained foods means that Sam is bored. He's doing just fine. Changing from baby food to table food is *not* a developmental task, like sitting or crawling. Yes, eventually you will have to try solid foods, but what's the rush? Once we chew up *our* food and it makes its way through the stomach, all food is baby food.

• *Feed carefully.* Watch your baby closely when trying new foods. There's no risk-free way to predict whether or not Sam will be able to gum Cheerios or bread safely. Give small pieces to start and sit with him while he eats. If you see him gag on a piece of bread, hold off for a few weeks and try again. Stay away from some of the more notorious **choking foods.** Each year, in hospitals all across the country, the following dangerous foods have to be fished out of babies' throats:

> Hot dogs
> Nuts
> Popcorn
> Hard pieces of meat
> Hard raw vegetables
> Grapes
> Hard candies

FOOD ALLERGY

Food allergy in babies is relatively common, occurring in approximately 5 percent of all children. Heredity plays a big part. If his parents have allergies, a child is much more likely to be allergic — although not necessarily to the same allergens. Allergic reactions to foods can start anywhere from minutes to hours after eating the allergenic food. A child who is only mildly allergic may get just a few hives anywhere on the body. Serious allergic reactions (called **anaphylaxis**) can lead to vomiting, diarrhea, swollen lips and tongue, wheezing, and a generalized rash. In some severe cases, future ingestion of the offending food can be very dangerous. Fortunately these reactions are rare.

A food allergy is the result of your body's immune system overreacting to food proteins called allergens. Normally, our immune system keeps us healthy by fighting off infections and by neutralizing any adverse response to a troublesome food. In children with food allergies, the immune system goes bonkers and produces too much of an antibody called IgE. When IgE is overproduced, it causes the release of histamines and other chemicals that result in rashes, swelling, and wheezing, as well as intestinal symptoms. If your baby does show signs of an allergic reaction to food, call your doctor right away.

MYTH: If a child has eaten a food with no problem, he can't become allergic to it.

TRUTH: Food allergy can be caused by foods that were previously eaten with no problem.

Food allergy occurs most often in children, but it can appear at any age. *A child may have no reaction to a food several times, and then develop an allergic reaction later on.* For example, your child might get away with eating shrimp for years and all of a sudden have a bad reaction to it. In fact, being exposed to a food frequently may even make a child *more* likely to become allergic to it.

Foods that are **most allergenic** for a child include:

Peanuts and peanut butter (reactions to these are the *worst*)
Eggs
Cow's milk
Soy
Wheat
Other nuts
Fish and shellfish

The friendly peanut (including peanut butter), because of its particularly potent allergen, is best avoided, along with all peanut products, until your child is at least two years of age. Obviously, any food may prove allergenic to your baby. If your child has experienced an obvious reaction, such as hives, stay away. Some food allergies can be outgrown, but there are enough foods out there to try without testing your baby's tolerance too quickly. If you're not sure about your child's reaction to a particular food, blood tests can confirm the existence of a food allergy.

Also, avoid giving your baby **honey** in the first year of life. Although not particularly allergenic, honey may contain spores that develop into the germ that causes botulism. Foods cooked with honey are fine, but avoid plain raw honey right out of the jar.

With these warnings in mind, let's discuss a few **good table foods to try:**

• *Pasta* is a great way to begin. Pastina, a tiny pasta star cooked like spaghetti, is a perfect starter pasta. Although he will probably like this just as is, you can mix in a bit of butter or margarine or some soft cheese (such as cottage cheese or ricotta). Your baby may be able to gum larger noodles as well, but remember to watch as he eats. If he seems to gag or spits out the pasta unchanged, he's not ready.

• *Cooked veggies* are another good choice. Steam, bake, boil, or microwave some carrots (make these very mushy), squash, or potatoes. If you microwave, remember to mix the food up well and check for temperature before you serve, to avoid burns. Also, try all the green veggies. Remember to allow a few days in between new offerings.

• *Shredded cooked meats* may be the first meats your baby will like, especially if you mix them with vegetables or noodles. Tiny pieces of chicken (without the skin) are usually well accepted, and if you make the world's best chicken soup (no, my mother does), now is a good time to try this. Chill it overnight first, to strain off the fat. Then mash up the chicken into little shreds and moisten it with a little broth. If you've added carrots, mash them well and offer these, too. As far as seasonings go, use modest amounts, but stay away from salt. The same goes for your prize-winning stew; if it lends itself to mashing, don't be afraid to let little Sam try some.

• *Soft mashed fruits* are also appropriate to try now. They're healthier than fruit juice, and you can offer all kinds, in cooked as well as uncooked form.

• *Fish* (but not shellfish, which you should avoid until after your baby's first birthday) is a healthy, high-protein choice. Carefully deboned flounder, sole, salmon, or most any flaky fish will do. Because of their mercury content, limit shark, mackerel, swordfish, and tilefish to no more than about 7 ounces per week. For other types of fish, including tuna, the FDA has advised that consumption be kept below 12 ounces per week.

• *Tofu* is another good source of protein. Offer this, seasoned and mashed, in place of meat. If you're a vegetarian and have discovered textured vegetable protein (TVP), seitan, or tempeh, let your baby try these as well.

• *Bread* and bread products are popular toddler foods, and now is a good time to introduce that all-American institution, the sandwich. Just break a grilled cheese sandwich or even a little pizza into tiny pieces. By a year of age or so, you will have turned your baby into the same fast-food freak that you are.

• As far as **snack items** go, soft cookies, such as arrowroot or graham crackers, and Cheerios are baby favorites. Biter biscuits are also okay, because they tend to form little messy grains as they're eaten, rather than breaking off in big chunks. Again, watch carefully as your baby tries a cookie or biscuit. If he gags, forget it for a few weeks and try again.

While the occasional snack is inevitable, keep in mind that nobody really *needs* snacks. They tend to fill babies up, making them less hungry for dinner, and even the healthier snacks tend to be less healthy than meals. Further, when offered as rewards for good behavior, snacks send the wrong message to kids. Eating should be something that a child does because he's hungry, not because he's a good boy. If you want to reward your child, do it with *real* hugs and kisses, not the Hershey kind. Nevertheless, some children will get hungry between meals. If a child has eaten his lunch, for example, and seems hungry, a healthy snack, such as a cracker or a half banana, is fine. Just try to avoid snacks within an hour or two of mealtime.

• *Eggs.* Another nonessential food that many doctors will introduce in the first year of life, eggs are a good source of protein. Unfortunately, they're also a really good source of cholesterol. Although we don't get too worried about cholesterol intake at this age, there's no reason to push it. Eggs are also very allergenic, especially the white part, or albumen. For this reason, most pediatricians start off with the yolk, even though it contains all the cholesterol, before introducing the whole egg, usually at a year of age. Hardboil an egg, mash up the yolk, and mix it with the baby's cereal and fruit at breakfast. Or separate the yolk first and scramble it. Either way, limit your baby's intake of eggs to no more than three per week, and if little Sam spits them right back at you, he's telling you to hold off for a while.

JUICE

MYTH: Juice is a good source of nutrition.

TRUTH: Fruit, yes. Fruit juice, no.

Juice is not a very important part of a baby's diet. Because it contains a lot of fruit sugars, too much juice is a frequent cause of diarrhea in babies. Also, a baby who is filled up on juice will not eat as much of his healthier foods at mealtime. Recently it has even been suggested that babies who drink lots of juice may grow up to become chubby, short kids. So keep juice to a maximum of 6 ounces daily, and avoid the trap of using a juice bottle as a pacifier for a noisy baby.

Nevertheless, with juice it's a good time to introduce a cup. Although there are all types of sippy cups on the market, it's also okay to start with a 1- or 2-ounce paper cup. Most babies will take weeks to even begin to get the hang of the cup, so don't think your baby is a dud because he prefers his bottle. Start off with an ounce or two of apple or white grape juice, and then move on to orange or any of the other juices, sampling each for the usual few days before moving on to another. Use either strained baby juice or regular juice diluted half and half with water—a cheaper alternative. Start with an ounce, and gradually increase to 4 to 6 ounces once daily. Juice may be given as a midmorning or midafternoon snack, along with a baby biscuit.

WATER

MYTH: Babies need lots of water, especially in warm climates.
TRUTH: Babies do need fluids, but they don't need water.

For the most part, your baby will get plenty of water from formula or breast milk. During an illness your doctor may recommend extra water, since babies use up water when fighting infection. In the first three months it's a good idea either to boil (and then cool, of course) any water you give to your baby or to use bottled water to cut down the risk of infection.

Some mothers use water to stall a baby who always seems to want to drink. If your baby suddenly decides he wants a bottle every hour when he's been content at three-hour intervals for some time, an ounce or two of water may enable him to last another hour. Of course, if the water doesn't satisfy him, it's okay to feed him his formula or nurse him again.

VITAMINS

MYTH: Babies who are breast-fed do not need any supplemental vitamins.
TRUTH: Breast-fed and bottle-fed babies both need extra vitamins.

Vitamins A, C, and D are inadequately supplied by formula or breast milk. For this reason your doctor will usually recommend a vitamin in the first or second month. The most common vitamin used at this time is a drop that consists of these three important vitamins. At 6 months your doctor will prescribe a more complete vitamin supplement, which includes the B vitamins. Your baby's vitamin can be dropped right into his mouth at any time once a day.

Some babies will require additional supplements. Premature babies, for example, often require additional iron, extra vitamins, and high-calorie formula. If your baby has had any special problems while in the hospital, your doctor will prescribe whatever additional supplementation is appropriate.

FLUORIDE

MYTH: Fluoride supplementation will rot a baby's teeth.
TRUTH: Too little fluoride is just as harmful as too much fluoride.

If your water supply is not fluoridated, that 6-month vitamin will also contain fluoride. Even if your water has fluoride, if you're using ready-to-feed formula and don't give the baby any additional water, you will still need to use a fluoride supplement. Much has been written about the perils of overfluoridation. It is true that too much fluoride can stain teeth, but too little fluoride is even worse. In fact, fluoride is necessary to ensure that your baby's teeth and bones are as strong and healthy as possible.

CHANGING FROM FORMULA TO MILK

When you do change over, at 1 year of age, it's a good idea to do so gradually. If you've been using a cow's milk formula, your baby will usually have no problem making the switch. If, on the other hand, you have used a soy formula or one of the more specialized formulas, a change to cow's milk may present a challenge to your baby's sensitive digestive system. In either case, begin making the change on the first day by adding 1 ounce of whole cow's milk to 7 ounces of formula, mixing the two right in the same bottle. The next day, in each bottle, use 2 ounces of milk to every 6 ounces of formula. By the third day, combine 3 ounces of milk and 5 ounces of formula in every bottle. Keep adding another ounce of whole milk to the bottle as you subtract 1 ounce of formula. To summarize:

Day	Ounces of Formula	Ounces of Whole Milk
1	7	1
2	6	2
3	5	3
4	4	4
5	3	5
6	2	6
7	1	7
8	0	8

Most pediatricians will recommend using whole milk from age 1 to 2 years. At age 2, many babies will be changed over to 1 percent or 2 percent milk. Again, this type of decision is an individual one, and some babies, especially the sleeker models, will do better with whole milk for longer than a year.

Expect some change in your baby's bowel movements when you make the change to milk. Stools may be softer or harder. Your baby may spit up a bit more for a while. Of course, if there is significant vomiting or diarrhea, call your pediatrician. Also, try not to make the change to milk, or *any* change in your baby's diet, when he is ill.

To tie this all together and to give you an idea of what a healthy 1-year-old might eat on a good day, here's a sample menu. Please keep in mind that this is only a sample. Rare is the baby who will eat three full meals on any given day. And remember to cut up all these solid foods into bite-sized pieces.

Breakfast:　　Cereal with sliced banana
or
Oatmeal with berries
or
Waffles with peaches
or
French toast with applesauce
or
Muffin and fruit spread
with
Whole milk

Lunch: Sandwich—cream cheese and jelly, tuna, grilled cheese, turkey, chicken, etc.; applesauce

or

Pizza; fruit

or

Salad with turkey, tuna, or cheese; breadsticks; vegetables

or

Fruit yogurt

or

Pasta and vegetables with tomato sauce; fruit

with

Milk

Dinner: Chicken breast or nuggets; baked potato; salad; dessert

or

Hamburger (chicken or veggie burgers are even better); bun; veggies; salad; fruit cup

or

Lentils, tofu, or beans; vegetables; dessert

or

Fish fillet; salad; noodles with margarine; frozen yogurt

with

Milk

Snacks: Once a day, if your child eats his meals and is still hungry, offer a cookie or two, or fruit; try to keep snack time separate from mealtime

You may notice that meat is not essential at every meal. It's not even essential every day. Your baby will get plenty of protein from dairy products, lentils, tofu, and beans. Remember also that your baby, like most of us, will have hungry days and picky days. Just try to make *most* of his choices healthy ones and let him decide how much he wants to eat, if anything, at mealtime. If one day's lunch ends up as a fruit-only meal, don't worry. Tomorrow's lunch may well be a pasta day. The next day may be a veggie day. Miraculously, when you visit the doctor, your baby will probably have gained just the right amount and be in great shape.

THE DINER SYNDROME

A good thing to avoid is what I call the diner syndrome. Don't make your house into the neighborhood diner, and don't make yourself into the neighborhood waitress. When we adults go to the local diner, we tend to have one or two "diner favorites" that we keep coming back to. For some it's the cheeseburger deluxe. For others, it's the large Greek salad, hold the anchovies. Well, kids can get into this habit as well. If little Sammy doesn't want his chicken one night, don't feel you must keep searching for other choices for that meal until you find one he likes. If he isn't hungry for the chicken, it's okay to wrap it up and put it away for later. Then, when he *is* hungry, try the same chicken. When Sam refuses the chicken, don't feel that you must start bringing out everything in the house until you find something on the menu that he likes. If you do, Sammy will quickly catch on and will hold out for his diner favorite— say, pizza bagels. Soon little Sam will want nothing *but* pizza bagels. You've conditioned him so that if he waits long enough, his favorite waitress will bring out his favorite item on the menu. Again, if he's not hungry, it's fine. Put the chicken away for later. And if he should go to bed without dinner (gasp), don't feel guilty. He won't starve. He'll just make up for it the next day.

Of course, allow Sam to have his own likes and dislikes. If he *always* gives you a hard time with chicken and eats *everything* else (not just pizza bagels), then he may really hate chicken. Fine. Stay away from chicken for a few months, and then try it later in a different form. If he hated chicken breast, retry chicken a few months later as chicken nuggets. Remember, tastes change, and Sam may like chicken in the future, especially in another form. Make smart meal choices and stick to them consistently; your little one will soon get the idea that the diner is closed.

KIDFIXER FREQUENTLY ASKED QUESTIONS

Q: *What can I do about my year-old baby? She eats nothing!*

A: The truth is, the amount of food babies need to grow and gain weight is a lot less than most parents would expect. Many babies at 1 year of age will eat only one good meal a day, often breakfast, and just pick at lunch and dinner. Miraculously, they manage to gain weight. This is because the table food you're giving now has a lot more calories than the baby food your child was eating a short time ago. Also, babies are a lot smaller than adults and therefore need only a fraction of what we need each day. Avoid counting your baby's calories. Let her eat as much of your healthy food as she wants, and if she's not hungry one day, that's fine.

Q: *My baby seems to want to feed constantly. What can I do?*

A: Some babies *will* feed more frequently than others, but are you sure your baby is really hungry? Remember, babies can't tell you what's on their minds. They can't say, "I'm hungry," "I'm wet," or "Hey, there's nothing to do by myself. Get over here and entertain me." In all cases, they just cry. Sometimes it's hard to interpret these different cries. After a while parents become pretty good interpreters, but for the first few months, it can be a bit confusing. Don't overrespond to your child's cries with food.

Q: *My 9-month-old daughter, Jessie, is not interested in her formula bottle, and I can't get her to eat any dairy at all. I know she needs calcium, but how much does she need and how can I get it into her?*

A: A child in the first 6 months of life needs approximately 400 mg (milligrams) of calcium daily. Between six months and a year, children need approximately 600 mg of calcium daily. Supplement the diet of your 9-month-old with the calcium-rich foods listed below and little Jessie will get all the calcium she needs. Below are the calcium contents of a variety of foods:

1 cup of milk or formula or breast milk	300 mg
1 cup of white beans	225 mg
½ cup of cooked broccoli	35 mg
1 ounce of cheese	200–250 mg
1 cup of cottage cheese	230 mg
8 ounces of most yogurt	250 mg
½ cup of cooked spinach	120 mg
1 cup of calcium-fortified orange juice	300 mg
½ cup of mashed sweet potatoes	44 mg
1 cup of tofu	300 mg
1 cup of soybeans	130 mg
1 cup of collard greens	360 mg
1 cup of bok choy	250 mg

Q: *I've heard that babies often get iron deficiency anemia and that this can cause learning problems. Is this true? I'm concerned because I'm raising my baby as a vegetarian, and I won't give her meats. What are some good non-meat iron sources?*

A: Iron is a very important mineral. Most of the iron in our bodies finds its way into red blood cells as hemoglobin, which is involved in transporting oxygen to all the tissues of the body, including a developing baby's brain. Although breast milk and formula have a small amount of iron (iron is better absorbed from breast milk than from formula), by 6 months most babies need a little extra boost of iron. Although meats (not just beef, but poultry, pork, and fish, too) are the best source, iron is also provided by non-meat sources. Here are some good **non-meat iron sources** for your baby:

Iron-fortified cereals
Tofu

Pinto beans
Sweet potatoes
Pumpkin
White potatoes
Spinach

Q: *My baby always finishes the jar of veggies we offer. What do I do?*
A: Give some more. Don't be a prisoner to ounces, teaspoons, or other artificial measures. Let your baby's appetite determine how much he will eat. If he finishes his carrots, offer more. If he gobbles up his fruits, open another jar. Feed him until he's full and he stops—or at least until he slows down.

Q: *Our 7-month-old, who has started solids, is drinking much less. How will he get his fluids and nutrition?*
A: Keep in mind that your baby gets plenty of fluids from his solid food. Fruits are 90 percent water and veggies are only a smidge less. And cereal is, of course, mixed with formula. Not getting enough fluid is seldom a problem. When he's thirsty enough, he'll drink. In the meantime, he's getting plenty of nutrition from his solids.

Q: *How do I get my 9-month-old to try table foods? He gags on everything but yogurt.*
A: Remember, your child's tastes are still evolving, and the foods he rejects now will readily be accepted in a few months. Some babies also take a bit longer to appreciate the consistency of solid food, preferring the smoothness of pureed baby foods. Finally, baby food is health food, so the longer he enjoys baby food, the easier your job as chef is.

Q: *My 5-month-old daughter is refusing all cereals. What can I do?*
A: Don't fret. Although your daughter is allowed to try cereal now, it's not really needed for another month or two. At that time, she needs the extra boost of iron from cereal. Until then, the addition of cereal is optional, and she's just saying, "Thanks, Mom, but no thanks." Try again in another week or two. Eventually she'll come around.

Q: *My 9-month-old daughter is a great eater. Can I switch from formula to milk now?*

A: Hold off a while, if you can swing the extra pesos. Even though she is such a great eater, it's best to continue formula for 12 months, since babies who are switched to milk too early can sometimes develop microscopic bleeding in their intestines and iron deficiency. Accordingly, the American Academy of Pediatrics recommends 12 months of formula.

Q: *My son is 9 months old. Is it safe to offer him foods that contain cow's milk?*

A: Although your child shouldn't switch from formula to milk yet, he is welcome to try foods containing dairy now. Cheese, yogurt, frozen yogurt, even ice cream are all okay. Milk as the *main* source of nutrition is still not complete enough for babies at 9 months.

Q: *My 9-month-old daughter had diarrhea with milk-based formula but is fine with soy formula. Can I try dairy products now? Will she have problems with these foods?*

A: Go ahead and try dairy products. First of all, these are usually better tolerated in babies who have had problems with milk formulas than the formula itself. Also, by nine months many babies will have outgrown their cow's milk problems. Offer only a little at a time, in case your baby still has a problem, but do give it a try.

Q: *Everyone says that your baby will tell you when he has had enough, but I don't think my Julius knows when to stop. He appears to have a bottomless pit for a stomach, and I believe he would eat the entire box of rice cereal if I let him. He just won't stop. Help!*

A: Julius's gargantuan appetite seems to belie the old adage that babies will stop when they're full. Some babies just never seem to get filled up. If this is the case with Julius, pay attention to his pace and note when he is slowing down. If he seems to be gobbling a bit more slowly, then stop there.

Q: *We're vegetarians. Will my little Monica miss out by not getting meat?*

A: As long as Monica gets enough total calories (she is gaining well at her checkups) and enough protein, then you're fine. Protein is supplied in all formulas and dairy products as well as breast milk. Monica will also get protein from such foods as tofu, tempeh, and textured vegetable protein.

PART III

LIVING
WITH BABY

The phrase "working mother" is redundant.

— JANE SELLMAN

8

BABY'S
APPEARANCE

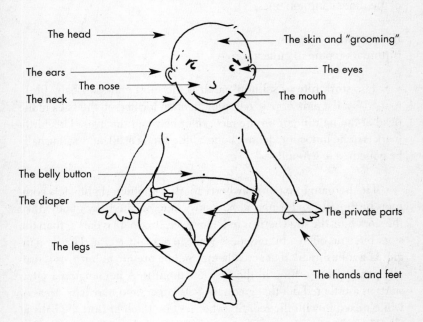

The head

The skin and "grooming"

The ears

The eyes

The nose

The neck

The mouth

The belly button

The diaper

The private parts

The legs

The hands and feet

No doubt about it, babies are strange-looking little creatures. When they're first born, their heads are usually cone-shaped from being squeezed through the birth canal. Noses are swollen from being shoved up against the wall of a uterus for nine months. Legs, also from being crowded into their little nine-month baby motels, are as bowed as Granny's. If that's not enough, babies are frequently born with all kinds of spots, rashes, and blotches.

So now is just about the right time to learn what your "package" consists of. In this chapter we'll take a head-to-toe close-up look at your new baby.

THE SKIN

A newborn's body can be an odd blend of spots, rashes, lumps, bumps, and bulges. Fortunately, the great majority of these are quite normal. Unlike that new DVD player, these aren't defects. Let's examine some of the more common ones.

Birthmarks
Birthmarks come in quite a variety.

• The **stork bite** or **salmon patch** is the most common baby birthmark. It's a flat pink or pale red splotch, often located on the back of the head at the hairline or on the face, right between the eyes. This birthmark is quite innocent, doesn't bother little Linda at all, and will usually be gone in a few months.

• The **hemangioma** or **strawberry mark** is another, slightly less common birthmark, and it may appear anywhere on the baby's body. Like the stork bite, the strawberry is red. However, this mark is darker than the stork bite and often a bit raised, so you can actually feel it. The hemangioma is a birthmark that actually may not be present at birth, as it usually pops up some time in the first few months. A hemangioma often starts as a little red dot that gradually gets larger, and may have areas of white mixed in with the red. Strawberries don't itch or hurt the baby at all. Though some never fade, a general rule is that 50 percent of hemangiomas are gone by age 5, 70 percent disappear by age 7, and 90 percent are gone by the time a child is 9. As you can see, this unwanted stranger can be a bit persistent, but most do fade away in time.
Because of their tendency to disappear naturally most dermatologists recommend leaving strawberries alone. Attempting to remove them surgically can be a bit tricky, since they are made up of thousands of little blood vessels and are more extensive below the skin than they appear on

the surface. Rarely, however, a hemangioma can be located in an unfortunate spot, such as on a baby's tongue or on an eyelid. If so, and if it enlarges greatly (also a rare event), then some attempt at treatment may be in order. Your pediatrician may refer you to a dermatologist or plastic surgeon, who may suggest medical treatment or laser surgery. Once again, the need for such an aggressive approach is quite rare. Hemangiomas are usually small, innocuous, and short-lived.

• The **café au lait** is another type of birthmark that may delay its appearance for weeks or months. For those of you who have forgotten as much high school French as I have, *café au lait* means "coffee with milk," which describes the birthmark's light brown or tan color. Café au laits are flat and can appear anywhere on the body, in any shape or size. Unlike the first two marks, café au laits are usually here to stay. Although permanent, and although they often enlarge a bit, they are rarely seen on the face and won't bother your little one at all.

MYTH: Café au lait spots are a sign of neurofibromatosis ("Elephant Man disease").

TRUTH: Most café au lait marks are just birthmarks and nothing else.

If your baby has several large café au laits, point them out to your doctor, who will test for a hereditary condition called neurofibromatosis, a rare syndrome that may be associated with fibrous lumps under the skin, curvature of the spine, and hearing or visual problems. Once again, the great majority of café au lait spots are just that: spots. Even if your child has several large café au laits, that does not necessarily mean that she has a serious condition.

• The **nevus** (mole) is another common mark, which again may or may not actually be present at birth. Usually small, brown or black, and often resembling a freckle, the nevus can appear anywhere on little Linda's body. It is quite harmless.

MYTH: Moles present at birth should be removed right away. They may be malignant.

TRUTH: Most moles can be left alone.

Moles are usually harmless. A few should be removed at several years of age because they have a slight chance of becoming malignant during adulthood. For example, a nevus that has an irregular shape or border, bleeds, is particularly large or is multicolored might be troublesome later on. Your pediatrician may refer you to a dermatologist, who will either recommend watching the birthmark or else suggest its removal. Remember, the great majority of these birthmarks remain quite innocent.

• **Mongol spots** are especially common in Asian and darker-skinned babies. These bluish or black splotches usually appear on a baby's back or butt and often will be mistaken for bruises by new parents. Relax. These are just temporary birthmarks and will fade some time late in the first year.

Dry Skin

Many babies arrive with dry, wrinkled "old lady" skin. They may even look as if they have some kind of skin disease, with chafing and peeling all over. Such dryness is normal and needs no treatment. Keep in mind that when you spend a lot of time relaxing in a comfortable bath, your skin gets dry and pruney. Multiply that bath time by nine months and you can easily see why Linda looks so dry. Rest assured that her dry skin doesn't bother her at all. She isn't itchy or uncomfortable. The only reason to do anything about such dry skin is for the sake of appearance. When Grandma comes for her first visit and you want to show off just how beautiful Linda can look, then by all means feel free to use a baby lotion to smooth her out. Just keep in mind that you're treating her cosmetically, not medically.

Dyshidrosis

Because the nerves that stimulate your baby's sweat glands are immature, you can expect her skin, especially on the hands and feet, to perspire. Such abnormal perspiration, called dyshidrosis, can make little Linda's skin dry, red, cracked, and even peeling. To avoid this, expose your baby's hands and feet to air by keeping them uncovered (footsie pajamas are notorious for causing dyshidrosis). Your doctor may recommend a moisturizer as well.

Intertrigo

Intertrigo is a red, macerated, often smelly rash found in skin folds under the chin, under the arms, and in the creases of the thighs. It affects zaftig newborns most, since they have lots of hidden areas that get little exposure to air. When skin surfaces rub against each other, the skin becomes inflamed. Sweat, milk and, when it gets into thigh folds, urine and stool can make intertrigo worse. Clean the area frequently, dry it well, and apply zinc oxide. If intertrigo worsens despite zinc oxide, there may be a secondary bacterial or fungal infection present, which your doctor will treat with the appropriate antibiotic or antifungal medication.

Erythema Toxicum

If, during Linda's first two weeks of life, you see tiny white or yellow pimples and red blotches spaced widely over her body, then she probably has erythema toxicum. Despite its ominous name and often disturbing appearance, erythema toxicum disappears, without any treatment, in a few days.

Baby Acne

MYTH: A baby with acne is being washed too often.
TRUTH: Neither overwashing nor underwashing causes baby acne.

Most babies will get baby acne at some time in the first few months. These pimples don't itch, and they aren't a sign that your baby has oily or dry skin. Baby acne disappears, with no treatment, in a few weeks or months. Just as teenagers get acne because of a surge in hormones, your baby can get baby acne because of all those maternal hormones she was exposed to in the uterus.

Milia

Milia are tiny white pimples that may appear on your baby's nose in the first few months. They represent tiny sebaceous cysts, are quite normal, don't bother your baby a bit, and will go away by themselves.

Miliaria Rubra (Heat Rash)

Heat rash consists of tiny red pimples, usually most pronounced on the chest and neck, especially on hot days or when your baby is overdressed. Simply dressing your baby in lighter clothing is all you need to do.

Eczema and Seborrhea

Two common rashes, seen frequently in babies with a family history of allergy, are eczema and seborrhea, mentioned together since they are often similar in appearance and often are present at the same time. Eczema, usually red, dry, scaly and in patches, is seen in babies most commonly on the cheeks, arms, legs, and chin. Seborrhea, yellowish and often greasy-looking or flaky, is most common on the eyebrows and on the scalp, where it's called cradle cap. When mild, these rashes can be left alone. If they seem itchy, though, you can treat them with moisturizers, mild anti-inflammatory ointments or, in the case of cradle cap, with a shampoo prescribed by your doctor.

MYTH: If your baby has eczema or seborrhea, she's allergic to something she's eating.
TRUTH: Not necessarily. These rashes often occur without a specific allergen.

Although eczema and seborrhea are often seen in children with allergies, they aren't always the direct result of a *particular* allergen. Some children just seem to have generally sensitive skin, and they break out in patches of eczema or seborrhea for no apparent reason.

On the other hand, if your baby has *severe* eczema, your pediatrician may suggest trying a different formula or removing certain allergens from your diet if you're nursing. Some babies with eczema seem to get redder and scalier when they're washed a lot, since frequent washing may deplete the protective natural oils in their skin. If your baby has severe eczema, try bathing her less often; every two to three days would be fine.

Hives

Hives (welts) typically occur after a child eats or drinks something to which she is allergic.

MYTH: You can only get a rash from something you are exposed to for the first time.
TRUTH: Your child can *develop* an allergy after several uneventful exposures.

After several innocuous PB&J sandwiches, we can suddenly become allergic to peanut butter. After eating Hershey bars for years we can (heaven forbid) become allergic to chocolate. It's not always the first exposure that causes hives.

Hives can also result from non-food allergies. Some children break out in hives when they are sick with an infection or when they are bitten by an insect. When the body recognizes something as foreign, such as a cold virus or mosquito venom, it releases histamine and other chemicals from skin cells that produce the typical hive, an itchy raised white bump surrounded by a red halo. Single or multiple hives can occur anywhere on the body and can be either large or small.

MYTH: If a parent is allergic to a drug, then a child will probably be allergic as well.
TRUTH: Although allergies "run in families," the specific allergen may differ.

If you have allergies—to foods, to inhalants, to drugs—then your child is somewhat more likely to have allergies as well, but not necessarily to the same foods, inhalants, and drugs.

Common causes of hives include:

• **Drugs.** Any medication can prove to be allergenic to a child, and again, a reaction need not occur on the first exposure. Also keep in mind that some drugs are "cousins" of each other, and if a child is allergic to one, she may be allergic to the other. Two such drug relatives are the antibiotic classes penicillins and cephalosporins. If a child is allergic to a penicillin (this includes amoxicillin and Augmentin), then she is slightly more likely to be allergic to a cephalosporin as well (such as Ceclor, Keflex, and Cefzil).

• **Foods.** Here are some of the foods most likely to cause hives:

Nuts, especially peanuts and peanut butter
Chocolate
Shellfish (including scallops, lobster, shrimp, etc.)
Tomatoes and tomato sauce
Berries (including raspberries, strawberries, and berries in jams and yogurts)
Pork (including bacon and ham)
Artificially colored food (especially red or yellow colors)
Fruits with pits, such as peaches, apricots, cherries
Egg whites (although healthier, they're more allergenic than yolks)
Cow's milk and other dairy products
Citrus fruits
Soy in any form, including tofu

MYTH: If a rash follows a dose of medication, a child is allergic to that medication.
TRUTH: That depends upon the rash.

Here's a very common scenario. A child is taking an antibiotic for an ear infection and, after a few doses, develops a rash of tiny red dots. The rash is not itchy and does not seem to be hives. Your first thought is that it is an allergic rash, but it might also be what doctors call a **viral exanthem.** The viral infection that preceded the ear infection can cause a rash that is unrelated to drugs. As we will see later on in this book, there are many viruses that feature a rash. In roseola, for example, a child can have several days of fever and then, when the fever leaves, will often develop little red spots all over. If that child happened to have been taking an antibiotic, let's say for an ear infection that she had along with her virus, a parent would assume that the rash is an allergic rash, when in fact it's just a part of the virus—a viral exanthem.

Other rashes can be confused with medication allergy as well. In scarlet fever, a strep throat with a rash, a parent might not notice the rash until day two or three of the illness. If by this time the child had been started on an antibiotic, the parent might very well assume that the rash is an allergy to the antibiotic, when in fact it's just a part of the infection. Finally, some antibiotics—amoxicillin most commonly—can cause a non-allergic drug rash. Such rashes aren't hives, don't itch, and aren't a sign of allergy at all. They look pretty bad, since they can cover a child with small red dots, but they're just side-effect rashes, not allergies. Using the same drug in the future may or may not result in a rash.

Contact Dermatitis

This is an allergic rash that usually follows skin contact with an allergic substance (an allergen), either immediately after exposure or, more commonly, in one to three days. Exposure to a contact allergen results in a rash that is itchy, red, raised, scaly, streaky, and occasionally oozing. As is the case with hives, your child may do just fine after several exposures to a contact allergen only to end up with a rash after a later exposure.

Although any child can be allergic to any allergen, some of the more **common skin allergens for children** include:

- Laundry detergents and fabric softeners that go into the dryer
- Perfumed soaps, lotions, shampoos, sunscreens, and skin softeners
- Plants and weeds (poison ivy is the most famous contact allergen)

- Lemons and limes (these cause a brownish "stain" when dribbled from the mouth)
- Latex (from rubber gloves)
- Nickel (an alloy that's mixed into gold jewelry)
- Acrylics, woolens, unwashed new clothing

Contact dermatitis usually responds well to simply eliminating the allergen—change your detergent, soap, etc. If it doesn't respond quickly, your doctor may prescribe a mild anti-inflammatory ointment.

Jaundice

Many babies will look a little yellow in the first week of life. This coloring is called jaundice and is usually brought about by the changeover your baby makes from fetal blood to regular blood. All the baby's fetal red blood cells, which are different from our red cells, must be destroyed and disposed of by the body. A result of this blood breakdown is a waste product called bilirubin, a yellow-colored chemical excreted by your baby's body. Some of the bilirubin is temporarily deposited in the skin and in the whites of the eyes. The result of all this chemistry is that your baby will look a little yellow for the first few days.

Don't be too concerned about jaundice; that yellow coloring is only temporary. As long as your baby is getting plenty of breast milk or formula, the bilirubin will be washed away. There are times, however, when there is too high an accumulation of bilirubin. For example, if your blood type and Linda's blood type differ (you are type O and she is type A, for example), Linda's blood may be broken down too quickly, and there may be more bilirubin than she knows what to do with. If you think your baby looks extremely yellow, call your doctor. He can do a simple blood test to check the level of bilirubin.

One way to get rid of bilirubin is to wash it out of a baby by feeding a bit more often. In some rare cases, a baby's bilirubin will be very high and more serious steps will be needed to eliminate the jaundice. Some babies, for example, need to spend a day or two receiving phototherapy—"sunbathing" under special "bili-lights" at the hospital. Light, especially light of certain wavelengths, can rid the body of bilirubin. In the most extreme cases of newborn jaundice—and these are, thankfully, quite rare—an exchange blood transfusion must be done, in which donor blood is gradually and safely exchanged for your baby's high-bilirubin blood. Again, such steps as phototherapy and exchange trans-fusions are the exceptions. The rule is that newborn jaundice is innocent and harmless.

There are numerous other birthmarks, rashes, and skin conditions, but fortunately these are rare. A good general rule is this: if you see any-thing on your baby, you're not sure what it is, and it doesn't disappear in a day or two, call your pediatrician or point it out to him at your next visit.

GROOMING YOUR BABY

Now that you understand a bit more about your baby's skin, let's see how we can keep her looking bright and shiny. There are a few skills you will need to master. Don't worry, they're a lot easier than programming that DVD player.

Bathing

Until the umbilical cord falls off, keep Linda clean with a sponge bath. Once the cord is gone, you can use a baby tub or, as long as you hold on tight and place a large towel in the bottom for traction, the sink or bath tub.

Assemble all of your bath supplies. You'll need a towel, a washcloth, and some baby soap. If you're using a baby tub, have the water in before you go and get Linda. Once you start the bath, you don't want to have to run back into the next room for supplies. Which brings up another issue:

NEVER LEAVE YOUR BABY ALONE IN THE BATH!

Even a few inches of water can drown your slippery little girl, and ba-bies do drown, most commonly after the first 8 to 9 months, when they can sit by themselves and parents feel confident leaving their infants ei-ther alone in the bath or with an older sibling "in charge." If the phone or the doorbell rings, wrap your baby in a towel and bring her along with you. Better still, let the phone ring. They'll call back. Five-gallon buckets are another notorious site for baby drownings, so keep these out of your house.

Pick out a gentle soap. Baby soap is usually fine, as is a mild hypoallergenic soap such as Dove, Neutrogena, Cetaphil, or Basis. Make sure the water is *comfortably warm*—not too hot and not too cool. Baby skin is a bit more sensitive than our own, so avoid that nice steamy bath that you enjoy. Put 4 or 5 inches of water in the bottom of the tub; that's plenty. Cradle your baby in the crook of your elbow, elevating her head above her body, and lower her body into the water, keeping her head above the water. Try to keep at least some of Linda's body in the water so that she won't feel chilled. If necessary, from time  to time gently splash a little of the tub water on her body to keep her wet and warm. With your free hand, put a little soap on a wet washcloth and wash her all over. For her hair, use either the same soap that you use on her body, or baby shampoo. When she is all soaped up, rinse the washcloth off with water and wash the soap off your baby. Immediately dry her by wrapping her in that soft baby towel. That's it!

There are different ideas about how often to bathe.

MYTH: Don't bathe a baby every day or she will get dry skin.
TRUTH: Bathe your baby every day if you like, as long as her skin isn't very dry.

Although you can bathe your baby every day, washing her hair as you bathe her, don't feel that you *must* bathe her each day. If you skip a day, perhaps because you were too busy with other chores, that's fine. Unless she's the world's youngest construction worker, chances are Linda didn't get too dirty today. She can wait a day for her next bath.

Cutting Your Baby's Nails

Babies have cute soft little nails, but even these baby nails can scratch their faces. So when Linda's nails get long, you will have to cut them — in most babies, this will be necessary every week or two. Use a baby scissor or nail clipper and place the index finger of your nondominant hand (your left hand if you are right-handed) inside your baby's hand. The baby has a grasp reflex and will hold on to your finger. With your other hand, use the baby scissor to cut the nails of the safely curled hand. This way the baby won't grab the scissor and cut herself. If you're a little shy about cutting your baby's nails, feel free to use a nail file instead.

THE HEAD

The Fontanelle (Soft Spot)

At birth, your baby's skull is made up of several different bones that meet in the front and back of the head in little soft spots, called fontanelles. At birth, the back or posterior fontanelle will usually be closed (it may be open in premies), but the front (anterior) fontanelle won't close for another six to eighteen months. Although the fontanelle is a soft spot, there is more than just a thin layer of skin protecting your baby's precious brain. Several layers of covering (called meninges) lie between the skin and the brain. You may notice that your baby's anterior fontanelle often pulsates as arteries under the fontanelle make it move up and down in the same rhythm as the heartbeat.

Bumpy Heads: Caput and Cephalohematoma

Babies often look like little coneheads. As their cute little coconuts are squished in passing through the narrow birth canal, they become a bit pointy. This cone-shaped swelling (called a caput) will, in a few months, smooth out nicely and your baby will be left with a nice round head. Occasionally a head will be very swollen and will feel "mushy" on one side. This is a cephalohematoma and represents bruising of one bone of the skull from the birth process. Caput and cephalohematoma are harmless, have no effect on your baby's brain, and will round out by a year.

Flat Heads

MYTH: If your baby has a flat head, let her sleep on her belly.

TRUTH: It's not worth the risk of crib death to have a baby with a rounder skull.

Some babies have asymmetric (uneven) or flattened heads. Now that most babies spend their sleeping hours, along with most of their waking hours, on their backs, it's not uncommon to see a baby with a very cute but very flattened head. A baby's skull is made up of several bones, and until a year or so of age, when these bones have fused, your baby's head can assume odd shapes. As with most things in babyland, such flattening is innocent. In time that lumpy or flattened head will smooth out nicely. On rare occasions, when a head is particularly flattened, some babies require what are known as molding helmets, adorable little devices that round out an extremely flattened or asymmetric skull.

Rarer still is a condition called craniosynostosis, in which the spaces between the bones in a baby's skull (these spaces are called sutures) close too early and the baby's skull assumes an extremely flattened or asymmetric shape. Although rare, craniosynostosis is serious since all sutures must remain open long enough for a baby's skull to grow evenly and to allow for proper brain growth. Craniosynostosis is treated by a neurosurgeon.

THE EYES AND VISION

Babies are born with very poor vision—newborn vision is often 20/200, which means that babies need to be 20 feet away to see what adults can see from 200 hundred feet. Gradually, vision becomes normal.

Strabismus and Pseudostrabismus

One common source of parental anxiety is pseudostrabismus, or false squint. Quite often parents think their babies' eyes are crossing—the eyes actually seem to be turning in. Most of the time this is just an optical illusion. Your baby's nasal bridge is totally flat (take a look!) and there is a little fold in the inner corner of her eye. These two characteristics cause the iris (or colored part) of a baby's eye to seem "hidden" near the nose, and her eyes actually look crossed. As the nose becomes less flat and as those folds go away, however, her eyes can now be seen to be right in the middle.

Of course, some babies' eyes actually do turn in or out. Known as strabismus, a baby's eyes can either turn in (esotropia) or out (exotropia). One way to tell if that squint is real or false is to shine a flashlight in your baby's eyes. The light should hit both of the baby's pupils (the black center of the eye) in the same place. That is, if you see that the light in one eye hits the center of the pupil but the light in the other is off center, then your baby may have strabismus. If you're not sure, just ask your doctor to check for strabismus at the next visit.

It's important to pick up strabismus because a baby with one eye turned in or out will find it difficult to focus. After a while the baby's brain will actually "turn off" the vision in one eye to focus better. **Amblyopia,** a potentially permanent difference in vision between the two eyes, can result if strabismus is not picked up early. Once again, if you're not sure if your baby is focusing properly, a visit to your pediatrician or a pediatric ophthalmologist will determine whether that squint is real or false.

Retinoblastoma
Retinoblastoma—a rare tumor of the retina of the eye—can also be indicated by a squint or by a white or yellow reflection in the pupil of one

eye. This malignancy is an important one to pick up early so that it can be treated effectively.

Blocked Tear Duct

When a baby is born, the ducts that carry tears away from the eye are often not fully open. Such blocked ducts cause the eye to fill with tears, and your baby may look as though she is crying all the time. Your doctor will show you how to massage the tear ducts to improve the flow of tears. Sometimes the sludging of tears results in a mild infection. If your baby's eye seems red or swollen, let your doctor have a look. He may prescribe an antibiotic drop or an oral antibiotic. The blocked tear duct usually resolves in a few months. Very rarely, the blockage persists longer, and an ophthalmologist will have to open the ducts surgically.

THE NOSE

Sneezing

Sneezing is quite common and does not necessarily mean that little Linda has a cold or an allergy. It's just her way of clearing those tiny nasal passages of the normal amount of mucus inside.

Stuffy Noses and Noisy Breathing

Babies are noisy little critters, and their breathing sounds can really add to the "noise pollution" of your home. The reason Linda is so noisy is that she's so very petite. Babies have small nasal and bronchial passages—all it takes is a drop of mucus to plug up a nose or partially block a bronchial tube.

   In the winter, your heating system can dry out the air and make nasal and bronchial mucus that much thicker. If your baby is a noisy breather, try using a warm mist vaporizer to loosen the mucus in her nose and chest. "Normal saline" nose drops, which are ordinary salt water drops in the same concentration as tears and other body fluids, are also great at dissolving mucus. A drop or two in each nostril, as often as every two or three hours if needed, can quickly open up a blocked nose. Since babies with stuffy noses need to breathe using their mouths, your baby may feed less with a stuffy nose. For this reason, a good time to use those nose drops is right before a feeding.

While we're on the subject of noises, a word about another common and innocuous sound: **hiccups.** Hiccups in newborns are absolutely normal and represent an immaturity of your baby's digestive system. They can occur at any time and may persist for several minutes. If you do nothing, they will stop on their own. If you want to speed things up, try giving your baby an ounce of cooled boiled water or bottled water.

THE EARS

Ear Wax

Here's some advice about removing ear wax: don't do it! Wax protects the ear by trapping dust and debris before they move further into the ear canal. If your doctor sees that your baby's ear is totally blocked with wax, he may try to remove it with an ear wax curette (scooper) or may suggest a wax loosener (such as Debrox). Sometimes a doctor or nurse will wash out the ear canal in a quick, painless procedure called a lavage. On the other hand, if you attempt to clean out your baby's ears using a Q-tip, you will usually accomplish one of three things: you will either injure the ear canal, puncture the ear drum, or push the wax farther in. If you see wax sitting at the very end of the ear canal, feel free to clean it out with a washcloth or piece of gauze moistened with water or hydrogen peroxide. Leave the rest of the ear cleaning to your doctor.

THE MOUTH

Teething and Tooth Care

Teething is blamed for almost everything that a baby does, so let's begin by dispelling some common teething myths:

MYTH: Teething causes diarrhea.
TRUTH: Teething never causes diarrhea.

MYTH: Teething causes a runny nose.
TRUTH: Never, never.

MYTH: Teething causes fever.
TRUTH: Only in never-never land.

I'm amazed to see teething blamed for all these problems, even in books about child care written by nurses, who should know better. In fact, teething causes none of these problems. How, then, can it be that such myths are so well accepted? It's because of the difference between coincidence and causation. When a child cuts a new tooth and then happens to get a cold the next day, Mom will assume that, since the cold followed the tooth, the cold was *caused* by the tooth, when in fact it was a coincidence. If you stub your toe and it rains later that day, did your toe stubbing cause the rain? You probably wouldn't think so, but what if it rained on the day after you stubbed your toe three times in a row? That might get you thinking. The same applies to teething. Twenty times over the first two and a half years a baby gets a new tooth. Factor in at least a half dozen colds and you can see that there are going to be plenty of times when that new tooth will be coming through when there is a cold germ around. This is coincidence—it looks like more because of the large number of times the two events happen around the same time, but coincidence is all it is.

The only things that a new baby tooth causes are:

• *A bit of drooling.* Even this is not always due to teething but is often a result of the development of the salivary glands—your baby now has more saliva than she knows what to do with.

• *Minor discomfort and fussiness.* Want to know how much it hurts to have a new tooth break through? Ask your 6-year-old nephew. He'll tell you that it doesn't hurt much at all.

To treat the minor discomfort of teething, a teething ring is usually all that's needed. A local gum anesthetic, such as Baby Orajel, may help a bit, although it gets washed away in a minute or two. Tylenol can be used but is seldom necessary.

There is great variation in the emergence of little Linda's teeth. Her first tooth may emerge as early as 4 months or as late as 1 year. Also, dif-

ferent babies get teeth in different sequences. The most common order
for the emergence of primary teeth is this:

Lower central incisors
Upper central incisors
Upper lateral incisors
Lower lateral incisors
Upper or lower first molars
Upper or lower canines
Upper or lower second molars

Remember, your baby's teeth may emerge in a completely different
order. Also, the number of teeth to expect at a particular age is even
more variable and of interest only to Grandma, who seems to celebrate
the emergence of a tooth as though it's the signal of permanent world
peace. Getting teeth earlier or later is of absolutely no concern to your
baby, to her doctor and, hopefully, to you as well.

Even before your baby has teeth, wash off her gums with a piece of
gauze and water after each bottle to prevent decay. Starting at about 6
months, assuming that she has teeth, use a drop of baby toothpaste (the
size of a pea is enough for her whole mouth) and gently brush her teeth
each morning and evening.

Remember not to prop a bottle in your baby's mouth when you put
her to sleep. **Baby bottle mouth,** a general decay of the baby teeth due
to exposure to the sugar in formula, is the awful-looking and quite common result of propping a bottle, and it can leave a baby with badly rotted teeth.

Thrush
Babies often have white coating on their tongues, which makes sense
when you consider that their main source of nutrition is breast milk or
formula. However, a white coating of the tongue can also be the sign of a
mild yeast (fungus) infection called thrush. The fungus that causes
thrush (called monilia or candida), is the same yeast infection that
women frequently get after taking antibiotics, and is the same yeast that
pops up in diaper rashes. In babies this pest finds the inside of the mouth
a particularly inviting place to live. When thrush is present, instead of a

little white film inside your baby's mouth, you will now see a thicker layer of white. Also, if it's only breast milk or formula causing the coating, you will easily be able to scrape it off with your finger. If thrush is present, the coating will not come off so easily. Finally, milk won't usually leave a persistent residue inside the lips and cheeks, whereas thrush will.

Thrush is easily treated with medication. Your doctor can recommend an oral drop (nystatin is a common choice) to use several times each day to fight off the fungus. If you're nursing a baby with thrush, she most likely "contaminated" your breasts with the fungus, and your nipples or areola may be a bit red or sore. Apply a few drops of your baby's thrush medication directly to your breasts after nursing. If your baby is a pacifier addict, get a fresh pacifier, since thrush can also thrive right on the pacifier. It's even a good idea to put a few drops of the thrush medication right on the pacifier before giving it to your baby.

Pacifiers

MYTH: Babies need to use pacifiers because they need sucking time.
TRUTH: They get plenty of sucking time when they're feeding.

I've never had that much of a problem with pacifiers. Sure, they're messy. Yes, babies look silly with pacifiers hanging out of their mouths. My main problem with pacifiers is that they make more work for parents. If your baby is a pacifier addict and can't sleep or even nap without one, then you tend to spend lots of your valuable time running back into her room to put the pacifier back into her mouth. All of a sudden she won't nap without it, won't go to sleep at night without it, won't spend any time at all without it. The pacifier falls out, so you have to run in and put it back in her mouth. The pacifier falls on the floor, so you have to wash it off.

All things considered, I'd much rather see a baby develop a dependency on her thumb than a pacifier. Linda can find her thumb herself, it won't fall on the floor, and if she wakes up at night and expects her thumb in her mouth, she can pop it back in without your help. Also, most (unfortunately not all) kids will give up a thumb-sucking habit on their own when they become more interested in grabbing for toys. Pacifier babies sometimes wind up with those silly pacifier necklaces even while playing with toys.

Another reason to avoid developing a pacifier addict is that babies who regularly use pacifiers are more likely to get ear infections. So if your baby doesn't have a pacifier, don't buy one.

THE NECK

Torticollis (Wry Neck)
Some babies are born with a subtle tilt of the head to one side, with the chin pointing toward the other side. Called torticollis, such rotation is often due to a fibrous thickening in a muscle of the baby's neck, which pulls it to one side. Wry neck is treated with stretching exercises that lengthen the tightened neck muscle.

THE BELLY BUTTON (UMBILICUS)

When changing your newborn's diaper, drop a bit of rubbing alcohol right on the belly button. The alcohol will help keep the small stump of umbilical cord clean and help it dry up and fall off, an event that can be expected anytime within the first few weeks. Try to keep the diaper folded below the belly button—this will also help the cord dry out. Once the cord separates—no, it doesn't hurt—you may see a bit of blood in the navel. Again, alcohol will keep the area clean. Let your pediatrician know if there is a strong odor from the navel or if the skin around the navel is particularly red, both indications that the navel may have become infected.

Umbilical Granuloma
In many babies, when the umbilical cord falls off, there is a small shiny "button" of pink tissue in the navel called an umbilical granuloma. This common little irritation represents an incompletely healed belly button and doesn't hurt your baby, but it may ooze or even bleed a little. The

granuloma requires no special treatment, may be washed in the bath, and does not have to be covered. Point it out during your next visit to the doctor. He will gently cauterize the tissue with a chemical called silver nitrate.

Umbilical Hernia

Many babies will have a bulge from the navel, which becomes even larger when they cry, laugh, or strain. This is called an umbilical hernia, and no, it doesn't mean that your baby will need surgery. Unlike the more familiar inguinal or groin hernia, the umbilical hernia will almost always go away by itself in a number of months or even a few years. Although Grandma will no doubt remember that her doctor treated umbilical hernias by taping a coin over the belly button, no "belly band" treatment is necessary. The umbilical hernia does not hurt your baby, and you need not worry that the bulge really balloons out when she laughs or cries.

THE DIAPER

Changing a Diaper

As an experienced diaper changer, for my own kids as well as the many babies who have had the audacity to poop on my office examining table, let me first say that it's no big deal. To help move things along quickly, be prepared. Have all your supplies ready, clean up quickly, and get out of there. Think of it as though you're performing a military maneuver in a highly radioactive area. Have all your troops and supplies ready, hold your breath, get in and get out. That way, you limit your exposure to the nuclear waste.

Here's what you'll need:

• *A small basin of water or baby wipes.* Water is cheaper; wipes are easier; take your pick. Some babies do get diaper rashes from baby wipes, but most tolerate them with no problem. If your baby does have a diaper rash, however, then don't use wipes, only water. If you use water instead of wipes, you'll also need something to use for wiping. Cotton balls, tissues, or a washcloth will all do fine.

• *A fresh disposable diaper.* As with wipes, take your pick of the diaper brands. Buy in bulk if you can—the cost adds up. Make sure the diaper is big enough so that your baby will be comfortable, but not so large that you're finding stains on your sheets and your carpet.

• *Vaseline or some generic bland cream or ointment.* Vaseline is probably the best thing to use if your baby has no rash. If she has a rash or is irritated, there are other ointments to use, which will be discussed later.

• *Powder.* Though we love the smell of baby powder, you can usually do without it. First of all, you might accidentally get the powder into the baby's face, and talc, the main ingredient, is harmful to babies' lungs. If you *do* use it, step away from the baby, shake a little on your hand, and then pat it on the baby.

With your supplies assembled, it's time to get down to business. Dip a cotton ball or washcloth in water (or use a wipe), quickly wash away any stool or urine, and *dry the area well* with cotton or a cloth. Dab a little Vaseline all around the genitals (if some gets inside your baby girl's vagina, it's safe), put on a new diaper, and you're finished. With girls, always wash and wipe from front to back (from the vagina toward the rectum, not from the rectum toward the vagina) to avoid bringing stool into the clean vagina and urethra.

Diaper Rashes

No baby makes it through the first year without a few good cases of diaper rash: a flat red rash over the buttocks, lower part of the belly, inner thighs, and labia (in girls) or scrotum (in boys). No matter how clean your baby is, expect to face this problem at some time.

 **MYTH:** Diaper rash occurs because of an irritant in a baby's diet.
TRUTH: Diet is seldom the cause of diaper rash.

MYTH: Babies get diaper rashes because they're not cleaned often enough.

TRUTH: Even the cleanest of babies can expect an occasional diaper rash.

Urine and stool in the diaper combine to make the skin overly hydrated and underacidic (breast-fed infants are less often troubled by diaper rash since their stool is more acidic). A dark, wet, airless, and nonacidic environment is just what bacteria and yeast love, and these bugs are, along with other irritants in the stool and urine, largely responsible for most cases of diaper rash.

To **prevent diaper rashes,** it's important to do the following:

• *Change diapers frequently.* The longer bacteria, yeasts, and irritants are in contact with a baby's bottom, the greater the likelihood that a diaper rash will result. Of course this doesn't mean running in every two minutes to see if the baby is wet. An occasional feel for that familiar warmth at the baby's bottom will quickly tell you that it's time for a change.

• *Dry the diaper area well with each change.* Exposure to water can cause diaper rashes.

• *Avoid strong soaps.* If you use soap and water to wash your baby after a poop, use a mild soap such as Dove, Basis, or Cetaphil. Most babies do well when cleaned with baby wipes, but if your baby has a diaper rash, switch to one of these mild soaps and water and hold off using wipes.

• *Wipe from the vagina toward the rectum* when cleaning girls, not the other way around. The vagina and the nearby urethra, or opening of the urinary tract, are relatively sterile areas. The rectum is loaded with little bacteria and yeasts. If you wipe from the rectum to the vagina, you can give little Linda a bad diaper rash, vaginitis, or even a urinary tract infection.

• *Avoid using perfumed wipes and ointments,* especially if your baby seems prone to rashes. Stick to a bland ointment, such as Vaseline, zinc oxide, Triple Paste, Balmex, or A&D.

Of course, in spite of all parents' efforts, most babies will get a diaper rash at some time. In that case, call your pediatrician. He may be able to recommend an ointment, cream, or medicated powder over the phone. A visit is in order for a a rash that is particularly persistent or severe. However, if the rash doesn't look too bad and you would like to try something yourself, here are a few basic **at-home treatments for diaper rash:**

• Stop using wipes and switch to water and a mild soap.
• After your baby has been changed, leave the diaper off for a few minutes to expose the skin to air.
• Use an ointment with zinc oxide (Triple Paste is particularly effective).

In some cases a diaper rash is more than just an irritation. If there are large areas of redness with little red dots near the edges of the rash (like little islands off the coast of a country on a map), then Linda may have a **yeast** (candida) **infection.** If your doctor determines that Linda has a yeast infection in the diaper area, he may prescribe a medicated cream. Diaper rash can also be caused by a bacteria, such as staph. Bacterial diaper rashes often have little pimples or crusts mixed in with the redness and are usually treated with an antibacterial ointment or oral antibiotic.

THE PRIVATE PARTS

Inguinal Hernia
More common in boys than girls, an inguinal hernia is a weakness in the muscles of the groin that allows tissues under the muscle to bulge out. A telltale bulge in the groin will help you and your doctor make this diagnosis. Although not usually painful, an inguinal hernia in a child should be repaired surgically, since the tissues that force their way through this muscular weakness can become trapped (incarcerated), causing a strangulation of enclosed tissues—an emergency situation.

Hydrocele

Sometimes a baby boy is born with a seemingly huge scrotum. This painless accumulation of fluid is called a hydrocele. By a year of age the fluid is usually absorbed into the body. When a hydrocele persists past a year, it is often accompanied by a hernia. A visit to a pediatric surgeon or urologist is a good idea if your child has a hydrocele that lasts past his first birthday.

Hypospadius, Epispadius, and Chordee

Most baby boys are born with straight penises, with the meatus (hole) located right at the tip of the head of the penis. Some babies, however, have a meatus located underneath the head of the penis, sometimes as far south as the shaft. This is called hypospadius. Alternatively, some boys have the hole located too high up on the penis—epispadius. Finally, some are born with a "bent" penis, caused by a band of tissue, called a chordee, that pulls down the head of the penis. None of these conditions is painful and your baby will be able to urinate just fine. Nevertheless, for future cosmetic reasons, a urologist should be consulted. If you plan to have your son circumcised, this consultation should occur before the circumcision, since it will affect the procedure.

Undescended Testicle

In about 3 percent of all newborn boys, a testicle will not have dropped from inside the abdomen, where it sits for most of pregnancy, into the scrotum. Your doctor will usually be able to feel a testicle higher up in the groin. Especially common in premies (where the incidence is about one in three), the undescended testicle often drops into the scrotum by itself, from the groin or the abdomen, over the course of the first few months of life. However, this condition becomes more serious as time passes. A testicle that has not dropped into the scrotum is at risk for:

- **Infertility.** The scrotum is cooler than the groin or abdomen and sitting around at a higher temperature, even if only a degree or two higher than normal, can affect fertility.

- **Malignancy.** A high testicle is more prone to developing malignancy. In addition, self-examination is more difficult in a high testicle, which hinders cancer detection.

• *Psychological reasons.* What kid needs one more thing to be teased about?

A testicle that has not descended by a year of age will rarely descend at all, so most doctors suggest bringing down a high testicle surgically by this age. If your doctor cannot feel your baby's testicle at all, a surgeon may suggest a laparoscopy (insertion of an instrument under the skin) to make sure the testicle is present.

Once a child has had an undescended testicle brought down surgically, there is still a slight increase risk in that lowered testicle for:

• *Infertility.* If the undescended testicle is treated before age one, then the risk for infertility is much less—but still higher than someone whose testicle was in the scrotum to start.

• *Malignancy.* Even after it has been brought down into the scrotum, the surgerized testicle is slightly more likely to develop a malignancy later on in life. Even the other, completely normal testicle is at a slightly increased risk.

• *Torsion (twisting) of the testicle.* Rarely, a testicle becomes twisted around its stalk, causing a painful emergency. If the testicle is not quickly "unwound" surgically, then its blood supply can be choked off and the testicle will become gangrenous (rotted) and will have to be removed. Torsion is more common in the testicle that was undescended at birth.

• *Hernia.* Inguinal hernias are frequently found when undescended testicles are lowered. They can be repaired at the time of surgery.

Labial Adhesions
Sometimes the two sides of a baby girl's vagina will stick to each other, resulting in a narrowed vaginal opening. Such labial adhesions usually separate naturally and are not painful for your child. Occasionally, however, the adhesions will be more complete, closing the vagina completely and even obstructing the flow of urine from the urethra. If your baby's vaginal lips seem to have closed off her vagina, point this out to your pediatrician. He will either manually separate the labia or else prescribe a hormonal ointment to aid the separation process.

The Circumcision

These days, the great majority of baby boys are circumcised, but the decision to circumcise your baby is, of course, yours to make. Some **reasons to consider circumcision** include the following:

• Boys who have been circumcised tend to have fewer urinary tract infections. A circumcised infant boy has about a 1 in 1,000 chance of developing a urinary tract infection in the first year of life; an uncircumcised infant boy has about a 1 in 100 chance. The foreskin that is left in place in uncircumcised boys appears to be a bit of a breeding ground for germs.

• Studies tell us that circumcised males also have a slightly reduced risk of sexually transmitted diseases, such as gonorrhea, herpes, and AIDS.

• Uncircumcised adults appear to have a greater chance of getting cancer of the penis, a type of malignancy that is, fortunately, quite rare and occurs very late in adulthood.

Reasons to consider *not* circumcising your son:

• Many parents decide against circumcision because of the discomfort involved, even though many circumcisers nowadays will use an anesthetic cream to reduce the pain.

• Many dads who are not circumcised prefer to have their sons look the same way.

Again, the choice is yours. Rest assured that most baby boys do just fine either way.

If you decide to have your baby circumcised, this can be done right in the hospital by the obstetrician. Jewish parents may elect to have the procedure performed by a trained mohel or religious circumciser. Your obstetrician or pediatrician can give you the name of an experienced mohel.

Care of the Circumcised Penis

The area of circumcision will heal well within a few days. Keep the gauze on as long as instructed by the doctor or mohel. After removing the gauze, you may notice a yellow discharge around the head of the penis. This is not pus and does not indicate an infection; it is simply fluid from the healing tissues and will go away by itself. Vaseline will prevent the sensitive circumcised penis from sticking to the diaper. Let your pediatrician know if your baby does not urinate normally within six to eight hours after the circumcision or if there is persistent bleeding or redness around the tip of the penis that gets worse after three to four days.

Care of the Uncircumcised Penis

Keep in mind that the foreskin may not fully retract for several years. Don't force it back during cleaning. Simply wash the genital area normally while bathing. There is no need for special cotton swabs or soaps. Later, when the foreskin fully retracts, boys should be taught how to wash underneath the foreskin every day.

THE HIPS AND LEGS

Since babies are pretty crowded in their little nine-month condos, they can look quite bowlegged and pigeon-toed at birth. Fortunately, a baby's hips, legs, and feet will gradually straighten out after six months in the roomy comfort of a crib. Sometimes, however, that odd-looking leg or that unusual foot can represent something more than just crowding.

Hip Dysplasia
Most common after breech deliveries, and frequently familial, is dysplasia (failure to develop) of the hip. Our hip joints are made up of a ball and socket—the head of the thigh bone (femur) is the ball and the acetabulum (shelf) of the pelvis is the socket. In babies with dysplastic hips, the socket is too shallow to hold the femur in place, and the hip easily dislocates. You may notice that one of your baby's knees seems higher than the other when she is placed on her back or that the skin folds on one thigh look different from those on the other. More commonly, your pediatrician will feel a click as the ball falls outside the socket when he opens and closes your baby's hips. Dysplasia of the hip is treated with a special splint or harness that holds the femur in the acetabulum. The earlier a dysplastic hip is diagnosed, the more easily it can be treated.

Tibial Torsion (Incurved Legs)

When a baby's tibia (this is the larger of the two bones extending from the knee to the ankle) twists inward as it travels down toward the foot, this is called tibial torsion. The most common cause of childhood pigeon-toe, tibial torsion usually resolves by a year with no treatment at all.

THE HANDS AND FEET

Metatarsus Adductus (Incurved Feet)

Another common cause of intoeing is metatarsus adductus, an incurving of the front of the foot. Like tibial torsion, metatarsus adductus often resolves by itself, with no treatment. Occasionally a severely incurved foot may need treatment with a special shoe.

Acrocyanosis (Cold Blue Hands and Feet)

Because her circulation is not so robust as yours, little Linda's hands and feet may appear cold and blue. This doesn't mean that she is too cold or uncomfortable. If you warm up her room in an effort to make her hands and feet warm, it will be too warm for the rest of the body. As her circulation matures, usually by several months of age, Linda's hands and feet will no longer appear quite so cold.

KIDFIXER FREQUENTLY ASKED QUESTIONS

Q: How can I keep my child's head from flattening?

A: Position your baby so that the head does not rest on the flattened side. Try turning her crib around or changing the side where she keeps her teddy bear. Also, when she isn't sleeping, let her have some tummy time.

Q: *How do I know if my child's birthmark needs to be removed?*

A: There's no sure way to know without visiting your pediatrician. Sometimes the size, the shape, or the coloring of a birthmark will reassure your doctor that a birthmark is innocent. Sometimes he will need the help of a dermatologist. Fortunately, the great majority of birthmarks seen in babies are innocent and are only of cosmetic significance.

Q: *What can I do about my baby's eczema? He's scratching himself all day.*

A: There are some general steps to take to treat severe eczema in babies. First, you might consider bathing him every second or third day instead of every day, and only for a quick dip. This will help stop his skin from drying out. Next, use a mild soap, such as Dove, Basis, or Cetaphil. Keep his nails short, cutting or filing them often, so that he doesn't scratch himself, since scratching actually makes the skin more inflamed. Your doctor can recommend a good moisturizer and can even prescribe an anti-inflammatory ointment. These should be used sparingly, since they can cause skin to become even more irritated if used too often. If you are nursing and your child's eczema is particularly troublesome, your doctor may recommend eliminating some of the more allergenic foods from your diet, such as chocolate, shellfish, berries, egg whites, nuts, tomatoes, citrus fruits, and dairy.

Q: *What can I do about my peeling 1-week-old?*

A: Do nothing. He's peeling because he just got out of a nine-month bath and his skin is a bit dry. The peeling will go away all by itself, and it won't itch at all.

Q: *Alan, my 4-month-old, appears to have developed some sort of rash around his mouth. I wonder if it could just be the result of getting it wet all the time while sucking his thumb. I have been putting baby lotion on it, but that does not seem to be helping. Any ideas?*

A: Chafed skin around a baby's mouth, known as perioral contact dermatitis, is a common and persistent problem. A baby's skin is a sensitive covering, and is protected by natural oils that keep the skin soft, clean, and moist. When this covering is exposed to an excess of water, from drooling or thumb sucking, those protective oils are washed away and the skin begins to dry out. Eventually, the dry skin will crack, itch, become red, and even become infected. Pacifiers, which keep a baby's drool in constant contact with the skin, can make the drying-out process worse. Certain chemicals from the plastic of the pacifier can further irritate the skin. If Alan has perioral contact dermatitis, make sure you get rid of his pacifier. Avoid using strong ointments or perfumed lotions. Simple zinc oxide can help as well.

Q: *I accidentally gave my 9-month-old son, Roberto, some of my peanut butter and he did fine—no rash, no problem at all. Now that I know he's not allergic, can I continue to give him peanut butter? He really loved it, and I know that it's a good source of protein.*

A: Sorry, Roberto. Even though you enjoyed your accidental treat, that doesn't mean you'll be as lucky next time. It's not always the first exposure that gets you. It might be the second, third, or fourth. Also, with such strong allergens as peanuts, being exposed during early childhood actually makes it more likely that you will become allergic later on. Best to save those PB&J sandwiches until at least two years of age—many allergists recommend waiting until age 3.

Q: *I love using fabric softeners in the dryer. Not only do my clothes get softer, but they also smell great. Can I still use softener sheets in my dryer for my husband and me but not use them for my baby daughter?*

A: This isn't a great idea. The chemical from those dryer sheets is often allergenic and tends to stay in the dryer for several loads, so your baby may get a reaction even when it's not specifically added to her load.

Q: *How hot should my baby's bath be?*

A: Keep the baby's bath water between 90 and 100 degrees. In general, the hot water heater in your house should be kept at 120 degrees, to prevent accidental scaldings.

Q: How can I make my baby's bath less slippery? I'm always afraid that she will fall when I bathe her.

A: Place a large towel in the bottom of the tub. This will make the surface much less slippery.

Q: My daughter is 10 days old and her umbilical cord is still attached. What am I doing wrong?

A: Nothing. The umbilical cord often doesn't separate for two or three weeks. Just expose the cord to air by folding down the diaper and apply alcohol to the cord several times a day. This will help the cord dry out and fall off.

Q: My baby has a little oozing from the belly button. Is this a problem?

A: Not necessarily. If there is a small amount of oozing, the liquid that oozes does not smell particularly foul, and there is no redness or swelling around the cord, then this is probably normal. Redness, a bad smell, or a large amount of discharge can mean that your baby has an infection of the umbilicus. Also, a particularly large amount of oozing can, on rare occasions, be a sign that there is an abnormal connection between the belly button and the bladder.

9

SLEEP (HELP ME MAKE
IT THROUGH THE NIGHT!)

Remember the good old days?

You know, the days when the only person you had to take care of was yourself. When the only mouth to feed was your own, and your only job was a nine-to-five, with a paycheck at the end; when you slept at night.

Sleep. You never really appreciate a good night's sleep until you no longer have it. Ever since our children were born, I've developed a great respect for those golden hours of rest. After all, my kids were the worst sleepers in the world. To put my older child to sleep, we first had to sing a bedtime song while rocking him on our laps. After an hour of singing "Mary Had a Little Lamb" or the unbelievably repetitive "Itsy Bitsy Spider," he would settle at last into a snooze. Of course, this was just a tease. No sooner had we placed him in his crib than the crying began. Up my wife or I would jump for fifty choruses of "Farmer in the Dell." This would go on throughout most of the night, until we gave in and brought him into our bed, crowded together like sleep-deprived sardines. When 5 a.m. rolled around, the master decided it was time to get up. Miraculously, after only five hours of sleep he was fresh and frisky, ready for another day of play. Oh, and lest you think he made up for it with nice long naps, know this: no Altman child has *ever* taken a nap. Ever. (Until high school, that is. Then, teachers tell us, they napped quite well.)

In retrospect, I'm amazed that we made it through those early sleep-deprived years (son number two was no better). We tried every way imaginable to get those guys to sleep, and took everyone's advice. Some moms and dads favor constant contact with a child—to the point of sharing their bed with baby. Others believe in rocking a child until he becomes drowsy and then slipping him quietly into the crib. We listened to everyone and tried every way. Every way, that is, except the right way. In the following chapter, we'll discuss the basics of your baby's sleep. I hope this will enable you moms and dads to gain a few extra hours of rest and benefit from what my wife and I learned the hard way.

NORMAL SLEEP

Most newborns sleep fourteen to sixteen hours a day. At first, a baby's sleep periods are spread out evenly, with about eight hours during the day and eight at night. After the first month or two, most babies will develop our day-night rhythms and sleep more during the night than they do during the day. Of course, if you keep waking little Clarisse for midnight feedings, certain that she must be hungry, she will not develop a normal day-night cycle until much later. Unless you've brought home a little premie peanut, once the sun sets let your baby sleep. By 4 to 5 months of age, the majority of babies are able to sleep through the night without a feeding.

NORMAL AROUSALS

While babies sleep, they make all kinds of movements, grimaces, sounds, and weird little gestures. This doesn't mean that they're in distress, gassy, or hungry; it's just normal newborn sleep. These normal arousals are natural, not just for newborns but also, to a lesser extent, for all of us. Several times during the night babies will awaken briefly, look around, reassure themselves that they are where they're supposed to be, and quickly go back to sleep. Again, they don't awaken because they're hungry, in distress, or gassy. How do we know this? Simple. They go right back to sleep, without relief of the supposed distress, without gas medication, and without a feeding. Such restlessness is normal newborn sleep, not a sign of distress or hunger.

This interrupted normal baby sleep is one reason why we advise, if at all possible, keeping your baby out of your bedroom at night. There's no reason for a sleepy mom or dad to wake up with a start just because Clarisse is grimacing, gesturing, or even having a brief nocturnal awakening. What you don't know about your baby's late night activity won't hurt you—and it certainly won't hurt her. If you have no bedroom for Clarisse, put her crib in the den or living room—a far better choice than trying to ignore her sounds, grimaces, and brief awakenings.

MYTH: If you separate from baby at night, you are missing out on "night parenting."
TRUTH: You do plenty of "day parenting" without adding more work at night.

Many "night parenting" advocates claim that to maintain mutual trust between parent and baby, it's just as important to provide comfort during the night as it is during the day. To these experts I say: aren't the hours of the day, when you and your baby are awake together, enough to form a trusting relationship? Any "expert" who claims there aren't enough daylight hours to bond with a baby either has never had a baby or else had lots of help raising one.

Taking care of a baby is a wonderful, enriching, fulfilling experience, but it's also extremely tiring. With a baby there's no nursery or elementary school to give you a break for a few hours. After sixteen hours of being a mommy, you are *entitled* to a few hours of sleep. So enjoy your baby during the day and enjoy your rest at night. Keep in mind that little Clarisse needs her rest too. She's had plenty of you during the day.

MYTH: If your baby cries at night, immediately run in to her. She needs you.
TRUTH: Take your time. She may stop crying before you know it.

There are many well-intentioned sleep "experts" who advocate running in to a baby with her very first cry. If she's crying, the logic goes, something must be bothering her. Therefore, when you hear your baby cry, immediately run in and pick her up. If you have no problem with carrying your baby around twenty-four hours a day, then go ahead. If, on the other hand, you'd like to sleep an hour or two each day, or even spend a few minutes eating a meal or speaking to your spouse, your baby may have to learn to **delay gratification** for a few minutes.

Children need to learn that even if a cry is not answered immediately, help will arrive eventually. A little patience is not a bad trait to develop. Of course, I'm not saying that you must make your newborn baby wait some artificial amount of time before feeding her or changing her wet diaper. What I am saying is that a child who has *every* cry answered *immediately* will eventually expect all of life's little problems to disappear just as quickly. The baby who has never waited a few seconds to be picked up may well become the impatient child who whines when a toy or cookie is not presented quickly enough.

So now you've got it: my official pediatrician's blessing to let your baby cry a little. If it's bedtime, you've fed and changed her, the cat is not nibbling her toes, and she's not burning up with fever—in other words, if she's not in trouble—it's fine to let her cry briefly when you put her to bed. The sooner she learns to sleep alone, the sooner *your* life will get back to some semblance of normality. You'll be a happier parent, and certainly a more patient and understanding one, if you get a good night's sleep.

TIPS FOR DEVELOPING A GOOD SLEEPER

• *Caffeine.* If you are nursing, limit caffeine intake from coffee, tea, and sodas. Caffeine is not only great at keeping us awake, it passes into breast milk and does the same for babies.

• *Back to sleep.* Put your baby to sleep on her back. This will greatly reduce her risk of sudden infant death syndrome (SIDS). If she spits up, she will not suffocate; she'll just become messy.

• *A dark room.* Put your baby to sleep in her crib in a relatively dark room (a night-light is okay). It's important that, when Clarisse has her normal arousal, she is in a familiar environment. If she is used to falling asleep in a bright room and then you switch off the light once she's asleep, she will expect that light during her normal arousals.

• *The bedtime ritual.* Establish a bedtime ritual. Children who have the same bedtime ritual each night actually begin to feel sleepy during that last brief bedtime story or quick lullaby. Let's take a closer look at this very important topic.

THE BEDTIME RITUAL

If you haven't heard of Dr. Richard Ferber and his book, *Solve Your Child's Sleep Problems,* you should. Dr. Ferber has taught thousands of parents (and almost as many pediatricians) how to get babies to sleep well at night. He believes that, by establishing a good bedtime ritual, almost all babies can be trained to sleep well. He also assures us that infants who have been made poor sleepers by poor bedtime rituals can be retrained to become good sleepers.

Why Is a Proper Bedtime Ritual Important?
Since babies have frequent normal arousals, it's important for a stirring baby to see the same conditions during an arousal that she sees when she goes to sleep. If you were to awaken from sleep and find yourself on the bathroom floor, you would recognize this as an unfamiliar sleeping situation, get up, and walk back into your bedroom. When a baby awakens during one of her normal arousals and sees that she's in a different situation, she can't make that trip herself; she must ask you to help her. How does she do this? She cries. If, during her arousal, the setting is the same as the one from sleep time, she may fuss a bit, turn her head around once or twice, or even cry for a minute or two, but she will quickly settle herself and get back to sleep.

The Correct Ritual
Most babies, in the first several weeks, haven't developed a reliable pattern of sleep. Some days they may drop off at 6:00, other days not until 7:00 or 8:00. Nevertheless, by 3 months you will know when little Clarisse is ready for bed. Her eyes may seem to be droopy or she may get a bit fussy. Now it's time for that bedtime ritual. Such a routine might be

a last bottle or nursing, followed by a quick diaper change, a minute or two of cuddling, a few rocks in a rocker, accompanied by a lullaby, and then down we go. In time your baby will become conditioned to expect sleep to follow this pattern. To instill good sleeping habits, don't hold her until she falls asleep and then slip her into her crib. She will never learn to settle herself this way, and when she has her normal arousal, she won't know how to settle down again. Take your drowsy but still awake baby, place her in the crib, and leave. If she starts to cry, it's perfectly okay to let her go for a few minutes before going back in. You may find that she'll quickly stop crying on her own, but if not, wait five minutes until you reenter for a reassuring rub. If leaving causes another wailing session, wait another five minutes before going back in to calm her. After a few of these five-minute sessions, Clarisse will fall asleep. You do the same.

The Wrong Ritual: the Sneaky Approach

It's time for bed. Little Clarisse is finishing that last bottle of the day and her eyes look heavy. Rather than "disturbing" her by placing her, awake, in her crib, you decide to hold her on your lap or rock her until she's completely asleep. Then, holding your breath, you carefully place her in her crib without waking her. If you're careful, you think, you can slip her into her crib and she'll never notice that you're no longer holding her. What's the problem with such an approach? Little Clarisse **never learns that she sleeps alone;** as far as she knows, she sleeps with her mom (or dad). If Clarisse falls asleep on Mommy's lap, she will expect to be on that lap when she has her normal arousal. If she is used to falling asleep while being rocked by Daddy, when she awakens she'll wonder where the rocking is. Also, while some people routinely share their beds with their infants, doing so not only ensures that Clarisse will expect to be in that bed with Mom and Dad when she rouses, but it also puts her at risk; scores of children are suffocated each year by sharing their parents' beds. Put Clarisse to sleep alone—not on Mommy's lap, not in Daddy's rocking chair, and not in the family bed.

THE GOOD SLEEPER WHO BECOMES A BAD SLEEPER

Believe it or not, some kids come home from the hospital already sleep-trained. Miraculously, they become drowsy in their cribs and sleep, uninterrupted, for a good ten or twelve hours. Lucky parents, beware: you may not be home free yet! A child who sleeps well from the start may become a poor sleeper later on. Some babies will begin to have sleep problems at 7 or 8 months of age. A child who previously slept from 9 p.m. to 9 a.m. will now awaken at 2 a.m. for no reason. Parents will speculate: "It's the teeth." But emerging teeth do not awaken a sleeping child. Is it an ear infection that's keeping Clarisse up? If her crying is unaccompanied by a cold or by fussiness during the day, then an ear infection is unlikely as well. There are, of course, other medical, rather than behavioral, reasons for a baby to awaken each night. A quick visit to the doctor will usually reassure you that your baby is fine. In general, the previously good sleeper who now awakens in the middle of the night usually does so for *no* reason.

HOW TO CONDITION A BAD SLEEPER TO BECOME A GOOD SLEEPER

Whether you've got a baby who slept fine for the first few months but is now driving you crazy, or your child was conditioned improperly with the sneaky approach and expects to sleep with Mom or Dad, you will need to do something to recondition her. Dr. Ferber has developed a very good system of training a child to learn to sleep through the night; one that is effective and appropriate for any healthy baby over the age of five months. Although it involves several nights of conditioning, the success rate is very high.

Using the proper ritual discussed above, put your drowsy but *awake* child on her back, in a dimly lit room, in her crib and leave. Since she's not used to sleeping in this way, she will cry. Look at the clock in your room and allow Clarisse to cry for five minutes. If she's still crying after five minutes, go in to her and calm her down. Don't start rocking her and don't give her a bottle. Just calm her down and leave. If you can't get her to stop crying after a minute or two, leave anyway. Now, allow her to cry for ten minutes before that reassuring pat. Next time wait fifteen minutes before your *brief* comforting appearance. Then, for the rest of that first night of conditioning, wait fifteen minutes between every trip in. On the second night, *start* at ten minutes, then wait for fifteen minutes and then twenty each time she cries. On the third night, start off with a fifteen-minute crying period, then twenty, then twenty-five each time. The next night, it's twenty, then twenty-five, then thirty each time. Even with the toughest of sleepers, rarely will it take more than three or four nights of such conditioning to succeed.

To summarize:

Day	Waiting Time (Minutes)
1	5, 10, 15, followed by 15-minute intervals
2	10, 15, 20, followed by 20-minute intervals
3	15, 20, 25, followed by 25-minute intervals
4 and subsequent days	20, 25, 30, followed by 30-minute intervals

Although you're in for a few difficult days, the reward of a good night's sleep makes it well worth the effort.

KIDFIXER FREQUENTLY ASKED QUESTIONS

Q: *On average, how much should an 11-week-old baby sleep during the day? I feel as if my son is always sleeping.*

A: Some newborns sleep very little, while others are sleepyheads and spend all their time, other than feeding times, asleep. My advice:

enjoy it while it lasts. There is no problem with being "too sleepy," just as there is no problem associated with being awake much of the time. Both patterns represent normal newborn variability.

Q: *Won't my baby girl be lonely if we're separated at night?*

A: Sleeping alone is a good way for your baby to begin to learn the process of separation. Throughout your baby's developing years, she will gradually spend more time away from her parents as she develops self-reliance and independence. Sleeping in her crib alone at night is where it starts.

Q: *My 6-month-old daughter, Belle, has already developed bad sleeping habits—my husband rocks her for hours and sings "Beauty and the Beast." Is it too late to change?*

A: Fear not. Even after several months of poor habits, Belle can be reconditioned to sleep beautifully. Develop a good ritual and stick to it. It will rarely take more than a week to retrain a child who has learned a bad sleep ritual.

Sometimes a **transitional object** can help. Let Dad rock Belle while also holding a safe soft stuffed doll. After just one chorus of "Beauty and the Beast," have him place Belle, still awake, in her crib along with the doll. Belle will surely howl when Dad leaves, but be brave. Remember, she's not in pain here; she's just been given a new bedtime routine, and she's a little confused. If Belle's crying persists, employ the conditioning method (discussed above), visiting her at increasing intervals. After three or four nights of conditioning, she should be sleeping well.

It is difficult work—nobody likes to listen to a crying baby for thirty minutes at a time—but the rewards are great. After a good night's sleep you'll soon forget the torture of the preceding nights. You'll be happier and, believe it or not, so will little Belle.

Q: *What about nap times? Do I use the same techniques there?*

A: Yes, with two exceptions. If an hour has passed and your child is still awake in her crib, forget that nap and try again next time. Also, if she gets tired and drops off while in the playpen or on the floor, that's okay. Eventually, once the night sleeping has straightened out, she will realize that the crib is a pretty cool place to sleep, and she'll expect to nap there, too.

Q: *Can teething be waking my baby at night?*

A: Unlikely. Teething may cause a little discomfort, but not enough pain to awaken a soundly sleeping baby. If there is really something physically wrong causing your baby to awaken at 3 a.m., whether it's her teeth or her tummy or her ears, would she stop so quickly when you pick her up? Would she be fine during the next day?

Q: *I've tried this method of conditioning, but I just can't do it. I give up. I can't take the crying. What now?*

A: Although the Ferber method seems to work for most families, some parents just can't bring themselves to put up with the howls and shrieks. They either camp out on the baby's floor or else go through the Disney songbook several times each night. Eventually, at age 2 or 3, you can reason with your child. At that age, there are other things you can do to recondition your child to sleep alone, such as using a star chart or some other little reward system.

Q: *When I try to condition my daughter to sleep by herself at night, she cries so hard that she makes herself vomit. What can I do?*

A: If you hear your daughter vomiting in the middle of the night, go in and clean her up quickly and without much fuss. Change the sheets, change her PJs, and out you go with the usual quick pat on the back. If you spend a lot of time soothing her or giving her a bottle to calm her down, then you are, in effect, rewarding her for vomiting. Before you know it, she will have discovered just how to make herself vomit in order to get you back in there with her. So make your trip a quick one, or else cleanup will become a regular part of your bedtime ritual.

Q: *We have an older son. While we are conditioning our newborn baby girl, is it fair to expect him to put up with her crying?*

A: Your older child may be sacrificing a few hours of sleep, but he'll be fine. Think of this as a family project. Besides, he's probably fed up with his sister's sleeping problems and will be relieved when she finally sleeps through the night. As far as him developing bad sleep habits of his own, this is rare for older children. If your son shares his baby sister's room, consider giving him new temporary quarters for a few nights. For example, fix up the couch in the den like a little tent. Even a sleeping bag on a mattress in the living room will do, and it can be fun for an adventurous child.

Q: Who should do the conditioning? Is this a mommy job or a daddy job?

A: Share the "fun." How you split up the quick trips in for a pat on the back is up to you. Maybe you'd prefer to alternate: Mom, then Dad, then Mom. Or else it might be better for you to split the night in half, Dad getting the first few hours, then Mom finishing up. Sleep conditioning is a tough job, and sharing the load is important. Even if you're a family where only the husband has a job outside the home, he should do his share. Remember, Mom has a new occupation too—raising this little troublemaker—and it's as tough as any 9-to-5 job.

Q: My year-old son, Vince, has been grinding his teeth a lot over the past month when he sleeps. Should I be concerned about this or is it something he will outgrow?

A: Tooth grinding (bruxism) is one of a group of normal behaviors common at night—sleepwalking is another—known as parasomnias. At one time it was felt that bruxism was a sign of tension. It's not that at all, but just a normal sleep variant. Fortunately, it will usually disappear by itself.

Q: My year-old son, Harry, has been getting up earlier and earlier every morning—5:00! Is there any way to train a child to sleep later?

A: There's not much you can do to train him to sleep in, other than just allowing him to cry for a few minutes until he settles himself back to sleep. If he were waking at 2 or 3 a.m., then you might try the Ferber method, but a 5 a.m. waking time is, unfortunately, not unusual at his age. Over the course of a few months, many kids will, on their own, delay their waking hour.

Q: I put my 8-month-old daughter to sleep on her back, but in the morning I find that she has flipped over onto her belly. What can I do?

A: This is a bit of a dilemma. Although we know that back sleeping is safest for babies, since it greatly reduces the risk of crib death, many babies will start to flip over by 6 or 7 months of age. If your daughter has flipped over and you can quietly and gently flip her back, go ahead. If, on the other hand, she quietly flips to her stomach and does so without awakening her mom and dad, then there is nothing you can do but leave her on her belly. There is a school of thought that says that the baby who flips over while sleeping is probably not very likely to smother and be subject to SIDS anyway. This makes sense. Also, by 8 months the risk of SIDS is much lower than in the first few months.

10

THE MONTHLY CHECKUP

Most doctors see babies for routine well-baby checkups at least every month or two during the first year. At each well-baby visit, your pediatrician will perform the usual poking, listening, and looking that your own family doctor does when he examines you. In addition to the examination, at 2 months of age your baby will begin the immunization and screening schedule.

IMMUNIZATIONS

From time to time newspaper articles and tabloid TV shows scare people by hyping the terrible consequences of "unsafe" vaccines. Several years ago, for example, the common DTP vaccine (diphtheria-tetanus-pertussis) was blamed for causing brain damage, a claim that was later disproved. Though DTP is now universally accepted as a safe vaccine when given to healthy babies, the media made no retractions. It seems that reassuring stories are not so newsworthy as frightening ones.

Similarly, a doctor from England recently aroused fear when he claimed that the MMR vaccine (measles-mumps-rubella), when given as a three-in-one immunization, predisposed children to developing autism. Although some children were indeed diagnosed with autism within a few months of receiving the MMR vaccine, there was no evidence that the vaccine actually *caused* autism. It's easy to see how this temporal relationship could be thought of as a causal relationship. Though children developed autism shortly after the vaccine, the occurrence was, in fact, coincidental. While the relationship between the MMR vaccine and autism has been disproved, the fear remains, since news of the vaccine's safety never made it to the front pages the way the original "shocking" story did.

The best person to ask about immunizations is your pediatrician. Trust him and you will trust his judgment about your child's immunization schedule. If you don't trust him, don't look for answers on TV or in the tabloids; get yourself a doctor you *do* trust. Above all, make careful, considered decisions. If you would like to know more about a particular medication or immunization, ask your doctor where you can find reliable information.

In the next few pages we'll discuss immunizations that currently make up a typical immunization schedule. Keep in mind that recommendations regarding vaccines for children are constantly changing. New vaccines are added periodically and the required frequency of booster doses (subsequent injections of a vaccine to "boost" immunity for later years) changes every few years. Because of the changing nature of recommendations, and because your pediatrician will adjust schedules to fit into your child's regular appointment routine, I won't give specific times for each vaccine; guidelines will be general. As always, consult your pediatrician to find out just what schedule is correct for your baby. As an appendix to this book, you will find an immunization chart that will allow you to keep track of all the vaccines your baby receives.

The Polio Vaccine
In the 1950s thousands of children died or were paralyzed due to polio, a disease of the spinal cord. Polio vaccine, an injection of inactivated virus, is administered in a total of four doses spaced throughout childhood—three doses in the first year and a booster dose before starting school. Polio vaccine is quite safe and rarely has any side effects at all, other than a slight swelling at the site of the vaccine, which is common with any immunization. Some children also develop a low-grade fever within the first few days after receiving the polio vaccine.

The DTaP Vaccine
The DTaP vaccine, given three times in the first year of life, again in the second year, and once more before school, protects against three real killers: diphtheria, tetanus (lockjaw), and pertussis (whooping cough).

Before the discovery of the vaccine, diphtheria was a common bacterial cause of death in children, attacking noses and throats with a suffocating blanket of pus. With this vaccine, which is a toxoid (toxin treated so that it has no negative effects on the body but can still provoke the formation of antibodies), cases of diphtheria are, fortunately, rare, but still may surface in children who have not been immunized.

Like the diphtheria part, the tetanus part of this three-in-one vaccine is a toxoid. It protects against the disease tetanus, a severe, life-threatening spasm of muscles seen most often after a crush injury or a cut from dirty metal or wood.

The pertussis component of the DTP vaccine, a combination of immunogenic proteins, is responsible for most of the injection's side effects. Fortunately, in the DTaP version the pertussis fraction has been modified to make it less reactive (the *a* in *DTaP* refers to acellular pertussis—a weaker form), and reactions are much less frequent and much less severe than in the past. After his DTaP shot, your baby may be irritable or sleepy, and you may notice a warm lump at the site of the injection. In some cases a mild fever might be present for a day or two.

MYTH: Nobody gets whooping cough anymore, so why give the vaccine to my child?
TRUTH: Wrong! There's plenty of whooping cough out there.

In pre-vaccine days pertussis, or whooping cough, was an epidemic killer, and there are still many cases of life-threatening pertussis in unimmunized babies. Also, the immunity provided by the vaccine for pertussis often wears off, and we see cases rather commonly in previously immunized teenagers and young adults. The good news, though, is that a teenager struck by whooping cough who received his DTP shots as a baby will have a much milder case. In contrast, an unvaccinated baby who contracts the whooping cough germ is very much in danger.

On rare occasions your doctor may choose to eliminate the pertussis part of the vaccine and give your baby only the DT vaccine, a decision usually reserved for babies who have had an unusual reaction to their last DTaP vaccine, such as a prolonged high temperature or an all-day crying spell, and for children known to have certain neurologic problems.

The HIB Vaccine
The HIB vaccine is a lifesaver that protects against a bacterium called Hemophilus influenza B (no, this is not related to the common influenza or flu virus). Until the HIB vaccine, this nasty bug was the most common cause of childhood meningitis, a deadly infection of the tissues that surround the brain and spinal cord. Now that the routine immunization schedule includes HIB, cases of meningitis in children have decreased dramatically. Rare now as well is another life-threatening Hemophilus infection called epiglottitis, a dangerous swelling of a flap of tissue directly above the windpipe. Hemophilus is also a cause of severe bloodstream infections, pneumonia, and potent joint infections.

The HIB vaccine is usually given three times during the first year of life, and then a booster dose is added in the second year. The HIB vaccine is not a live vaccine, but consists of a sugar prepared from the capsule of the germ. It rarely causes any reaction, but a low-grade temperature or swelling at the site of the shot may be present for a day or two.

The Hepatitis B Vaccine

The hepatitis B vaccine has, over the last several years, joined the list of immunizations now recommended for all babies. This vaccine, produced by modern DNA technology (ordinary baker's yeast is genetically altered to produce noninfectious hepatitis proteins), is also given three times during your baby's first year. It rarely causes a reaction, but a mild temperature may occur or your child may have a swelling at the injection site.

The virus, hepatitis B, causes a severe infection of the liver and increases the likelihood of developing cirrhosis of the liver or liver cancer later in life. The most common way to catch this infection is from blood products or from sexual relations, but newborns can also contract it via an infected birth canal. If a pregnant woman has recently acquired hepatitis B and is unaware of it, her baby is at risk.

MYTH: I don't have to give my baby the hepatitis vaccine, since he's not about to have sex.

TRUTH: He may already have been exposed to hepatitis, from his mom.

Even your innocent baby could be at risk for hepatitis B. First of all, if you've acquired hepatitis B during your pregnancy, you may not yet test positive for it, and you can pass it along to little Zack while he's in your uterus before you even show any signs of illness. Second, if Zack ever requires a transfusion, he would be at risk for acquiring hepatitis B through the transfused blood. Although blood is screened for hepatitis B, no screening procedure is absolutely foolproof. Third, although hepatitis B is acquired primarily by way of birth, sex, or blood, a significant number of cases occur each year where the method of transmission is unknown. Finally, it's easier to get this immunization series over right away, since you won't have to drag Zack, kicking and screaming, into the doctor's office when he's older (and stronger).

The Varicella (Chicken Pox) Vaccine

Chicken pox is a truly annoying illness. Covered with blisters, feverish, and itchy, the poor infected child must be isolated from humanity for at least five days. Not only can chicken pox be annoying, but on rare occasions it can spread to the brain, causing a dangerous encephalitis or brain inflammation. Some cases of pox have even been complicated by secondary infections of the skin, the so-called flesh-eating strep infections. Admittedly, these are rare birds, and we pediatricians seldom see them. Nevertheless, when the chicken pox vaccine was released and extensively tested, we all breathed a sigh of relief. The vaccine, now routinely recommended for all 1-year-olds, is a weakened live virus that may, rarely, result in a low-grade temperature, some swelling at the site of the shot, and, even rarer, a few noninfective pox days or weeks later.

MYTH: After the chicken pox vaccine, a child is more likely to develop shingles.
TRUTH: The chicken pox vaccine does not make shingles more likely.

Shingles, or Herpes zoster as it's known to physicians, is actually a recurrence of the chicken pox virus later in life. In some people, instead of the pox virus infecting a patient and then disappearing in a week, it lies dormant on nerve cells in the body. When it reappears along those same nerves later, for a variety of reasons, the virus shows itself in a limited area, such as an isolated patch of blisters on the side or back. Contrary to speculation, Herpes zoster is *not* more likely to occur after the chicken pox vaccine than after a natural case of chicken pox.

MYTH: I'm not giving my child the chicken pox vaccine. I'd rather he catch it naturally.
TRUTH: Catching the illness is no fun and also puts your child at risk of complications.

If you give little Zack his chicken pox vaccine, he probably won't have to get sick at all. True, no immunization yields 100 percent immunity. Measles cases erupt despite the measles vaccine, and mild cases of whooping cough occur despite the immunization, which can wear off. Similarly, the chicken pox vaccine does not eliminate all chance of contracting chicken pox. The difference, though, is that a breakthrough bout of chicken pox occurring in an immunized child will be much shorter, milder, and much less likely to have serious complications.

Because it is a live-virus vaccine, some children with reduced immunity, including those with AIDS or certain malignancies, do not receive the varicella vaccine.

The Pneumococcal Conjugate Vaccine

This inactive vaccine consists of the sugar coating of seven strains of the pneumococcus bacterium. Pneumococcus is a truly nasty little bugger that is now the number one bacterial cause of pneumonia, as well as a common cause of meningitis and bloodstream infections. A member of the strep family (but not the strep that causes strep throats), it is also the culprit in many cases of childhood ear and sinus infections. Given four times in the first two years of life, pneumococcal vaccine may cause a low-grade fever after a few days, and your baby may seem a bit fussy for a day or two.

The MMR Vaccine

Although occasionally given separately, measles, mumps and rubella (German measles) immunizations are usually administered together as MMR, a weakened live-virus vaccine given once between a year and 15 months of age and again before starting kindergarten (age 4½ to 5 years).

Although we pediatricians are lucky that measles is rare, thanks to the MMR vaccine, occasional cases still pop up from time to time. The rare baby who contracts measles can expect a cold, cough, fever, red runny eyes, and red spots all over his body. Mumps, another rarity in areas where kids are fortunate enough to have adequate supplies of MMR vaccine, usually shows up as a swelling of the salivary glands on the side of the face. Rubella (German measles) is often confused with measles but is usually milder and is also characterized by swollen glands (lymph nodes) behind the head or ears. Of much more concern is congenital rubella, acquired by a baby whose unimmunized mom came down with German measles during pregnancy. Such unfortunate newborns can suffer from a host of serious medical conditions, including hearing loss, visual disturbances, heart disease, and neurologic problems.

Reactions to MMR immunization include swelling at the site of the vaccine within two to three days of the injection and, less commonly, low-grade fever and a generalized rash one to two weeks after receiving the vaccine.

As is the case with other live vaccines, children who have severe problems with their immunity should not receive the MMR vaccine. Also, because measles vaccine is prepared in eggs, children with *severe* egg allergy should not receive the MMR vaccine.

SCREENING TESTS

Along with all those vaccines, babies are subjected to a variety of screening tests during the many well-baby visits in the first year.

The Newborn Metabolic Screening Panel

Even before little Zack comes home from the hospital, he will most likely have had his first screening blood test. The metabolic screening panel is routinely performed once within a day or two of birth, and then repeated either before discharge or in your doctor's office. A drop of blood from the baby's heel is tested to ensure that he doesn't have one of a number of extremely rare inherited diseases. The conditions tested vary somewhat from state to state but include such illnesses as sickle cell disease, cystic fibrosis, phenylketonuria, tyrosinemia, biotinidase deficiency, homocystinuria, maple syrup urine disease, galactosemia, HIV, and thyroid disease. Again, most of these conditions are extremely rare, but if your baby has an abnormality in any of these tests, your doctor will be notified by the state's laboratory and will want to see your baby for a confirmatory test.

Hearing and Vision Screening Tests

Many hospitals now routinely screen for hearing problems in newborns. Also, some doctors screen for visual problems in the first year of life with a handy little camera called a vision screener, which can pick up such visual disturbances as farsightedness, nearsightedness, astigmatism, and strabismus (a condition in which the eye turns in or out).

The Urinalysis, Blood Count, and Lead Screen

Later in the first year, a routine urinalysis will ensure that your baby does not have a silent urinary tract infection, diabetes, or kidney disease. Also late in Zack's first year a blood count (hemoglobin or hematocrit) will make sure that he is not anemic (low in iron). A blood test for exposure to lead will also be done at this time. Lead can find its way into your child from old lead-based house paint, from environmental dust and soil, and from lead-containing pipes, and can lead to reduced growth, learning problems, and kidney damage.

The PPD Test

Finally, babies are usually screened around nine months for exposure to tuberculosis. A minute amount of noninfectious tuberculosis protein (called PPD, purified protein derivative) is placed just under the skin on your baby's forearm. In two or three days, simply look at the area around the injection. If you see a big welt (like a mosquito bite), notify your doctor. Once again, this test determines whether your baby has been *exposed* to tuberculosis. A positive test does not mean that he is *sick* with tuberculosis.

KIDFIXER FREQUENTLY ASKED QUESTIONS

Q: *My child is due for an immunization today, but he has a cold. Can he still get the vaccine? Will he get sicker? Will the vaccine not "take"?*

A: Although most doctors refrain from giving vaccines to babies who have a high temperature or a serious illness, the common sniffle is no contraindication to getting a routine vaccine.

Q: *My child is way behind on his vaccines. Do I have to start every-thing over? Have I "wasted" the shots he's already gotten?*

A: Don't worry. Even the best-intentioned parents can fall behind on im-munizations. Sometimes you're planning a vacation and don't want to spoil it by giving a vaccine that may result in a fever. Many babies fall behind because they have a bad infection at the time an immuniza-tion is due and must delay the vaccine. Frequently immunizations are back-ordered, and your doctor may have to wait for his supply. Have no fear. Those early vaccines were not wasted because the series wasn't completed in the usual period of time. Your doctor can still catch up and finish off your child's vaccine series. Also, most vaccines can be safely combined, so more than one shot can be given at the same time. Your doctor will be able to prepare a catch-up schedule for you.

Q: *Is it safer to wait until a vaccine has been around for a few years, rather than to be the first one to try it out? Shouldn't I let others get the vaccine and make sure there are no unexpected problems or complications?*

A: If vaccines were just thrust upon the market with no testing, then yes, it would be safer to wait. Fortunately, this isn't the case. Before that new vaccine is released to the public and recommended by the American Academy of Pediatrics for routine use, it has been tested and retested until the vaccine has been shown to be safe. The ques-tion to ask your pediatrician is this: has this vaccine been recom-mended by the American Academy of Pediatrics for routine use in children? If his answer is yes, then there should be no hesitation on your part. Some vaccines are only recommended for special groups, or in certain circumstances. For example, hepatitis A vaccine is usu-ally given only to people who are at risk for acquiring this illness, such as those traveling to underdeveloped countries. Other than these special-circumstance vaccines, all those that have been recom-mended by the Academy of Pediatrics are appropriate for *all* kids.

Q: *Can we be certain that the protection from one dose of chicken pox vaccine will last forever? What if they say, after a few years, that my child needs a booster shot? Isn't it better just to get the disease, since getting the disease will make my child immune for life?*

A: Not really. Although right now one dose of chicken pox vaccine is all that is believed to be necessary for lifelong immunity, there is no guarantee that somewhere down the line a second dose may not be needed to boost a child's immunity. This was what happened with the measles vaccine, originally a single immunization but now given twice. If a booster dosage is later suggested for chicken pox, it's a small price to pay to avoid a week of misery or a serious complication.

Q: *I've heard that some vaccines contain mercury. Isn't mercury dangerous?*

A: In the past, most vaccines used a very small amount of thimerosal, which contains traces of mercury as a preservative. Now mercury has been eliminated from most vaccines and mercury levels are greatly reduced in those few vaccines still preserved with thimerosal. Speak to your pediatrician to make certain that he uses mercury-free vaccines.

Q: *Is it safe to use a shot that combines two or three different vaccines?*

A: Quite safe. To save your baby from many different pokes, there are now such combinations as hepatitis B and HIB as well as DTP, polio, and hepatitis B. These have been thoroughly tested, are no more likely to cause reactions, and are just as effective as vaccines given separately.

11

THE PORTABLE
BABY

After you've had a new baby there's a tendency to feel a bit blue. New moms sometimes have a hormonal imbalance that causes a nasty, if temporary, depression. Dad isn't exempt either, what with the added pressures of a new family member and new child care responsibilities. Add in a lack of sleep and you have all the ingredients for a nice case of cabin fever. It's time to get out of the house.

MYTH: It isn't safe to take a baby outside in the first few weeks.
TRUTH: You can go out whenever you like after the first week—sooner if you must.

Unless you're taking home a small premie or a baby with special health issues, there's no reason to remain cooped up in your house or apartment. Full-term babies adapt to changing temperature quite well after the first week of life. Contrary to popular belief, they aren't put at risk by a brisk winter day or even a bit of rain. So go for that walk and, as long as the weather is not too extreme, make it a nice long one, too.

MYTH: You *must* take a baby out every day for fresh air.

TRUTH: This is a baby we're talking about, right? Not a dog?

There's no law saying that you *must* go out every day. Babies don't have to be let out for an "airing." If you have something to do around the house, or you're a mom who does office work from home, don't feel that every day must include a walk. Not feeling up to par? Prefer to spend one day in the comfort of your home? Go ahead; little Ruthie won't mind. Also, Ruthie would just as soon stay indoors when the thermometer soars up into the 90s or drops into the teens. If you're uncomfortable outside, chances are your baby will be uncomfortable as well.

That little bundle you schlepped around for nine months wasn't exactly sitting still. When you jogged down the street, rode in your car, or climbed the steps to your apartment, who do you think was riding along with you? Although they are sheltered from sudden changes in motion by a nice cushy uterus and the shock absorption of amniotic fluid, babies are real movers and shakers before they're born, and they usually handle travel quite well after they're born. Of course, now you're not providing the same cushy and shock-reduced environment that you supplied for nine months, so you'll have to be a bit more careful about those sudden starts and stops.

Most destinations are fine, but **avoid the following:**

• *Crowded places.* Malls and department stores are not great choices for the first two months. Although most of the infections that Ruthie picks up will come from her own family members, there's no sense in tempting fate. Below two months of age babies' immune systems are not fully developed, so why expose your newborn to a sea of germs while she is still susceptible to infection?

• *People with obvious infections.* Although there is no way to know for sure if someone is incubating a germ, it still makes sense to stay away from that coughing guy on the corner or that kid down the block with the green runny nose.

TRAVEL

MYTH: Babies are too fragile to travel during the first six months.
TRUTH: Babies can handle a long car ride, train trip, or flight just fine.

Our many adoptive parents have brought home newborns from as far away as Asia with no problem, so don't feel you must wait until Ruthie is a big girl before she visits her grandma out west. As far as a vacation trip, feel free to include your baby after those first two susceptible months.

Of course, travel with a baby imposes its own little hardships and special considerations. To make your travel experience as enjoyable and stress-free as possible, keep the following **travel tips** in mind:

CAR TRIPS

• *Make frequent stops.* If you're taking a long car trip, stop at least every three hours, or else you'll have a cranky, wet baby screaming in the back.

• *No loose objects.* Make sure that your overloaded car has no loose objects that can hit the baby if you stop short.

• *Drive slowly!* You're now entrusted with a very young and very precious life. Let that annoying guy get ahead of you, and if he cuts you off, let him go.

• *Bring along your baby's favorite toys.* Play her favorite CD. If you have a minivan with a VCR, let her watch her favorite cartoon — again.

• *Bring a portable crib*; the motel may not have one.

• *Bring medications.* If you're going somewhere that may not have your child's medicines, bring them with you.

• *Don't forget that car seat!*

FLYING WITH BABY

Here are some tips for making that airplane trip easier.

• *Reserve a separate seat.* The safest way to fly with a child is to reserve a separate seat and put little Ruthie in her own car safety seat. As expensive as this may sound, it's the safest policy and will also make it more likely that she will sleep for part of the trip—you may nap, too. Most airlines give a 50 percent discount on seats for children two years of age and under.

• *Food.* Some airlines have baby meals, but call ahead to double-check your airline's policy. Bring along some baby food, drinks, and snacks, just in case.

• *Permission needed?* If only one parent is flying out of the country with a baby, many airlines require a notarized letter stating that both parents give permission for the infant to travel.

• *Diaper bag.* Incorporate your diaper bag into your travel bag. Make sure you have extra diapers, wipes, toys, and an extra shirt for you—in case of spills.

• *Bring a bottle.* To prevent that annoying ear popping, let Ruthie drink something when the plane ascends and descends. Swallowing provides the same relief from pressure that adults get from chewing gum.

• *Fly at night.* A night flight, if convenient, might ensure better sleep, for both you and your baby.

TRAVEL OVERSEAS

Before you and Ruthie head for Zanzibar:

• *Current medications.* Make sure you bring any medication that your baby regularly uses. If she is a wheezer and requires a nebulizer,

bring it with you, along with the medication that is used in the nebulizer. If she has a skin condition and uses a special ointment, bring that as well. If you're going for more than a few weeks, bring along her vitamins.

• **Bring along a supply of medication that she might need.** If she gets frequent ear infections, you might want to ask your doctor to write a prescription for a medication that works well for her and that she takes without too much of a fight. That way you won't be at the mercy of an unfamiliar pharmacy.

• **Make sure that she's up to date on her regular immunizations,** such as DTaP, polio, and so on. Diphtheria is still endemic in some areas, but three doses of DTaP will provide effective protection for your baby. Many countries have high rates of measles. If Ruthie is going to such a place, she will need an early measles vaccine (this is usually given after a year of age but can be given earlier if travel plans necessitate). She would then need another measles vaccine at the usual time.

• **Special immunizations.** There are some countries for which special immunizations are recommended and for which preventative medication is required. For example, a hepatitis A vaccine is recommended before traveling to certain underdeveloped countries. Other countries suggest malaria prophylaxis, others a typhoid vaccine. Such recommendations change depending upon what outbreaks are occurring at a particular time. How is one to know what is needed? This is one time when your pediatrician probably will *not* know the answer. The best policy is to get in touch with the Centers for Disease Control and Prevention (CDC), either through their Web site's travel page (www.cdc.gov/travel)

or by phone (888-232-3228), a few months before you travel, and then again within one month of travel.

• *Insect repellent.* If you're off to a place with lots of creepy-crawlies, bring along an insect repellent with 30 percent DEET, the one effective insect repellent.

• *Pack a sunblock,* with an SPF of at least 15 (see the FAQ section below).

• *Traveler's diarrhea.* Travel to many countries involves a risk of traveler's diarrhea, a bacterial infection of the intestines. In such areas as Central America, Africa, the Middle East, and Asia stick to bottled water and eat only fruits that can be peeled. Avoid salads and uncooked vegetables, as well as ice cubes, all of which may be contaminated. Your doctor may suggest a specific antibiotic (such as Bactrim or Septra) to treat the bacteria that cause traveler's diarrhea.

• *Your child will need a passport.*

KIDFIXER FREQUENTLY ASKED QUESTIONS

Q: *I'm never sure how to dress my baby for a walk. How much warmth does she need?*

A: Other than small premies, after the first week of age dress your baby the way you're dressed. If you're wearing a sweater, your baby doesn't need two sweaters. If it's summer and you're wearing a T-shirt, your baby can wear a T-shirt as well.

Q: How about a sunny day? Does my baby need sunblock?

A: Your baby should be protected from the sun, just as her parents should be. Children are more susceptible to sunburn than adults, and a severe sunburn that occurs during childhood is more danger-ous, in terms of later risk of skin cancer, than a sunburn that occurs during adulthood. Use a sunblock with an SPF of at least 15. Try to find one without PABA, a chemical that can be sensitizing for babies.

Q: Can I give my baby something to make her sleep for the whole flight?

A: This isn't usually a great idea. First of all, most babies do just great on a flight. The gentle vibration and movement are a lot like those familiar movements from inside the uterus. Also, there's no guaran-tee that your child will sleep when given medication. Many babies will drop right off after a dose of an antihistamine, such as Ben-adryl, but many others will become fussy or hyper from the same medication.

Q: Is it a good idea to give my 5-month-old daughter a decongestant to prevent ear-popping before she flies?

A: A decongestant usually isn't necessary. Drinking a bottle or nursing during ascent and descent is usually all that's needed. If your child has a stuffy nose, use mild children's nose drops or spray (children's Neosynephrine, for example), on ascent and descent.

Q: My 6-month-old, Ralphie, has a cold. Do we have to cancel our trip to Disney World?

A: Not necessarily. It would probably be a good idea to have your pedi-atrician take a look at Ralphie's ears, just to make sure he has no ear infection, before you leave. If she gives you the go-ahead, enjoy the trip. Just remember to give Ralphie a drink on ascent and descent (and maybe a shot of children's nose drops as well).

Q: We have a boat. Are there any special precautions I need to take for my 7-month-old daughter?

A: First of all, make sure she's wearing the smallest life jacket you can find. It might also be a good idea to bring along some children's Dramamine, an over-the-counter medication that reduces nausea. Of course, *never* leave her unattended on the boat.

Q: *I like to ride my bike. A friend bought me this really cute little trailer that attaches to my bike for my 8-month-old Lucie to sit in. Is this safe? I bought her the cutest little helmet!*

A: Sorry, but that helmet and trailer will have to wait. Until her first birthday, Lucie's little neck isn't quite strong enough for that kind of travel.

12

BEHAVIORAL
ISSUES

The way you act toward your baby is at least as important as the things you do for him. It's not always easy being a good parent, but it's vital to raise your child in an environment of love, patience, and support. This chapter will deal with some of the ways in which some well-meaning parents fail to live up to this ideal, and will provide some guidance to help you stay on the right track.

THOSE FIRST FEW WEEKS

Bringing a baby home from the hospital is an amazing experience, but it's also a time of stress and anxiety. After having to push a bowling ball through a pinhole—isn't that what delivering a baby is like?—and now handling hormonal changes that would try a saint, you may not be at your very strongest. Insurance companies are very considerate; they allow new moms to spend two full days to recover after a delivery. How generous of them. For most parents, there are also new financial pressures to face (a crib costs *how* much?).

Through the years, many parents have expressed the concern that they don't sense the instant overwhelming love for their newborn babies they expected. Instead, they often feel guilty or inadequate because all they really want to do is *rest*. What I tell them is this: Your feelings are normal. Love is not something that suddenly appears, in full force, when a baby is delivered. Love grows. Delivering a baby, whether by vaginal delivery or by cesarean section, is an operation. It takes an awful lot out of a woman and requires several weeks of recuperation. It's perfectly normal, in those first few weeks, to be as concerned about regaining your energy as you are about "meeting" your new baby. As you recover, mentally and physically, from childbirth, and as your baby starts to develop his own personality, a gradual bonding process will take place. You are sure to find that little Jason, with his smiles and coos, is becoming less of a job and more of a friend.

THE SLEEPY BABY AND THE JITTERY BABY

Not only can babies look very different, but they can also act in very different ways. Consider, for example, the sleepy baby and the jittery baby.

If your baby seems to spend the entire day sleeping, you may well wonder, "Is this okay?" Relax, it really is. Many babies are truly sleepy babies. They nurse or bottle-feed, fall back to sleep, awake for a poop and a change, and then back to sleep they go. Some babies sleep twelve hours at night and still take several healthy naps during the day. Again, this is not a problem, as long as little Jason is alert, active, and feeds enthusiastically when he's awake. Such sleepiness is just his own pattern, learned in the uterus, and he will soon spend a lot more time awake.

Some jittery babies look as though they are nervous as soon as they get home from the hospital. They seem to be constantly jumpy, moving, and trembling. As long as these movements are limited to the legs or arms, there is nothing to worry about. Babies with jittery extremities are just showing us that their newborn neurologic systems are not fully mature; they're acting the way fetuses do in the womb. Of course, if your baby is shaking all over, then give your doctor a call. Some babies with low blood sugar or low blood calcium in the first few weeks of life will actually tremble all over and should be seen by the pediatrician.

TEMPERAMENT AND RESPONSIVITY: IT'S NOT YOUR FAULT

Let's clear one thing up right away: **not everything is your fault.** Just as different adults have differences in temperament, so do different babies. Some infants are quiet and passive, others noisy and on the go. Some babies seem generally happy most of the time, while others are moodier and unsmiling. Some infants are more likely than others to cry when frustrated, tired, or slightly uncomfortable. The same quick bath that one child finds pleasing can set off a bout of screaming for another. Pediatricians appreciate that, just as there is a normal range of length, weight, and even developmental achievement, there is a normal spectrum of baby fussing and crying, what child neurologists call responsivity. At one end of the spectrum is the tranquil noncrier. At the other end is the infant who fusses and cries more than most. It's important to recognize that there is nothing wrong with such a crying baby, just as there is nothing wrong with the infant who is easily satisfied. Once your doctor has ruled out the many causes of a crying baby, discussed throughout this book in different chapters, you just may have to accept the fact that your baby is a crier—that he's hyperresponsive. Rest assured, such behavior usually lessens by 6 months of age.

If your baby's temperament is much like your own, then it will be easier for you two to get along. If not, this transition will be more difficult. Yes, your genes did have a large role in making your baby the unique individual that he is, but your special gumbo of DNA left plenty of room for individuality. Just as you were unable to order blue eyes, athletic ability, an IQ of 150, and good study habits, you were similarly at the mercy of whatever temperament came out of the personality hopper. And, once you discover that you and your child are very different people, there's not much you can do to change that personality; you're just going to have to live with it. New moms and dads too often feel guilty if their babies are difficult to console or if they spend more time fussing than their friends' infants. As Richard Olsen assures us in his fine article about infant temperament in *Contemporary Pediatrics,* "The tendency to blame parents has the potential to increase parental guilt and decrease parental feelings of self-worth and efficacy. It also fails to account for differences in the behavior of young infants. Parents' ability to console a crying infant has an impact on their feelings of competence. If the infant is difficult to console, parents need to understand this is an innate characteristic of the infant, not a result of their inadequacy."

Again, it's not always your fault.

DISCIPLINE AND PARENTAL TEMPER

Now that you've been given "dispensation" for your baby's occasional foul moods, let's discuss how to respond when your child *is* acting up.

MYTH: It's okay to discipline a child by gently spanking him.
TRUTH: It's never acceptable to hit a child.

This doesn't seem too tough, does it? Why would any parent hit an adorable and innocent little baby? Yet it does happen, every day. Consider this example.

Mrs. Smith wanted desperately to have a baby. She and her husband had been trying to conceive for several years, and when she finally did become pregnant, she did everything right—no smoking, alcohol, or caffeine, lots of healthy food.

After Smitty junior was born, Mrs. Smith had a brief period of depression, but then returned to her old buoyant self. She kept Smitty junior neat as a pin, and he seemed to thrive, gaining weight well at each checkup. At the monthly exams, however, I noticed that she seemed a bit more upset by Smitty's crying than one would expect. Several months later, Mr. Smith brought his son in for a sick visit because he had "fallen off his changing table" and bruised his back. Such a story is not unusual; kids are slippery little critters, and the first time a child rolls over, he often rolls onto the floor. The only problem with Mr. Smith's story is that by 7 months most parents have experienced just how quickly their kids can make that dive and are usually more careful. This was an age-inappropriate accident, and I was a bit suspicious, especially because Smitty senior seemed a little fuzzy on the details. When I examined Junior, I noticed some suspicious older bruises, including one on his arm that looked a lot like a handprint.

Soon Dad admitted, with relief, that his wife had a temper problem, and that day she had confessed to having slapped Smitty several times. She knew that slapping Smitty junior was wrong, but she couldn't control her temper.

This is an all-too-common story; many parents have trouble controlling their tempers. Make no mistake about it, hitting your baby is child abuse. A recent American Academy of Pediatrics study showed that

- More than 3 million children are abused or neglected in the United States each year.
- Three children die each day from abuse and neglect in the United States.
- One-third of all Americans have seen an adult physically abuse a child.

Are these parents all bad people? I would not judge Mrs. Smith as a completely bad person. She's a good wife, a fine neighbor, and a caring daughter to Smitty junior's grandparents. She does, however, have a problem controlling her anger and is now getting help from a family therapist. Many parents have this same problem. What should you do if you feel you're in danger of losing it when your baby just won't stop crying, or spitting up all over your nice clean house, or breaking your beautiful antique porcelain figures? Consider these tips, designed to help a parent manage the inevitable frustration and anger that is part and parcel of parenting:

- **Take a break!** Ask Grandma, a sitter, a friend, or your hubby to watch your baby for an hour. Get out of the house and get some separation from him. You'll see just how trivial that "terrible thing" he did really was and you will have a chance to cool down and get control.

- **Babyproof your house.** Not only will you make things safer for your baby, but you won't have to watch him like a hawk to make sure your valuable possessions are safe. Take all those fragile things that mean so much to you and that your baby seems set on destroying and put them away until he's older. Similarly, babyproof your wardrobe. Take Mom's silk blouse and Dad's cashmere sweater and save them for your night out together.

- *Ask for help at home.* Even if you can't get away, have Grandma or a friend come over and help you feed that spitter or bathe that squirmer. Getting squirted or splashed can be maddening. Watching it happen to someone else is very funny.

- *Look out for signs that you may be losing it.* Are you smoking more? Are you drinking more? Are you resorting to your Xanax more frequently? Do you find only frustration instead of fun in activities you used to enjoy doing with your child, like shopping or walking in the park?

- *Get professional help.* It's no sin to recognize that you have a problem with temper control and to ask your doctor if he knows the name of a good therapist. Recognizing that you have a problem can be difficult, but your doctor will understand and will be glad to help you find help.

- *Don't hit; it can become a habit.* Even when you're not angry, don't slap your child to discipline him. Hitting a child doesn't "teach him a lesson." It just teaches him to hit others, and it can become a bad habit to break. If you do it while you're under control, because you think you need to discipline your child, you will do it even more when you lose control. There is *no* time when hitting a child is acceptable behavior.

- *Don't scream at your baby.* It will only frighten him. If you feel that you must scream to let off some steam, put the baby in his crib or playpen, go into another room or step outside for a second, close the door, and scream away.

- *Don't discipline—yet.* Before 2 years of age discipline is meaningless. Babies learn by example and by copying their parents' behavior. If you care for your child in a patient and calm way, you will have a patient and calm baby to care for. Once your child is 2 years of age, use a two-minute time-out to discipline him.

- *Avoid the most stressful situations.* Do you lose it when you have to bathe your baby? Make that Daddy's job, or skip it altogether on those days when you're tired or grouchy. Is it that trip to the supermarket that gets you, since you have the combined stress of a crying baby and the disapproving looks of those old biddies who forgot how hard it is to be a parent and who expect babies to act like librarians? If so, save the shopping trip for when the sitter comes, or else have the sitter shop for you; or shop after dinner, when Daddy can watch the baby and you can treat yourself to a nice cup of mocha latte as you scan the aisles.

• *Keep your baby's cranky times in mind.* Know when your child is losing it and avoid stressful activities when he tends to be fussiest. If he always gets cranky at 3:00 in the afternoon, don't choose that time to go shopping or to give him a bath. That's a good time to let him have a nap or to let him cry it out in his playpen if nothing will console him. It's also the perfect time for a little support from a neighbor or friend.

BREATH-HOLDING SPELLS

As Drs. Jane Anderson and Daniel Bluestone relate, in their article entitled "Breath-Holding Spells: Scary but Not Serious," this is one of the many times when something a child does is scary, but not serious. The typical scenario: Jason cries after a fright or some minor injury. He exhales, and then you hear nothing at all coming from him—no cry, no sound, not even a breath. Soon he's pale or even blue. He may even pass out or, most frightening of all, start shaking his arms and legs—just like a little convulsion! After a few seconds he's conscious, pink, and his old self again. What was *that*? Was it a seizure? Did he hurt his head? No, this was a breath-holding spell, and as scary as it is, it's actually quite common and totally benign.

Although we don't know why some children have breath-holding spells and others do not, they seem to occur because the circulatory system in breath holders is more sensitive to nerve stimulation than in kids who aren't breath holders. Typically, breath-holding spells first occur between 6 and 18 months of age, and a child who has had one such spell is likely to have more. They are completely involuntary—this isn't Jason's way of getting back at you—and, although frightening, are harmless and usually resolve by 5 years of age.

What to do while your child is having a breath-holding spell:

• *Keep your breath holder safe.* Hold him in your arms or lay him on his side on a bed or a carpeted floor.

• *Calmly wait for the spell to stop.* This usually happens in a few seconds.

Finally, don't try to prevent a breath-holding spell by avoiding situations that might make your child cry. Kids need limits, and a breath-holding spell is no reason to change the way you parent your child.

LOVE, LIMITS, AND LEAVE THEM ALONE

This classic phrase, which is one I've borrowed, offers good advice for parents. What does it mean?

• *Love.* As a pediatrician, I've been humbled by the way someone with a difficult infancy and early childhood can turn out to be such a super school-age kid and such a terrific teen. A child who had several rough illnesses or behavioral problems in school may become the brightest and sweetest kid around. Often, I am left with the conclusion that such a child made it through those early tough years because he had the most caring and loving parents around. That doesn't mean that his folks did everything perfectly. All moms and dads make some mistakes—I know that I sure did. But for every criticism I wish I hadn't made, for every scolding I wish I hadn't given, and for every spelling mistake on a homework assignment I wish I'd overlooked, there were plenty of hugs and kisses, and there was a lot of praise. In short, there was a lot of love. **Kids are smart enough and sensitive enough to forgive us our trespasses—as long as they are equipped with love.** Don't be afraid to pick up your baby and hug him. It may seem obvious, but tell your child that you love him, and praise him often.

• *Limits.* As your baby becomes a child, and later a young woman or young man, there is a tendency to want to be a friend. When they were babies, I enjoyed playing with my sons more than doing just about anything. As they got older, we swam together, camped together, and biked together. Today they're grown up and are pretty much out of the house, but my sons are still my best friends. Sometimes, however, in the effort to be a best friend, we forget that we're parents, too. Although a good friend will always try to make a pal happy, sometimes a parent has to make tough decisions that will make a child unhappy. Sometimes we have to say no to that extra cookie request, or deny that unsafe toy. You will, no doubt, one day hear something like this coming from your child's bedroom: "But why do I have to wear a helmet when nobody *else* is wearing a helmet?" Or else "But Jennie's mom lets her go to the mall, why can't *I*?" We all make mistakes. Not all of our decisions will prove to be correct. Yet even though it may make us temporarily unpopular with our children, we must set consistent limits. Even if our children see our actions as arbitrary and even if they say that magic phrase, "I hate you," we have to be their parents.

• *Leave them alone.* When our children are very young, we have nearly absolute control; they're within our grasp, physically, almost all the time. Soon we share control with other caregivers—a nanny, a babysitter, eventually a teacher. With the loss of control comes independence on little Jason's part. Without his mommy and daddy around to make every decision for him, he will have to learn to fend for himself. As a small baby, when Jason's cries are not met with an instant response, he learns to delay his gratification. Later on, as he creeps and crawls and cruises around the family room, he will learn how to get that toy all by himself. As you leave him alone, he will learn new skills that will allow him to develop into a fully functioning young boy and, eventually, a responsible young man. **It is by allowing our children to fend for themselves that they learn how to cope with life's challenges and difficulties.** Sometimes this is difficult. It's tough to allow a child to hand in a homework assignment with the word *president* spelled with a *z*. But if we quickly respond to every need, rather than allowing our kids to learn from their mistakes and to find solutions to their problems all by themselves, they will never learn to solve problems.

SIBLING RIVALRY

Let's face it. You and your older child, Jason, have been pretty good buddies for the three years of his life. You've spent countless hours reading him stories, pushing him on his swing, and in general satisfying every whim. Now along comes the new baby, Jenna. Suddenly Jason's best pal and playmate is out of action. Jason's relatives and family friends are equally traitorous. All they want to do is pick up little Jenna and give her toys. It's no wonder that Jason has gotten just a little fed up with his new baby sister. Can you blame him?

Although some degree of rivalry is to be expected in all older siblings, some jealous older brothers or sisters carry it to extremes and harm their new siblings. Admittedly, such an extreme is rare, but if your older child seems to be just a tad too rough with those hugs and "affectionate" little love pats, then keep a close eye out for any possible harm.

How can you **limit the amount of jealousy** your older child feels toward this new baby you have thrust upon him?

• *Don't force the baby on your older child.* If he wants to take part in helping you care for the baby, go ahead and let him. Just use the word *gentle* every two or three seconds. If, on the other hand, Jason has decided that he'd rather play with his toys alone, by all means allow him to do it.

• *Enough about the baby!* Don't feel that you must continually say how cute and wonderful the new baby is. Jason can see just how cute she is—that's the problem!

• *Remind him that he's special to you.* Emphasize that even though you love to play with Jason, you need to spend some time with baby Jenna as well.

• *Use time-outs when necessary.* When your older child tests you by acting like a baby—after all, if the baby gets all that attention by simply pooping in a diaper and crying, why not do the same?—try not to overrespond. If you respond to his regressive behavior with a long tirade or a long lecture, he'll just act that way again. After all, Jason just wants your attention. He doesn't really care if that attention is positive or negative. If acting like a baby gets him a long lecture, he'll just do it some more. To discourage such "baby" behavior, give him a brief time-out—a few minutes in his room without you will eventually dissuade him from such behavior.

• **Remember to use time-in as well.** When you do have a minute to spend with your older child, make a fuss about how happy you are to be able to do big-boy things with him. When you notice him acting mature and helping you in the house, give him a time-in by reading a quick story to him or by coloring with him for a few minutes. This is positive reinforcement.

KIDFIXER FREQUENTLY ASKED QUESTIONS

Q: *If slapping is a no-no and if time-outs are for older kids, how do I discipline my year-old daughter?*

A: Until time-outs come into play, usually after age 2, we teach our children by example and by positive reinforcement. Babies tend to imitate the behaviors they see in their parents—they even imitate their moods—so set a good example for your little one. Also, use positive reinforcement (praise, hugs, kisses, time-in activities) to encourage good behavior.

Q: *I know I shouldn't have done it, but I slapped my 9-month-old son yesterday for getting into my makeup. I feel terrible. I've never done it before, and I know I'll never do it again. He seems just fine—it wasn't much of a slap—but I feel terrible. Have I emotionally scarred him for life? Will he grow up hating me?*

A: Although it's never okay to hit a child, you're not an ogre, he won't hate you, and he's not scarred for life. We all make mistakes and lose our temper at times. Forgive yourself and rest assured that your son will forgive you as well. Just as it's foolish to think that bonding to a newborn is an all-or-none process at birth, it's silly to think that one minute of temper will undo years of love and affection. If, on the other hand, this is something you do repeatedly, then consider meeting with a therapist to learn better ways to channel your anger.

Q: *I've babyproofed my house, but there are still times when my 11-month-old daughter gets into things she shouldn't. Saying no doesn't seem to work—she just laughs. What can I do?*

A: After a while, just saying no is not enough. First of all, when you say no, also physically remove your daughter from the object she's handling. If she's crawling around your child-safe family room and she scoots over to your coffee table and starts eating the TV remote, say no, pick her up, and move her to another part of the room. Also, try to distract her with a more appropriate toy—fish something out of the toy chest that she hasn't seen for a month and offer that as a substitute. Redirecting a child with a new toy can save you from having to replace a lot of remotes.

Q: *My older child, Carrie, always got along with her baby brother, Justin. Now that Justin is 8 months old, Carrie has become a terror. If this is sibling rivalry, why is it just starting now? Have I done something wrong?*

A: It's not you, it's Justin. Until now he was no threat to his sister. He just napped in his crib, ate his baby food, and played with those boring plastic keys. Now that he's a big boy, he's sitting in his sister's high chair, eating her cookies, and playing with her toys. Justin has become a threat, and Carrie's retaliation is inevitable. Respond by spending a few minutes whenever you can doing grown-up things with Carrie that Justin can't do—like reading a story together or doing a puzzle.

PART IV

GROWTH AND DEVELOPMENT

Children are like fingers: some long, some short.

— OLD CHINESE PROVERB

13

MY, HOW
YOU'VE GROWN!

I wish I had a nickel for every time parents or grandparents (especially grandparents) asked me if their child or grandchild was too small. "She looks so much smaller than all the other babies who are 6 months old," is a typical complaint. "Why isn't she growing faster?" is another.

MYTH: Babies are supposed to gain 1½ to 2 pounds every month.

TRUTH: Babies are very different and gain at different rates. They also can't add.

On average, babies in the United States gain about 1½ to 2 pounds a month. But this is just a statistic. It takes into account the following facts:

- Nursed babies often tend to gain a bit more slowly.
- Many babies gain little or no weight for two months, then catch up the following month.
- Babies of different cultures often grow at different rates.

The 1½ to 2 pounds a month is just an average, not a requirement. Babies, just like real people, have days when they seem hungrier than

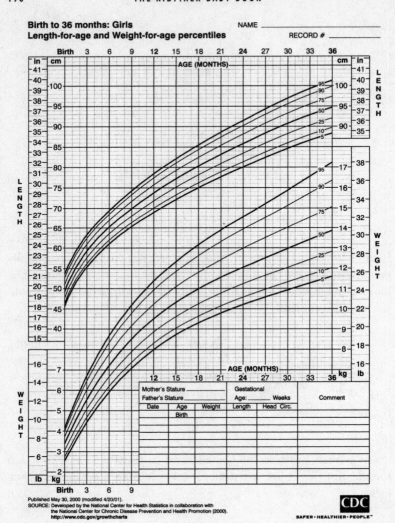

A baby girl growth chart

other days. They have weeks when they eat less than other weeks. They have months when they gain more than other months.

So, if babies all gain at different rates, how do you know that your little Cruella is gaining and growing normally? That's where your doctor's growth chart comes in handy. Growth charts for babies look something like the chart on page 190.

On this chart, your pediatrician will plot your baby's length and weight at every visit. Her length and weight curves, if she is an average-sized baby, will be near the middle of the graphs. If she is on the small side, her own curves may be closer to the bottom; if bigger, near the top. She may even change the curves she follows, shifting from one near the top, for example, to one closer to the bottom. Eventually, however—and this may not occur until she's 2 or 3 years old—Cruella will start to follow one of the arcs on the chart. Once she has established her growth curve, as long as she follows it reasonably well, then there is usually no problem with growth. If she was a 50th-percentile 3-month-old (that is, her length and weight each visit for the first three months always seemed to land near the 50th-percentile curve), and lately she is following the 25th-percentile curve, that's okay, as long as she now is tracking along this new curve and not falling off the chart completely. This all may seem a bit complicated, and at times it is. Just ask your pediatrician to explain your child's growth chart progress the next time you make a trip to his office. He'll be happy to show you how Cruella is doing.

Here's another myth that many parents have repeated:

MYTH: Babies double their weight at 6 months and triple it at a year.
TRUTH: Again, every baby is different (I'm certain that no baby knows how to multiply).

Again, although many babies will double their birth weights by 6 months, many will not. For example, a baby who has been sick a great deal in the first few months may not have doubled her weight by this time. Conversely, many babies will have doubled their birth weights earlier than 6 months of age and will more than triple their weights by their first birthdays. Remember, these generalizations are just statistical averages. If you take all babies in the country and average their birth weights, then compare these figures to their average weights at 6 months and 1 year, yes, you will find that these *averages* seem to approximately double by 6 months and triple by 1 year. However, within these millions of babies are all kinds of numbers that go into making up the averages. Although Cruella's weight and length will be one small part of the millions of numbers that make up these averages, her weight and length themselves will most likely be above or below the average numbers.

Also, don't get too hung up on your baby's weight. Your job as a parent is to make sure that your child is *offered* the right food, which for the first several months is just breast milk or formula and later on includes baby food and soft table foods. How much your baby *takes* is out of your  hands. Yes, you can determine what your baby is offered, but no, you have no control over how much she takes. As long as you're not filling her up between meals with junk or juice, then relax. And if she only takes a little at one meal, she'll make up for it during the next meal or the next day. Don't count your baby's calories; just offer lots of healthy food, a minimum of junk and juice, and sit back and watch her eat—or sit back and watch her throw the food at you. When she's hungry enough, she'll eat.

Also, don't be too concerned about her exact percentile. This is not Weight Watchers. If she has a month where she gains more than you expected, she'll probably gain less the next month or the month after. If she gains nothing one month, or even if she loses a few ounces, don't panic. Doctors look at long-term patterns, not at one or two figures. If your doctor, after plotting your baby's weight on the growth chart for a few months, feels that she is gaining too much, he will give you ideas about how to gradually correct this trend. He may, for example, suggest that you give food that is a bit lower in fat. If your doctor is concerned that little Cruella is gaining a bit slowly, he will suggest other modifications, such as choosing food that is richer in calories. On occasion, he may even recommend a formula that is higher in calories than the usual 20-calories-per-ounce formula.

If you have a premature baby, you can't expect her to follow the same curves as a full-term baby. To get a better idea of your premie's level of growth, you must take into account her prematurity. If she is 5 months old but she was two months premature, then compare her to other 3-month-olds, not to your friend's full-term 5-month-old.

FAILURE TO THRIVE

Pediatricians use the term *failure to thrive* for any less-than-obvious condition that causes a child's weight gain to be considerably less than expected over a period of several months. This isn't the child who had been gaining nicely but whose weight has slowed down a bit over the past month or two. As we've discussed, children often need to "find their percentiles" for several months before they start to track along one of those lines on the growth chart. The weight of a child with failure to thrive is consistently less than the fifth percentile and is dropping. Sometimes this inability to gain weight is so severe that length and head circumference can be affected as well.

About 10 percent of all children will be diagnosed with failure to thrive at some time in their childhoods. As described by Dr. Rebecca T. Kirkland in *Oski's Textbook of Pediatrics*, failure to thrive may be caused by any of the following:

• *Poor feeding technique.* A nursing mom who is not drinking or eating for two, or a new dad who is underfeeding from a bottle because he's afraid to give too much, can deprive a baby of adequate calories. Less commonly, a baby with a cleft palate or with severe nasal obstruction may have trouble drinking and breathing at the same time.

• *Fruit juices.* The baby who gets several bottles of juice a day may fill up, but a lot of those calories will run right out into the diaper. Juice babies can either be skinny or, if they hold in the calories, quite chubby. In either case, they're not getting the *proper* calories.

• *Vomiting.* The baby with severe gastroesophageal reflux or with pyloric stenosis (discussed in Chapter 17) may be vomiting up too many calories to allow for proper growth.

• *Drugs, alcohol, smoking.* Babies whose moms used drugs or alcohol during pregnancy or smoked during pregnancy are more likely to be born small and have failure to thrive.

• *Congenital syndromes.* Kids with certain rare inherited conditions such as Turner's syndrome (a chromosomal abnormality) are more likely to gain and grow poorly.

• *Congenital heart disease.* As discussed in Chapter 19, some babies who are born with heart abnormalities, especially those with cyanosis (blue babies), may have difficulty with growth.

• *Neurologic causes.* Babies who have reduced muscle tone or who have abnormal swallowing due to neurologic problems may fail to gain weight adequately.

• *Chronic or hidden infection.* Children with AIDS or other diseases of immunity may burn up too many calories fighting off infection to grow or else may have poor appetites because of their infections. Other congenital infections passed on from moms, such as toxoplasmosis, can also limit weight gain. A urinary tract infection, one of the most common causes of failure to thrive in babies, may have no signs other than poor weight gain.

• *Tumors.* One uncommon cause of failure to thrive is a malignancy, discussed in Chapter 19.

• *Chronic diarrhea.* Whether due to infection, formula intolerance, or to malabsorption, diarrhea causes food to pass through the intestinal tract too quickly for nutrients to be absorbed into the bloodstream. Diarrhea is discussed further in Chapter 17.

• *Liver disease.* The liver is essential for metabolism of food, and any disease that affects the liver, such as hepatitis and cystic fibrosis, can cause a child to fail to thrive.

• *Metabolic diseases.* Such rare birds as hypercalcemia (too high a level of calcium in the blood), storage diseases (a hereditary abnormal buildup of fat or carbohydrate in the liver, bone marrow, and other tissues), and many other congenital metabolic illnesses (some screened for when your child is a newborn) can all be causes of failure to thrive.

• *Endocrine diseases.* An overactive thyroid gland, an underactive adrenal gland, or a pituitary gland that isn't putting out enough growth hormone are all causes of failure to thrive, though rare.

• *Anemia* can prevent proper weight gain, since red blood cells are essential for the metabolism of food.

There's an old saying: "If it neighs, eats grass, has four legs and a tail, think of horses, not zebras." This is a good policy in pediatrics as well as parenting. If a child is not gaining weight adequately, the cause is much more likely to be something common, like diarrhea or poor feeding technique or a urinary infection, than it is to be caused by a tumor or an inherited metabolic disease. Faced with a baby who's not growing, your doctor will ask some important questions about your feeding technique, about the baby's bowel habits, and about any other symptoms that your child may have. He will do a careful physical examination and possibly a simple laboratory test, such as a urinalysis or blood count. In most cases, these steps will be all that is necessary to get to the bottom of this very common problem. Of course, if no easy answer emerges, then there are the zebras to consider.

KIDFIXER FREQUENTLY ASKED QUESTIONS

Q: Why is my baby falling off her growth curve? She was always in the 50th percentile, and now she's only in the 25th.

A: Children often have to "find their percentiles." A baby might follow the 50th percentile for the first few months and then shift to the 25th percentile. That same child may later zoom up to the 60th percentile. By around age 2 to 3, most kids will start to follow more closely along a specific percentile arc on the growth chart. This will often be a curve that she follows until her adolescent years, at which time a growth spurt might thrust her into a higher percentile. This is one reason why it's not smart to get too caught up in percentiles, especially for the first two years.

Q: *My friend's doctor said that she can tell how tall her year-old son will be. How does she do it?*

A: She guesses. From time to time a mathematical formula will appear that promises to predict the adult height of a baby or child. Invariably, they all end up being unreliable. I remember one particularly long equation that used the height of a 2-year-old and the height of his parents to predict the adult height of the child. By the time this formula appeared in a medical journal, my kids were already fully grown. Curious to see how close they came to what the equation predicted, I looked back through their charts. How accurate was the formula? Well, according to the equation my sons should have been 6 foot 6 and 6 foot 9. Not even close.

   The only way a doctor can make a good estimate of adult height is with a calculation made from an X-ray of the wrist, called a bone age. With a child's age, height, and bone age, a trained doctor can usually come within two or three inches of the adult height. Of course, even *this* estimate can only be made once a child is school-age or older. So next time you hear about one of these mystical predictors, make sure you ignore their theories—along with any stock tips they may have.

Q: *My daughter, Sadie, was 22 inches at her 2-month checkup. She's still 22 inches at 3 months. How can this be?*

A: It can't—and isn't. The problem with measuring a baby's length is that there is no truly accurate way to do it. Whether your doctor uses a simple tape measure or the fancy table with the built-in ruler, Sadie's length measurements are only approximations. There simply is no good way to flatten out a baby to measure her height. Babies tend to curl up, like a Slinky, and until they're old enough to stand up straight and be measured against the wall, any length measurement is merely an estimate.

Q: *My baby measured 31 inches lying down at her 11-month check-up and this month, when she was measured standing at her 1-year exam, she was only 30 inches. Why is my baby shrinking?*

A: She's not. Standing height will usually be an inch to an inch and a half lower than lying-down height, and it's usually more accurate. In other words, the 31-inch measurement at 11 months was probably falsely long and the 30 inches is probably more accurate.

Q: *My 4-month-old baby, who is exclusively breast-fed, seems to be rocketing up in weight. Does she need a diet?*

A: Your baby is getting exactly what she wants, which is exactly what she needs. A baby who is breast-fed should be allowed to nurse as she likes. Some babies will be on the petite side and others will be on the hefty side, but they're both okay. Miraculously, if left to their own appetites, both babies will gradually find a percentile curve and follow it. For now, let her enjoy herself.

14

DEVELOPMENT:
GIFTED AND TALENTED

A common source of angst for new parents and grandparents is mental development. Let's face it, every parent would like to think that his or her baby genius is just that: a certifiable little whiz, just one step away from the Ivy League. In today's competitive world, parents frequently compare the intelligence of their own gifted and talented tots to that of their friends' kids. This is unfortunate, since little Sly has a tough enough job pleasing his new parents and grandparents without having to worry about little Robbie down the block.

Every child is special in his or her own way. Some children will develop striking artistic ability. Some will be musically talented. Others will be math whizzes. Still others will become world-class computer geeks. Every child will find his own way to shine, and discovering your little one's talent is one of the true joys of parenthood.

That said, there is still a place for quantifying your baby's brain power in the first year of life, if only to reassure yourself that all is well on the development front. To this end, pediatricians routinely screen a baby's development, much as they plot the baby's length and weight on a growth chart, with the **Denver Developmental Screening Test.** This chart assesses where a baby fits in various areas of development, such as fine and gross motor skills, language development, and social skills. Fine motor skills refer to a baby's ability to use small muscles (can Sly pick up a small object using his thumb and finger?). By gross motor skills, we mean a baby's ability to use large muscle groups (can Sly sit by himself and crawl?). Language development refers to Sly's ability to make baby sounds, and later to use real words. By social skills we don't mean dating; it's a category that includes such developmental tasks as smiling, laughing, and waving bye-bye. Like all such standardized tests, the Denver test is woefully limited in most cases, and is just a rough way of determining how your baby compares to others in several measures of development.

NEWBORN REFLEXES

The first type of development that pediatricians see is reflex development. These are little movements over which babies have no control—just like a knee jerk—but which let us know that all is okay with little Sly's brain. Babies in the first few months of life have certain involuntary behaviors that they do automatically. A few of these reflexes that your doctor will test and which you may actually play with include:

• The **Moro** or **startle reflex.** If you give your baby a little gentle startle, such as allowing his back to gently fall an inch or two to the crib mattress, he will throw his arms out, then quickly bring them back to the middle.

• The **rooting reflex.** As was discussed in Chapter 5, even when there's no bottle or breast around, your baby will still attempt to suck. If you stroke your finger on Sly's cheek right next to his mouth, he will turn toward your hand, seemingly searching (or rooting) for a meal.

• The **tonic neck** or **fencing reflex.** This is a cool one. Gently turn your baby's head to the right. You may notice, although it may be a bit subtle in some newborns, that he will extend his right arm out, as though he's wielding a sword. His left arm will curve up toward his head, just the way a fencer would do to keep his balance. Turn his head to the left and the left arm will "fence" while the right will curve up. Pretty neat, no?

• The **grasp reflex.** Place your finger inside your baby's palm and watch how he grips your finger tightly. This isn't because he's crazy about you, although we know he is. It's just another reflex.

• The **stepping reflex.** Hold your baby in your hands, with his head facing down, a little above the surface of a table. Let his feet gently drag along the table. Before you know it, if you're doing it correctly, he will make what looks like steps across the table.

These reflexes are all natural and healthy actions that your newborn will make with absolutely no thought. They tell your doctor that Sly's little nervous system is developing nicely. In a few months, however, these reflexes will go away and your baby will no longer have such cute and mysterious habits.

MYTH: If a child is a slow talker, he's probably slow in everything.
TRUTH: Not true. Each phase of development progresses at its own pace.

One thing an experienced pediatrician learns is that a baby may be accelerated in one area of development but slower in another. Thus, the baby who smiles by 6 weeks, beating out his neighborhood pal by a full two weeks, may decide he's too lazy to roll over until he's 6 months old, making him a poor second to the neighborhood motor champ, who has been rolling for weeks.

MYTH: If a child is slow in verbal development, he'll have trouble once he reaches school.
TRUTH: Not at all. He's got plenty of time to catch up.

The fact that little Sly talked before little Robbie doesn't predict that he will be any smarter in school, any more gifted, or any better at public speaking. These developmental tests and comparisons are notoriously poor predictors of future skill and of future performance. I remember one little girl whom I saw at a routine 8-month exam. The proud mom assured me that she was going to be a genius. "She talks already," Mom insisted. To my surprise, this cute chubby little prodigy actually did say a word or two when prompted. By the next month, she was saying four or five recognizable words, a level of language development we rarely see until 12 months of age. We couldn't wait to see what she'd say next. When the 10-month checkup came, however, she was still stuck on the same four or five words. Same story at the 11- and 12-month exams: no new words. By 15 months she had added another word or two, but, alas, her Harvard application was put away. To the disappointment of Mom, she was quite average in speech development, although she grew up to be a bright, happy teenager.

Keep in mind that your baby's brain, which went from pea-sized to fist-sized during pregnancy, is not yet fully developed at birth. Although intellectual development varies, we know that some of the following **developmental changes** are going on in Sly's head each month:

- *1 month.* A baby's vocabulary is mostly cries, but it's still a good time to start talking to your baby. He won't understand your words, but he'll be reassured by a calm tone. Babies at 1 month can lift their heads and turn them from side to side.

- *2 months.* Babies start to notice cause and effect. They see that if they cry, they will be picked up. A social smile will usually make its appearance, and many babies will follow you with their gaze.

- *3 months.* Some babies make little cooing sounds now, and speaking to your baby is even more important. Want proof? Watch how he often (but not always) stops sucking for a moment when he suddenly hears a change in your voice. Help your baby "learn" to speak by speaking slowly, speaking in a slightly higher voice, and by using small words. Babies also seem to listen better to words where the first syllable is emphasized. Also, your baby may lift up his chest a bit when placed on his belly. It's a good idea to give him a few minutes of tummy time while he's awake to allow him to practice his tricks.

- *4 months.* Your baby will now probably laugh—assuming you say something that he feels is funny. Sly's voice will also vary in inflection, rising and falling rather than remaining monotone. Since most babies are "midline-oriented" by this time (they no longer spend all their time looking to one side or the other, but can look straight ahead), the whole 180 degrees of the horizon are now open to his exploration. He may enjoy that mobile more. Most babies can now lift their chests higher when placed on their bellies.

• **5 months.** Some babies will try to imitate their parents' sounds, although this is quite variable—not all babies are good impersonators. Some babies will roll over by now, usually front to back before back to front. Some infants can sit with a little support from Mom or Dad.

• **6 months.** Babies will now make new vowel sounds. *Oohs, aahs,* and *ohs* appear, although most babies are not yet putting consonants in front of these vowel sounds. Many babies will now be turning over both ways.

• **7 months.** Grabbing toys, like rattles, is a favorite activity now that Sly has learned to purposefully grasp an object and transfer it from hand to hand. "Itsy Bitsy Spider" may be in your baby's top ten as he learns to expect what comes next in songs.

• **8 months.** Most babies can sit, at least for a second or two, when you prop them up. Many will imitate coughs and other sounds. Help your baby learn by speaking in real words rather than baby talk.

• **9 months.** Many babies will now add consonant sounds to their repertoires, most often starting with *b* and *d* sounds. As babies begin to creep or crawl, it's a good time to remember to make your house child-safe. Babies now begin to understand the concept of conservation— hide a toy and Sly seems to have an idea that it's not gone for good. He also realizes that Mommy will be right back from her errands or after dinner out with Daddy.

• **10 months.** Although you might swear that Sly is saying *mama* and *dada,* most babies are merely experimenting with sounds and are only accidentally calling you.

• **11 months.** Your little trickster may play peek-a-boo, wave, or go "so big" with his hands. Most babies are crawling by now, although some would rather just cruise around the furniture and have no interest in crawling.

• *12 months.* By now *mama* may mean Mom and *dada* may mean Dad—but not always. Many 1-year-olds, even though they understand what you say, won't yet respond in real language. Most kids are pretty mobile by now, crawling, cruising, and, for the real speed demons, even taking an unsteady step or two.

Again, these developmental steps are so variable that it's hard to compare one child to another. Believe me, if you have three kids, all three will do things at different rates. Still, there are certain **basic developmental milestones** that pediatricians use to ascertain that the little geniuses are "on target" in developing skills. Again, if your child passes some of these "tests" but not others, relax. If he is behind on all, then you might want to consult your pediatrician for reassurance.

Most babies will . . .

• Smile spontaneously by 2 months
• Follow things with their eyes by 3 months
• Lift up their chests and laugh by 4 months
• Sit with support, with a fairly steady head, by 5 months
• Roll over, at least one way, by 6 months
• Grasp and transfer objects by 7 months
• Sit, when propped up by you, by 8 months
• Sit alone, at least briefly, by 9 months
• Say nonsense sounds by 10 months
• Pull to a standing position by 11 months
• Play pat-a-cake or wave or play "so big" by 1 year
• Walk holding on (cruise) by 1 year
• Say two or three words by 15 months
• Walk alone, for a few steps, by 18 months

About the only time that a pediatrician may be a bit concerned is when a baby seems to be late in *all* areas of development. If Sly is a very late crawler, a very late verbalizer, if he isn't lifting his chest up off the table when he should—in other words, if he's very late in *all* areas of development—then there may be some cause for concern.

Even in this rare circumstance, however, the reason for such a universal delay may not be too serious. Some babies are just slow starters in all fields of development but catch up in plenty of time to shine in school. Also, keep in mind that, if you have a premie, he is expected to lag behind developmentally, just as he is physically, for the first year or two. To get a better idea of your premie's level of development, you must take into account his prematurity. If he is 6 months old but was two months premature, then you should be comparing him to other 4-month-olds, not to your friend's full-term 6-month-old (for more on premies, see Chapter 22).

Remember, comparing intellectual development among babies is very tricky, and an area with few meaningful conclusions. As long as your little Sly is progressing the way your pediatrician expects, don't compare him to anyone else's baby. There is an excellent chance that eighteen years from now they will both be in the same college, with different majors. There is also an excellent chance that twenty-two or twenty-three years from now they will both have finished that college—and will have moved right back into their parents' basements.

STRANGER ANXIETY

Toward the end of Sly's first year, you may notice a change in his behavior. Previously, he seemed friendly to just about everyone. He liked being held by you, enjoyed seeing Daddy, loved when Grandma and Gramps came by for a visit, and seemed to enjoy being tossed about among all of your friends. Lately, however, he has become much less of a social butterfly. He cries when his aunt and uncle pick him up, screams when Granny tries to to take him from you, and even wigs out when Daddy, an old favorite, tries to hug him.

Does this snooty behavior mean that someone has been mistreating him? Has he become a young depressive? Is he possessed? Relax. This is actually normal behavior. The great majority of 9-, 10-, and 11-month-old babies will pass through a stage called stranger anxiety. Your previously easygoing baby may, for the next month or two, only calm down when he's held by you, his mom and protector. Rest assured, this is only a temporary phenomenon. To help him pass through this stage quickly, just continue leaving him, as you always have, with people you trust and who care about him. When he sees that you always return home after leaving, he will begin to learn the important concept of conservation: when people (and things) go away, they don't disappear, but just come right back where they belong. As his confidence in your return grows, he will become more readily accepting of others.

SPEECH AND HEARING DEVELOPMENT

Normal hearing development begins in the uterus. That's right, those Bob Marley CDs you listened to throughout pregnancy to help you mellow out soothed little Sly as well. By the time he was born, Sly was responsive to your voice and soon developed his own cooing sounds. Babies even seem to respond better to familiar language. Studies tell us that Greek babies feed better when they hear Greek spoken to them, Spanish babies are more active when hearing Spanish, and baby pigs even prefer pig Latin (just kidding). Long before Sly says his first word, he's learning language. By 6 months a baby begins to understand much of what you say. Knowing that babies are such smarties means that it's a good idea to speak to them often. To **help your baby's language development,** try these tips:

- Stop the baby talk and speak to your child in real words.
- Speak at a slightly slower pace.
- Use short sentences.
- Speak in a slightly higher tone.
- Speak with appropriate emphasis to help catch a baby's attention.
- Once he begins to make words, repeat those words to help reinforce his speech development. For example, if he says "bottle," it's a good idea to repeat the word and add more. "Yes, Sly, that *is* a big bottle. You drink from a bottle. . . ."

Even allowing for individual differences, babies develop language skills in a somewhat predictable way, from month to month. Babies who don't seem to be developing language often fail to do so either because they don't hear well or because of a developmental delay.

How do you know if your child has a hearing problem? Certainly you should feel reassured if your child responds to a loud noise, like a car alarm or a slammed door. To test hearing further some parents will sneak behind their child and call his name, hoping he will turn his head in surprise in the direction of their voices. Reassured to see that he does, they then try to repeat the test, just to double-check. This time, no response. Do we have a problem? Actually, Sly is just fine. Although by 6 months most babies will turn toward a voice, they won't necessarily do it *repeatedly*. Just as adults will startle when they first hear a car alarm and then not even notice it after a few minutes, a baby will tend to ignore that voice after the first one or two times he hears it. Try again after a few minutes and he should respond.

Fortunately, many hospitals test a newborn's hearing before discharge, which enables parents to identify many congenital hearing problems. Once he goes home from the hospital, suspect **possible hearing loss** if your child:

- Does not turn to his name by a year
- Does not enjoy peekaboo or having someone read to him by a year
- Does not point to things by 15 months
- Has no words at all by 15 months

These are all very nonspecific signs, and many babies will show one or more of them at some time. For example, some babies have no interest in peekaboo simply because they think it's a silly game. Nevertheless, if your child shows several of these signs, or if you have some other reason to suspect that he doesn't hear you well, a trip to a hearing specialist is often a good idea.

Watch out for this one:

MYTH: Babies who have had several ear infections will have hearing problems.
TRUTH: Most babies handle ear infections just fine.

Although a baby with an ear infection will have trouble hearing clearly out of the infected ear *while he is sick*, his hearing most often returns to normal after the infection has cleared. Many doctors test a baby's ear drum with a test called a tympanogram after an ear infection has been treated. This easy and painless test can reassure a concerned mom that her child's ear is now fine, with no residual infection or fluid behind the ear drum. The baby with several ear infections in his first year of life does not usually have his hearing adversely affected by these infections, as long as the infections clear up within a few months time. For more on ear infections, see Chapter 18.

DEVELOPMENTAL DELAY

As I've said, the child who is right on task for most types of development but lags slightly behind in only one area rarely has a serious problem. The baby who smiles by 2 months, grasps and transfers objects by 7 months, and pulls to a standing position by 11 months but refuses to walk until 18 months may just need to work up the nerve to make those first tentative steps. At worst, if he doesn't shape up and walk by age 2, he may need a bit of physical therapy to work on his leg muscles. What about the child who is behind in everything? This is the child who is a very late talker, is late smiling and waving, lags in sitting and standing, and is behind in picking up small objects and using a spoon. If his progress in all areas is slow, then he can be said to have a general developmental delay. This doesn't mean that he won't catch up. He may very well turn out to be a world-class athlete or a famous writer or a great scientist. He does, however, need a visit with a child neurologist or an early intervention program to make sure there is no underlying neurologic problem and to develop a treatment program to help him catch up.

A word about **labels.** Most late bloomers are diagnosed—rather vaguely—with the term *developmental delay.* This can be frustrating for the dad who wants desperately to know why his little Sly is lagging so far behind. The truth is that most kids just don't fit into a neat diagnostic category. I try to tell such parents that titles and labels are not important. If Sly has a speech delay, it's important to address that issue with a good speech and hearing evaluation and, if appropriate, with language therapy. If he is a very late walker, then it may be important to get physical therapy. It's important, in kids with developmental delays, to **treat the specific delay.** It's not always important to tag such a child with a label.

MENTAL RETARDATION

Unfortunately, some children never do catch up. Although mental retardation is a diagnosis made after 1 year, I will mention it briefly.

Traditionally defined by an IQ (intelligence quotient) score of 75 or less, the overall incidence of mental retardation in the United States is estimated to be 1 percent. Most experts now forgo the IQ test in defining mental retardation and reserve the term for a child who needs support in several areas of adaptive function, such as communication, self-care, school performance, social skills, and safety. Obviously, there is variation within the spectrum of mental retardation. The child with an IQ of 78 who is able to feed and dress himself and who goes on to develop employable skills has less of a handicap than a child with an IQ of 50, who may be much more dependent on others.

Although the cause for a child's slowness is often a mystery, some **known causes of mental retardation** are:

• *Down syndrome.* This is a chromosomal syndrome (affected children have an extra chromosome number 21). In addition to retardation, Down syndrome kids have short stature and characteristic facial and physical features, and may have heart disease as well.

• *Fragile X syndrome.* Much more common in males, fragile X syndrome involves a mutation on an X chromosome. Affected children may have long faces and big ears, and boys may also have large testes.

The degree of neurologic involvement varies greatly, with some children, especially girls, having only mild learning problems.

• *Maternal alcohol and drug use.* As mentioned in Chapter 1, babies whose moms drink during pregnancy are often smaller than expected and may have small heads, small chins, small jaws, and other characteristic physical features, along with learning problems. Similarly, children whose moms use cocaine during pregnancy may have reduced intelligence.

• *Trauma.* Newborns who suffer from bleeding into the brain or young children who have serious trauma to the head, can have significant mental problems.

• *Lead poisoning.* Children who are exposed to lead, through old house paint, dust and dirt, and water from lead-containing pipes may suffer neurologic effects, kidney damage, and poor growth. Your doctor will screen your baby for exposure to lead at some time during the first year. If you live in a very old house, make sure that your paint is lead-free.

• *Infection.* Certain congenital infections (rubella, toxoplasmosis) can result in mental retardation, as can meningitis or encephalitis in childhood.

• *Inherited metabolic diseases.* Such rare inherited diseases of metabolism as Tay-Sachs disease, phenylketonuria, and galactosemia can cause retardation.

PERVASIVE DEVELOPMENTAL DISORDER (PDD)

The term *pervasive developmental disorder,* first used in the 1980s, includes many different disorders such as autism (a severe impairment in social interaction and language) and Asperger's disorder (characterized by social interaction problems without the severe language disability of autism). Most types of PDD have in common:

- Problems with social interaction
- Problems with speech and other types of communication
- Limited interests
- Actions that are repetitive or stereotyped

An estimated 1 to 2 children in 1,000 are labeled as having PDD. Such children vary from those with classic autism to those with only minimal handicaps. Because of this wide range, labeling a child as having PDD does little for the child and offers nothing, except a whopping dose of depression, for his parents. Also, attempting to make such a diagnosis too early can lead to mistakes and a great deal of unnecessary parental anxiety. I have seen children diagnosed with PDD who are now college students. I have also seen children diagnosed with PDD whose parents were later told that the diagnosis was an error. These children may have been late talkers who didn't play well with others and they were, for sure, unusual little kids. However, they did not have PDD or any other neurologic disorder. They are now speaking well, have plenty of friends, and are no more unusual than their parents.

In any case, no health professional should make a diagnosis of PDD in a child before a year of age, and probably not until much later. There is no reason to rush into a diagnosis, especially considering the great *normal* variation in childhood development.

KIDFIXER FREQUENTLY ASKED QUESTIONS

Q: My baby turned over from his back to his belly several times at five months but hasn't done it since. Why?

A: He doesn't want to! Once a baby has mastered such a task as rolling or crawling, he may lose interest for a time and decide to try something else. Also, turning over from back to belly has a particular disincentive for your baby. On his back, a baby of 5 months can see the world. On his belly, his field of vision is much more limited. In other words, it's boring on his belly.

Q: *My 11-month-old can walk already. Why can't he crawl?*

A: As smart as some babies are at 11 months, many just haven't noticed that their little friends learned to crawl first. Your baby learned it the other way around. This is very common. Many babies will learn to walk first. They take several steps and then plop down. After a few such crashes, many figure out that it's safer to stay close to the ground and begin to crawl. It's faster, too!

Q: *When I clap, my baby doesn't always respond. Does he have a hearing problem?*

A: Not necessarily. Babies are pretty smart little critters. They get bored, just as we do. If you clap once, your baby may respond with a blink or a startle. Do it again and he may not, because the startle value of the clap is gone. Wait a few minutes, surprise him again, and he'll usually respond.

Q: *Claudia used to love her grandfather. Now she seems afraid of him. Why?*

A: Tell Grandpa not to fear. This is typical stranger anxiety. Babies nearing a year of age often decide that they want nobody but Mom. Sometimes even a daddy is considered a stranger. In time Claudia will once again accept Grandpa and everyone else who's nice to her. Allowing her to spend time with her grandfather, with and without Mom around, will help her pass through this normal stage.

Q: *We're a two-language family, speaking Spanish and English. Will this confuse Marcia?*

A: Not at all. Babies, like little sponges, absorb everything around them. If you speak both Spanish and English at home, Marcia will learn to speak both as well. Just try not to eliminate the use of English in the house, since this is probably the language she will be speaking in school. So speak both languages to her. She won't be confused, and she'll probably thank you when she gets an A in high school Spanish.

Q: *One of my 4-month-old triplets tries to stand and walk all of the time. You can't hold her without her trying very hard to stand, and she will often become frustrated if you don't allow her to do so. The other two do nothing even remotely close to this. I've been told by a couple of friends not to encourage or allow her to practice this, as it is bad for the development of her legs. Is this true?*

A: What a good example of how kids develop differently—even kids who are not so very different genetically. Actually, let your little Speed Racer race. This "walking," which is actually her stepping reflex, won't harm her legs, her spine, or anything else (although she might make her siblings a bit jealous). In time, they'll all catch up and you'll have three times the fun on your hands.

Q: *My 9-month-old son, Aaron, bangs toys on his head and bangs his head against the crib mattress and floor. He doesn't seem to bang in frustration or as a tantrum; he just seems to enjoy it. We try to redirect him, but it's very difficult to distract him from banging. What can we do?*

A: Though disconcerting, head banging and other repetitive actions, such as head rolling and body rocking, are harmless and quite common among children of Aaron's age. These particular behaviors usually stop by 3 years of age, although repetitive actions are occasionally seen in older children and even in adolescents.

Some experts believe that repetitive actions actually stimulate a child's inner ear balance. They are not associated with damage to the brain or with developmental delay. In fact, one recent study showed that children who banged or rocked their heads turned out to have, on average, slightly higher IQs later on than those who did not have such behaviors. The conclsuion of that article was that the stimulation provided to the developing vestibular system in some way made brains function better!

Q: *Our daughter, Jennie, is 13 months old and is not talking yet. She tries to form words but usually only gets the first letter sound. For example, for* momma *she says* ma; *for* Barney *she says* ba. *Should my wife and I be concerned?*

A: Like most types of development, speech milestones vary greatly from child to child. By 6 to 10 months, most babies begin to understand simple single words, such as *ball* or *bottle*, although they cannot yet say these words themselves. By 12 to 15 months, many children will start to say a word or two. Frequently *dada* or *mama* is first, or sometimes *ba* for their bottle (or Barney). Although these words may be hard for anyone besides a parent to understand, they still count as words. By 18 months, many children will have five to ten of these baby words, although others do not seem to master speech until age two.

Since there is such a wide range of normal speech development, how can a parent know if there is a problem? In general, if a child Jennie's age can say one or two words (she can) and if, more important, she *understands commands*, then there is seldom reason to be concerned. For example, if you say to Jennie, "Where's the ball?" and she looks at her ball, that tells you she has good receptive language skills. If you combine receptive skills with the ability to say *ma* and *ba*, then there is usually nothing to be concerned about.

Regardless of when they start to speak, most children will begin to go through a **vocabulary spurt** at 18 to 21 months as they realize the power that language gives them to satisfy their needs and to express their feelings. The child who said a mere five words at 15 months of age may have a vocabulary of 50 words before her second birthday, and may even put two words together into a simple phrase ("Mommy up" is a popular one).

We expect that by the time she is 2, Jennie will be hard to quiet down. If she is not saying several words by age two, then you should consider having her hearing and speech evaluated further.

Q: *My 8-month-old has separation anxiety and I have been trying to find ways to help her feel okay when I am away from her—like playing peekaboo (which she enjoys and understands) or calling to her from the other room. She cries as soon as I step out of the room.*

I don't know whether to let her cry it out or go to her every time. I know that it is okay to allow her to get frustrated so that she figures things out on her own, but when is it too much?

A: The fact that your daughter doesn't want to see you leave means that you two have formed a nice, healthy bond. She's crazy about her mom (who wouldn't be?). However, just as it's healthy for her to *want* her mommy all the time, it's healthy for her to learn to separate from her as well. This separation anxiety is quite normal and, as she gets a bit older, her memory will comfort her. She will learn that when you leave, you always come back. Every time you leave and return, you are teaching her that you will be back.

Of course, knowing this is of little comfort to you when you have a screaming child every time you leave. Here are a few **tips for easing her separation anxiety** (and yours):

• **Prepare her.** Before you separate, tell her that you will be right back. Of course, she won't understand the words for a while, but she will learn the tone you use to say it and will be reassured by that tone.

• **Stay calm and casual.** If she sees her mom upset, she'll be upset. If she sees that Mom is smiling, she'll be less worried.

• **Practice "mini-separations."** When you go into the next room, say, "Where's Mommy?" When you come back, say, "Mommy's back!"

• **Don't sneak out.** It's tempting, but it will only make her more worried.

Q: **What is ABA therapy and is it appropriate for my year-old child who may have autism?**

A: ABA stands for *applied behavior analysis*, an aggressive teaching system whereby behavioral techniques (such as rewards for proper actions) are applied to teaching a child with a severe developmental handicap, such as autism. This somewhat controversial form of learning therapy has been found to be extremely helpful in many children with PDD. Although your child, at age 1, may be a bit young to have been labeled as having autism, a pediatric neurologist may feel that early treatment with ABA therapy makes such an early diagnosis important.

PART V

HEALTH AND SAFETY

When the children were babies . . . I used to get up at night and hold mirrors under their nostrils to make sure they were still breathing. I worried about their spitting out more food than went into their stomachs. I developed a "thing" about germs. When I changed diapers I washed their hands. When we went bye-bye in the car, it was like moving the circus. I had a fetish about the kids drinking their moo-moo from any cup that didn't have their name on it. Then, along came the thought-provoking slogan, "Don't sweat the small stuff," and my entire life changed.

— ERMA BOMBECK

15

GAS, COLIC, AND
THE WITCHING HOUR

"My baby has colic!"

Oh, have I heard this complaint!

Fact is, nobody is really sure what causes colic. We do know that some babies seem to spend a good part of every day fussing, crying, and repeatedly bringing their legs up to their chests as though in some kind of gas pain. Though we call these perpetually fussy, gassy babies "colicky," this is just a title, not a real diagnosis. Such distress seems to peak in most babies at around 6 weeks of age and then becomes much less frequent after four months.

The important thing to remember about true colic is that these poor kids (and their even poorer parents) are uncomfortable, with some type of intestinal distress, for a **major part of the day.** This is colic. There are many conditions confused with colic but are not. **Conditions that mimic colic** include:

• *Normal hyperresponsive babies.* As discussed in Chapter 12, many fussy babies have no intestinal problems at all but just represent one end of a spectrum of normal responsivity. Such babies do *not* have colic. They are not particularly gassy, although after crying for prolonged periods of time they have swallowed a bit more air and you can expect to hear that air being expelled from their rear ends. Most babies who are overly fussy will outgrow their objectionable personalities by 6 months of age.

• **Witching hour.** A baby who is crying from 6 p.m. to 8 p.m. every night but who is fine the rest of the day does *not* have colic. Such a baby is just another victim of the infamous witching hour or fussy period, when babies suddenly and for no apparent reason turn into little imps. They fuss, fret, pass gas, and generally go bananas, but they confine their satanic behavior to a limited number of hours in the evening or night. Many mothers tell us that before they gave birth they felt their babies kicking up a storm at just about the same time each day. Whatever causes a fussy period, it fortunately seems to go away by 4 months of age. Sometimes a little extra rocking or gentle music may relieve your baby's witching-hour fussiness. There are even CDs now with "fetal sounds." Do they work? Doubtful.

• **Gas passers.** A baby who passes gas all day yet is for the most part happy does *not* have colic. His farting may embarrass you at family functions, but he is not a colicky baby. The problem is not the baby who passes gas but the baby who *cannot* pass gas.

• **Diarrhea.** A baby who has chronic diarrhea does *not* have colic. The diarrhea may be due to a formula problem, overfeeding, an infection, or a number of other causes, but it is not colic.

WHEN IT REALLY IS COLIC

If little Bart does indeed seem to be cranky and uncomfortable all day, consult your doctor. If you are nursing, he may suggest that you eliminate some of these **suspicious foods and chemicals** from your diet, which might be responsible for Bart's distress.

• **Milk and dairy.** Yes, milk! Although milk is a good source of protein and calcium, both important for Mom's nutrition, it is also the most frequently cited item on a colicky baby's hit list. Remember, you don't have to drink cow's milk to make breast milk. Just drink plenty of other fluids (water is best) and maintain a healthy diet.

• *Gas-producing vegetables.* Lettuce, cabbage, onions, broccoli, cauliflower, garlic, and such exotic greens as kale, bok choy, and broccoli rabe are gassy not only for you but for many babies as well.

• *Allergenic foods.* Chocolate, shellfish, berries, egg whites, tomatoes, citrus fruits, and nuts are common food allergens that can cause a nursed baby to be uncomfortable for much of the day.

• *Caffeine.* Remember that caffeine is a drug. If you are drinking lots of coffee or tea, switch to decaf. Also, remember that many soft drinks contain caffeine, so read labels.

• *Medications.* Even nonprescription medications can upset sensitive little Bart. Cold medications, for example, contain stimulants that can make him fussy and uncomfortable. (And remember, if you're nursing, it's a good idea to speak to your pediatrician before you take *any drug.* Some medications can do a lot more harm than making a baby fussy.)

Let's assume that you've limited yourself to a bread-and-water diet and Bart is still fussy all day. Some **other causes of colic** may include:

• *Formula intolerance.* Bottle-fed babies have the added potential of suffering from colic due to formula intolerance. Such problems can be transient or chronic. For example, some babies will, after recovering from a stomach virus, develop temporary lactose intolerance. Lactose, the sugar present in most formulas, makes some babies whose sensitive intestines are recovering from a bad tummy bug gassy and fretful. After a few weeks of a lactose-free formula, they once again are able to enjoy their normal formula. Some babies will have true cow's milk allergy, which might not be detected until they are several weeks of age. When such an allergy is present, the milk protein in formula causes colic or may result in more severe problems, such as diarrhea, vomiting, or rashes. Again, there are plenty of substitute formulas for your doctor to recommend.

• *Gastroesophageal reflux (GER)*. As mentioned previously, reflux can be another cause of an uncomfortable baby. If your baby is spitting up more than usual, or if he seems to be writhing in pain as you feed him, then you and your pediatrician should consider reflux as a cause of his distress.

The great majority of the time, colic pops up for no apparent reason. The good news: it disappears the same way, usually by 3 to 4 months of age. Does this mean you have to wait patiently and helplessly while your baby is miserable? No. It just means that, no matter what you do (or don't do), Bart's distress will be short-lived. Often a colicky baby can be soothed by a few minutes of gentle rocking or by patting him on the back. There are also medications that on occasion will help a colicky baby. Many of these medications are antispasmodics—they may relax little Bart's active intestines. Such medicines are not without side effects, however, and your doctor will not rush to use them unless Bart is really uncomfortable. Other medications (such as Mylicon) help gas bubbles move along the intestinal tract more easily. Still others are antacids (Mylanta, Gaviscon) or acid reducers (Zantac), which limit symptoms of reflux. Remember, no matter what course you take, your baby will usually outgrow his minor digestive problems by a few months of age.

KIDFIXER FREQUENTLY ASKED QUESTIONS

Q: How about iron? Can the iron in my baby's formula be causing colic?

A: Not likely. Although it gets blamed for colic, vomiting, and constipation—for just about everything—that small amount of iron in formulas rarely causes a problem.

Q: *I've cut everything out of my diet except meat and potatoes and my Maggie still fusses all day. Other than using medications, how can I soothe her?*

A: There are many good techniques for soothing a colicky baby—or for helping any fussy baby. A few good **soothing techniques** include:

- Gentle rhythmic rocking in a comfy rocking chair is relaxing for both of you.
- Swaddling in a snugly wrapped blanket may feel just like that comfy uterus.
- Rolling her back and forth in a stroller for a few minutes may help.
- Take a short car ride; starting and stopping seems to quiet many babies.
- Monotonous noises on those baby-soothing tapes sometimes help a bit.
- A wind-up swing—especially one with music—is worth a try.

Q: *A friend recommended gripe water for my baby's colic. What is it? Does it work?*

A: Gripe water is an old remedy for colic that can contain many different substances, such as sucrose (table sugar) or herbs (commonly dill weed, fennel, or ginger). At one time gripe water also contained alcohol, but this has now been eliminated from most products. If gripe water helps at all—and this has never been proven—it's due to the sugar. Pediatricians have long known that sweet substances can have a mild sedative effect on some babies; that's one reason why religious circumcisers (mohels) use sweet wine before performing their procedure. The problem with such herbal remedies as gripe water is that they often contain other ingredients besides the sugar, some of which can be harmful.

16

FEVER PHOBIA

Fever—a very hot topic. In the 1980s, Dr. Barton Schmitt popularized the term *fever phobia* to describe the genuine fear many parents have regarding fever. Faced with a high temperature, many concerned moms and dads would bathe their children in alcohol, pack them in ice, and try all types of folk medications. Often, such steps made their children sicker than they would have been without treatment. In truth, fever is not a sign that something is going wrong, but an indication that something is going right. With the exception of the newborn baby, *fever means that the body recognizes an infection and is taking steps to get rid of it.*

NORMAL BODY TEMPERATURE

MYTH: Normal body temperature is 98.6 degrees.
TRUTH: Normal body temperature, measured rectally, is really anything up to 100 degrees.

Normal temperature varies, from as low as 96 degrees to as high as 100 degrees. Ninety-six degrees is not too low, and 100 degrees is not fever. In fact, **body temperature varies:**

• *Throughout the day.* It's not unusual for a baby's temperature to be a little lower in the morning than it is in the late afternoon or evening.

• *From person to person.* Some babies have an average temperature of 99.5. Others are usually around 97. Many newborn babies, especially if premature, haven't yet developed the ability to make fever to fight an infection. They often can become quite ill without showing any sign of fever.

• *With activity.* Just as a marathon runner might be expected to have a higher temperature in the middle of a race than the fan watching the race, the baby who has just been crying for several minutes may have a bit higher temperature than he did while he was resting comfortably.

• *With the method of measurement.* Rectal temperature, the gold standard for measurement, is usually a degree higher than oral temperature and may sometimes be *more* than one degree higher than a temperature taken under the arm. Nowadays, such devices as ear thermometers make temperature taking a snap. Unfortunately, they're not terribly accurate, especially in babies.

WHAT IS A FEVER?

So then, what is fever? Fever is anything over 100 degrees, measured rectally. Don't be concerned if your baby, who seems to have an average temperature of 98 degrees, now is 99.5 degrees. Yes, this is a bit higher, but it's not fever, and it is also no cause for concern.

Now that we've defined fever as anything over 100 degrees, let's talk a bit about it. If taking a temperature is such a variable thing, why do we take temperatures all the time? The answer: we shouldn't! I rarely take temperatures in my office. The only time I do so is when a mother asks me to, and even then, I usually do so out of politeness, rarely out of curiosity.

MYTH: Fever is a bad sign.
TRUTH: Other than in newborns, fever is actually a healthy sign.

Relax. Fever is produced by our own white blood cells as they attempt to fight off infection, not by invading bacteria or viruses. It is not a sign that something is going wrong, but that something is going right. Not convinced? Consider the lowly lizard. This poor cold-blooded fellow can't raise his body temperature by himself to ward off germs. So when he comes down with a case of lizarditis, he crawls onto a sun-warmed rock to simulate a fever. Take him out of the sun and he will actually become sicker. Luckily, unlike lizards, our bodies can produce fevers by themselves and we can forgo the toasty rock.

TAKING A BABY'S TEMPERATURE

So if fever is a sign that the body is resisting an infection, and if some doctors don't even bother to take temperatures in their offices, why should you, a new parent, bother to do it at home? Why not throw away those thermometers altogether? Here's why: sometimes a new parent does not yet know how to tell if a baby is sick. Maybe little Alfonso's nose is running and you're not sure if this is the start of a cold or just the effects of a crying spell. Perhaps he's a bit flushed. Are his cheeks ruddy because he's just been outside on a windy day, or is he ill? In these instances, fever can be a clue that there is an infection.

When you do want to know your baby's temperature, the rectal thermometer is the most accurate method. To take a baby's temperature rectally, lubricate a rectal thermometer with a little Vaseline. Shake it down so that it reads less than 99 degrees, insert it just inside the baby's anus, and squeeze the baby's buttocks to hold the thermometer in. Wait three minutes, take it out, and read the temperature.

To take an axillary (under-the-arm) temperature, put the thermometer under either arm and hold the arm down to keep the thermometer in the armpit. You can also treat yourself to an ear thermometer, a handy battery-operated device that displays the baby's temperature when you place it just inside the ear canal for a few seconds. Unfortunately, it's expensive and not terribly accurate in the first year.

HOW HIGH IS THE FEVER?

MYTH: The higher the fever, the sicker the child.

TRUTH: Fever is *not* a good indicator of the severity of an infection.

The fact that a temperature just rose from 101 to 102 usually means nothing. Babies will often have wide fluctuations in temperature for no reason at all. Also, when sick, **kids' temperatures are frequently higher than temperatures of adults** with the same types of infection. A child with an upper respiratory infection might have a temperature of 103 degrees. If Dad catches the bug, he'll often have only 101, or may have no fever at all. Although their temperatures tend to run higher, **kids tolerate fever much better than adults.** The child with a fever of 103 degrees may be happy and peppy despite the fever, whereas his dad may be lying there pathetically like a log, begging for Tylenol or sympathy, at 101 degrees.

An exception to the casual way we respond to fever is with the very young baby. Because babies in the first few months of life have not always developed their immune defenses completely, when they *do* run fevers they may be, on rare occasions, quite sick. For this reason, it's a good idea for you to let your pediatrician know when your very young baby has any fever. Certainly in the first four months of life, any fever should be reported to your doctor.

MYTH: Fever is the best indication that a child is seriously sick.

TRUTH: Behavior is much more important.

The most important indication, to you and to your pediatrician, that your baby is ill is not his temperature but his behavior. Does he feed well? Is he sleeping as usual? Is he spitting up more than usual? Is he fussier or drowsier than usual? You will quickly learn just what his normal behavior is and will become a heck of a lot more accurate in judging how sick he is than any thermometer reading. So relax about the temperature.

TREATING A BABY'S FEVER

First of all, keep in mind that there is no reason to treat a fever aggressively, since, as we've learned, fever is a healthy sign. In fact, the only reason to bother to treat fever at all is to make a baby feel a bit more comfortable. So if your baby has a cold and is happily running a slight temperature of 101, leave him alone. If, on the other hand, he is a sizzling 105 and is miserable, fever medication may make him feel a bit more comfortable.

The usual medication for fever is acetaminophen, which should be given no more often than every four hours and is available either in generic form or in such brands as Tylenol and Feverall. Different formulations come in different strengths; infant Tylenol (80 mg/.8 ml), for example, has a higher concentration than children's Tylenol (160 mg/5 ml). Stick to the dose your doctor prescribes or follow the directions on the bottle, which offer a decent approximation. Don't exceed the recommended dosage; too much Tylenol is more dangerous than the fever itself, and an overdose can upset a sensitive tummy.

MYTH: Good old-fashioned aspirin is the best drug to treat fever in a child.
TRUTH: Stay away from aspirin! It can be dangerous.

Aspirin usage can predispose some children to Reye's syndrome, a rare but serious disease of the liver and nervous system which can follow such viral infections as chicken pox and flu. Because of Reye's syndrome, aspirin no longer is used to treat fever in children.

Most important, once again, don't go crazy treating a fever. The best ways to help your baby when he has a fever are by keeping him well hydrated (give lots of fluids) and not overdressing him. Remember that you're only treating the fever to make your child feel more comfortable, not to cure him.

FEVER CONVULSIONS (FEBRILE SEIZURES)

Little Alfonso has started to run a bit of a fever but otherwise he has been acting normally. All of a sudden, he stares out into space or his eyes roll up into his head, with his arms and legs straight and rigid, or else jerking rhythmically back and forth. When you call out to him, Alfonso doesn't even turn toward your voice. This is not a pretty picture. In fact, Alfonso is freaking you out!

Nothing is more frightening to a parent than a fever convulsion, but believe it or not, your convulsing child is actually going to be fine. Seizures from fever are quite common, occurring in about 3 percent of children, slightly more often in boys than girls. They are seen most often between the ages of 6 months and 5 years, with a peak at 18 months. Fever convulsions also run in families; if his sibling or parent has had a fever convulsion, then Alfonso is more likely to have one as well. The good news about febrile seizures is that they cause no harm to your baby's brain. They also stop by themselves, with no treatment at all. The bad news is that if your child has had a fever convulsion, he has approximately a 1 in 3 chance of having another one in the future, especially if his first seizure occurred before age 1 and especially if a family member has had a febrile seizure.

The child with a fever convulsion may shake his arms and legs, may stiffen all over, may simply stare, may become limp, or may show these symptoms in a combination. Usually the whole seizure lasts only a minute or two, though to the frightened parent that minute can seem like an hour. If the seizure occurs during sleep, the whole episode may go unnoticed, a further example of how these events, although frightening, are essentially harmless. Not infrequently the seizure can occur in a previously cool child. That is, a fever convulsion is often the first sign that a child has any fever at all. Many times I've asked the mother of a baby with a convulsion if her child had been running a fever and have been told that the baby was perfectly fine and cool. When I went to examine the baby, he was febrile. That first rapid temperature spike often seems to be the one to do it. This is one of the reasons why temperature control methods are usually futile when it comes to preventing a febrile seizure. By the time you notice the fever, your child is often out of the highest risk period.

MYTH: Fever convulsions happen when the temperature gets very high.
TRUTH: It's not always the number, but often how fast the temperature rises.

A baby may be more likely to have a fever convulsion as his temperature quickly rises from 98 to 101 than if it gradually goes from 101 to 104.

MYTH: A fever convulsion is a definite sign that a baby has a serious infection.
TRUTH: A child can seize with a common cold.

It's often the most trivial infections that cause a fever convulsion. A child with a skyrocketing sudden fever often will turn out to have nothing more than a viral infection. You'll run in panic to your pediatrician, expecting lifesaving heroics, and leave with a bottle of Tylenol. As we've seen before, fever is no indicator of the seriousness of an infection, and neither is a seizure. It's frightening, but not an indication that your child is in trouble. Some viral infections seem particularly likely to cause a seizure. Roseola, for example, is a common viral illness precipitating 20 percent of febrile seizures.

MYTH: If your child convulses, put something in his mouth or he'll swallow his tongue.
TRUTH: Guess what—you can't swallow your tongue. It's attached!

Resist the temptation to do something dramatic. It's impossible to swallow your tongue, so don't rush to put something in little Alfonso's mouth if you see him convulsing. He'll only choke, and you'll turn a frightening but not very dangerous situation into a catastrophe.

What *can* you do to **treat your child during a febrile seizure?**

• First, *make sure your child has no food in his mouth.* If he does, quickly scoop it out with your finger, if possible. If his jaw is clenched, don't try to pry his mouth open. You'll have no success and will only make choking more likely.

• Second, either *hold your baby in a vertical position* in your arms or place him on his side on the floor with a pillow under his head so that he won't harm himself if his movements become too energetic.

• *Soak a large bath towel in tepid water* (not hot and not cold, but lukewarm) and wrap it around your baby to bring his temperature down.

• Once he's responsive and alert, *give him a dose of acetaminophen or ibuprofen.*

• Then *bring your baby to the doctor.* If this is Alfonso's first febrile seizure, the doctor will examine him to make sure that he has had nothing more than a simple fever-related convulsion, caused by a viral illness.

To **prevent future fever convulsions** in a child who has previously seized with fever, there are a few options.

• *Anticonvulsant medications* often prevent convulsions in a child who has had a febrile seizure, but most of these medications have to be given daily in order to maintain a high enough level, and they may cause drowsiness or other side effects. Most doctors will therefore not treat a child preventatively unless he has had several febrile convulsions or unless the convulsions are longer-lasting or more complicated than the usual fever seizure.

• **Rectal anticonvulsants** may act quickly enough to prevent the febrile child who has had seizures from convulsing. Of course, if your child has a seizure at the very beginning of an illness, then it will be too late to use such a preventative. Nevertheless, this is one option available to children who seize repeatedly with fever. Also, if a child tends to have a febrile convulsion that lasts longer than the usual two to three minutes, giving a suppository at the beginning of the convulsion can shorten its course.

KIDFIXER FREQUENTLY ASKED QUESTIONS

Q: *Is it okay to take my baby outside if he has a fever?*

A: Why not? If your baby has a slight temperature, acts fine, and is not going to be around a lot of other little ones to spread his germs to, and it's a nice day, go ahead. The trip outside will probably keep both of you from going stir-crazy. Of course, if it's twenty degrees below zero outside, or if he feels crummy and would seem to prefer to sleep a little more instead of going outside, that's fine, too.

Q: *My child's fever doesn't seem to be responding to Tylenol. What can I do?*

A: When a child is really feeling miserable with a high fever and you've seen the pediatrician and know he's not seriously ill, you may want to help cool him down with a tepid bath. The water temperature should not be icy, just a little cooler than that steamy baby. A few minutes in a lukewarm bath may take the temperature down a degree or two and make your hot tot feel a lot more comfortable.

Your doctor may also recommend another fever-reducing medication, such as ibuprofen (Motrin, Advil, etc.), which may keep fever down a bit better than acetaminophen. Because it is a stronger medication with more side effects, speak to your pediatrician before using it. Remember, fever is not something you have to fight or defeat. Don't feel that you're a failure because you can't get the fever down below 101. If you've seen the doctor and if your baby is acting just fine, don't worry so much about the temperature.

Q: Are all convulsions with fever just simple febrile convulsions?

A: Not always. Fortunately, most of the time when a baby has a fever and convulses, it's nothing more than a simple febrile convulsion. Although such episodes are scary, they're not very serious. On rare occasions, however, a seizure with fever may represent something more ominous. For example, a baby with meningitis can convulse because of the irritation to the brain brought about by such a serious infection. In this case, however, we're not talking about a happy and peppy baby who was laughing one minute and seizing the next. Babies with meningitis are sick little puppies. Of course, it's a good idea to have *any* baby with a seizure checked by the doctor. Together, you can usually determine if this is a simple febrile convulsion or something more serious.

Q: What clues would tell me if a seizure is something really serious?

A: As with most illnesses in kids, the best indicator that something serious is going on is your child's behavior. If your baby is eating and drinking as usual, is playful, is sleeping peacefully, and acts like his usual peppy self, then a brief seizure, although frightening, doesn't change the fact that he's probably not very sick. If he rebounds from this episode and is his old self in an hour or two, then relax. Also, typical febrile seizures usually last only a few minutes. If your baby has a convulsion that lasts more than five minutes, that may be an indication that his seizure is more than a simple fever convulsion. In addition, febrile seizures most often occur between the ages of 6 months and 5 years. If your 3-month-old has a seizure with fever, don't assume that it's an innocent febrile seizure. It may be innocent, but it may not.

Q: *My baby had a fever convulsion. Does this mean he has epilepsy?*

A: Epilepsy is a chronic illness in which a child (or adult) has repeated seizures. Unlike febrile seizures, these usually occur without fever. The great majority of children who have febrile seizures do not develop epilepsy. In fact, only about 3 percent of children who have had a fever convulsion later have a nonfebrile seizure.

17

TOILET TALK:
VOMITING, DIARRHEA,
CONSTIPATION

The reason pediatricians are so interested in subjects as yucky as vomiting and bowel movements is that they provide helpful indicators about a baby's health. After all, babies can't tell us when they have cramps. Signs such as vomiting, diarrhea, constipation, and weight loss are all important in assessing a new baby's health. To master the art of parenting, you will need to learn a bit about these "ins and outs."

VOMITING

Most healthy babies will spit up from time to time. Some will even spit up after meals once or twice each day. How, then, are you to know when you have a real problem? It's time to call your pediatrician if you see any of the following **vomiting warning signs:**

• ***Your baby vomits forcefully and repeatedly.*** Forceful (projectile) vomiting can be differentiated from normal spitting up by the way the vomit gushes from the baby's mouth. Sometimes the vomit will even come out through the baby's nose. Of course, even projectile vomiting *can* be normal. If it persists, however, call your doctor.

• *Your baby vomits after every feeding.* An occasional bout of vomiting can be quite normal. If *each* feeding results in vomiting, speak with your pediatrician.

• *Your baby vomits large amounts of milk at a time.* A little milk that's spit up with a feeding, especially with a burp, is okay. If, on the other hand, it seems that virtually all you feed is coming right back out, then make a call.

• *Your baby is vomiting more frequently than usual.* After a while you may find that your baby vomits once or twice a day. This may develop into her normal pattern. If she suddenly starts to vomit four or five times each day, consult your doctor.

• *Your baby is fussy, seems uncomfortable, or can't sleep.* If your baby is happy and peppy, gaining weight, and vomits once or twice each day, that's probably okay. If, on the other hand, she's not herself and starts vomiting, she may have a problem.

When you do call the doctor, he may be able to reassure you (and himself) over the phone that everything is fine. If not, he'll invite you to bring little Betty into the office. Once there he will examine her and look for **signs of dehydration,** which include:

• Dry tongue
• Wrinkled skin
• Lack of tears
• Recent drop in urine output

What if your baby is really going at it, with very forceful vomiting, or if everything that goes in is coming back? What are some **causes of vomiting?**

• *Pyloric stenosis.* If your baby is less than 3 months old, the doctor will feel the baby's belly for the presence of an olive-shaped mass, indicative of pyloric stenosis, a condition—slightly more common in first-born boys—that involves a thickening of a muscle at the end of the baby's stomach. If such a thickening occurs, it can lead to persistent vomiting and dehydration. Once diagnosed, pyloric stenosis is easily repaired by a simple surgical procedure.

• *Reflux.* Still other babies have a much more common condition that has been mentioned briefly, gastroesophageal reflux (GER), whereby the valve mechanism that allows food to go one way down into the intestines is not functioning properly and so food moves up into the esophagus or food pipe (and then out) instead. Babies with reflux can be messy. The vomiting may be a trickle or may, on occasion, be quite forceful, sometimes shooting right out of the baby's nose. It can occur at any time of the day and not necessarily right after a feeding. The little projectile that your baby graces you with can even occur two hours after a feeding.

Some babies will tolerate all this vomiting quite calmly, even smiling as they explode. Others, however, will be quite uncomfortable. Not only is the baby's breast milk or formula coming up, but stomach acid used to digest food is present as well. Although the stomach lining protects a baby from acid, the esophagus (food pipe) is more sensitive. Little Betty may be getting heartburn in addition to a messy bib. Many babies with reflux will, therefore, fuss during feedings. They may even twist their heads, as though they're asking you to stop feeding—a maneuver that probably acts to prevent food from refluxing up into the esophagus. Fortunately, reflux is usually outgrown in a few months without any treatment. At times, however, especially if your baby is not gaining weight, **reflux treatment** may be recommended, including:

• Thickening your baby's formula with a spoonful or two of cereal added right to the bottle to help keep the formula down
• Feeding your baby in a more vertical position
• An antacid, such as Mylanta or Gaviscon, to neutralize Betty's stomach acid
• A medication, such as Zantac, to reduce the production of acid

Again, most cases of reflux require no treatment at all, especially if you have a happy and growing (if messy) baby.

• *Intestinal obstruction.* On rare occasions, persistent vomiting might be a sign of a more serious problem, such as an intestinal obstruction. Obstruction occurs, for example, when a child's bowel becomes twisted—a condition called volvulus—or when one segment of bowel telescopes into another, intussusception. In duodenal atresia a small part of intestine, called the duodenum, fails to develop. All of these causes of obstruction have in common severe persistent vomiting as well as a decrease in stools.

• *Infection.* As discussed in more detail in the next chapter, gastroenteritis is a frequent cause of vomiting, usually seen in conjunction with diarrhea. Urinary infections can also cause vomiting.

• *Formula intolerance.* In Chapter 6 we learned that babies with intolerance to various components of infant formula can have severe vomiting, along with diarrhea, rashes, and other signs.

If your child has severe vomiting, make a trip to the pediatrician, who can help you determine the reason for the vomiting, and together you can formulate a treatment plan.

DIARRHEA

Great variation exists in what we call **normal bowel movements.** First of all, a baby's stool patterns change from week to week. The first movements, called **meconium,** are dark green in color and jellylike. Meconium stools are then usually replaced by soft yellow or tan seedy stools that look like mustard. In the following months, color can vary from brown through yellow to bright green. Likewise, consistency varies from formed through soft and mushy to loose and seedy. Breast-fed babies often have looser stools than bottle-fed infants. Even the number of stools that a baby has in a day may differ, from one every few days to several each day. Many babies move their bowels every time you feed them, due to an intestinal reflex called the gastro-colic reflex—when you stretch a baby's belly by feeding her, the intestines become active and a bowel movement soon follows. So if you're feeding your baby seven or eight times a day, as some mothers do in the first few weeks, you may be changing seven or eight poopy diapers each day. Some breast-fed infants will, after the first few weeks, go several days with no bowel movement at all. As long as they're not fussy and the stool, when it eventually passes, is soft, such a pattern is normal.

So, with such a wide spectrum of normal stools, **what constitutes diarrhea and what is constipation? Diarrhea** implies two things: First, it means that your baby's stools are looser than usual for her, and second, it means that the stools are more frequent than usual for her. **Constipation** means that her stools are firmer than usual for her and less frequent than usual compared to her normal pattern.

Notice two things about these statements. First, they are relative. What is considered diarrhea for one child may not necessarily be abnormal for another. Similarly, constipation in one can be perfectly normal for another. Second, these phrases tell us that *two* qualifications should be met to call a stool pattern diarrhea: increased frequency *and* increased looseness. Similarly, two requirements should be met before we say a child has constipation: decreased frequency *and* increased firmness.

For example, little Betty's normal pattern includes five to six seedy loose stools each day. Little Sondra moves her bowels once or twice each day, and her movements are usually like peanut butter in consistency. For Betty, two firm movements in a day could be considered a bit of a constipation pattern. For Sondra, a day with five or six loose movements would be considered diarrhea. Every child is different.

Diarrhea has many causes. Some of the more common ones include:

• *Infection.* Diarrhea often signals that a baby has a stomach virus or some other infection (see the next chapter for more information on stomach viruses).

• *Formula intolerance.* Diarrhea might mean that your child's formula is causing a problem (see Chapter 6). Formula intolerance can occur within days of beginning a formula, or it may not show up for weeks.

• *Diarrhea from medications.* Diarrhea is an unwanted side effect of many medications. Most common in babies is diarrhea associated with strong antibiotics. Although infants usually tolerate the looser stools seen with antibiotics, occasionally a medication will have to be changed if diarrhea is severe.

• *Toddler's diarrhea.* One of the most common causes of diarrhea in young children, especially those over 6 months of age, is toddler's diarrhea, also called chronic nonspecific diarrhea of childhood. Babies drink almost twice as many ounces of fluid per pound of weight as adults. Diarrhea can result when a child compounds this fluid load by drinking more than usual or when a baby is given too much juice or other high-sugar beverage (such as sports drinks). The high sugar content of juice and sports drinks actually draws water into the intestines, making looser, more frequent stools. Many kids with toddler's diarrhea grow well, act fine, sleep well, and happily pass their seven to ten stools a day with no complaints (other than the discomfort of a sore bottom). Others gain slowly and are fussier. Limiting fluids a bit and eliminating juice and sports drinks will usually help slow down toddler's diarrhea.

• *Malabsorption.* Less common but of concern are malabsorption illnesses, in which nutrients from specific foods simply pass through the intestinal tract without being absorbed into the bloodstream. The most common type of malabsorption is celiac disease, an allergy to gluten in wheat. In these kids, the addition of wheat to the diet (in cereals, cookies or pasta), causes severe diarrhea. Children with celiac disease often are fussy, gain slowly, and are frequently anemic from iron loss in diarrhea. Celiac disease is treated by eliminating wheat from the diet. Also, children with **cystic fibrosis** have fat malabsorption, in which dietary fat passes through the intestines without being absorbed. This is treated by replacing the missing pancreatic enzymes with artificial enzymes.

• *Inflammatory bowel disease (IBD).* Children with ulcerative colitis and Crohn's disease, two conditions more common in older children and adolescents than in babies, have diarrhea, often with blood in the stool, weight loss, and growth failure. IBD is diagnosed by the gastroenterologist, who examines a child's intestines using a flexible colonoscope.

CONSTIPATION

Although stool patterns vary greatly, some babies are plagued with hard, infrequent stools. **Constipation can be caused by:**

• *Inadequate intake of fluids.* The child who is not nursing enough or taking enough from the bottle can develop hard, infrequent stools.

• *Excess of binding foods.* Rice cereal is notorious for causing constipation, although most babies handle it with no problem. Bananas are also a bit binding.

• *Formula intolerance.* Though less often than diarrhea, constipation can be a sign of formula intolerance.

• *Functional constipation.* Most often babies become constipated for no reason at all other than an immaturity of the intestines. Think of your newborn as having to build up the muscles of defecation. A baby might squeeze and strain to pass a stool. If you think of that little baby as building up her muscles, then all that squeezing and pushing is nothing more than pumping iron to help her muscles develop. If your child is one of the many with functional constipation, your doctor can help devise a plan of treatment. Although some moms use the old tried-and-true rectal thermometer loaded up with Vaseline to induce a reluctant bowel movement, this can, on rare occasions, result in a broken thermometer in the baby's tush. Safer is the infant glycerine suppository, a little bullet of lubricant to get those lazy intestines to push out a stool. He may also suggest extra fluids or eliminating rice and bananas.

• *More serious medical (organic) causes.* Constipation, if severe and long-lasting, may signal a more serious digestive problem. In a rare condition called Hirschprung disease, the nerves that allow a baby's intestines to push food along aren't properly developed. These babies become extremely constipated, but usually the doctor can feel little or no stool in the rectum. Cystic fibrosis, celiac disease (both of which often cause diarrhea), and an underactive thyroid gland are also potential causes of constipation. Finally, babies with intestinal obstruction may experience constipation as well as vomiting.

Most reassuring is the fact that most of the time a baby's stools will eventually become regular on their own. Nature has a way of correcting most little problems that babies face and constipation and diarrhea are two good examples of the adage that when it comes to treating babies, time is often the best remedy.

KIDFIXER FREQUENTLY ASKED QUESTIONS

Q: My baby spits up a little after some feedings. Is this normal?

A: As long as she's happy and gaining weight well on the doctor's scale, you're okay. Note that I say "the doctor's scale." I do this to emphasize that you should not be weighing the baby at home each day, or *ever*, for that matter. As you know all too well, scales differ greatly from one place to another. Also, weights can vary at different times of the day. So don't be a fanatic about weight. Your visits to the doctor are frequent enough to weigh your baby.

Q: My baby's stools are yellow or green in color. Is this a problem?

A: A tan, green, or even yellow stool is fine. Inside our adult bodies, our stool is green, colored by bile. As stool passes along our digestive tracts, the green stool changes to brown. In babies, stools often make this intestinal voyage so quickly that there isn't time for the green-to-brown trick to occur, and out pops a green stool. It's fine.

Q: *My nursed baby, who usually has six seedy yellow stools daily, went three days before having a bowel movement but seems happy and the stool is soft. What do I do?*

A: This can happen with nursed babies. It is an exception to the rule that a dramatic change signals possible trouble. The key factors here are these: the baby seems fine, is nursing and sleeping well, and when she finally does move her bowels, they're still soft. You probably have no problem. If she is obviously uncomfortable all day and the stools are rock hard when they finally make their much-awaited appearance, then you may be dealing with constipation and should place a call to your pediatrician.

Q: *My baby has a streak of blood in her stool. What's wrong?*

A: Don't panic. Such a streak of blood usually just means that she has a small tear or fissure in the anus, caused by an unusually large or hard stool. Also, frequent loose stools can irritate her sensitive tush and cause a little blood to appear. Of course, if there's more than a streak, or if it persists for more than a day or two, call your doctor.

Q: *My daughter, L.J., is 6 months old. She used to have three or four bowel movements a day. Since starting solids, she now has one every few days, and she has to strain, grunt, and push to get out her hard poop. What can we do?*

A: At 6 months many babies become constipated. This is a combination of several things, including physiologic constipation (in other words, it's normal for that age) and the introduction of binding cereals. Try avoiding rice cereal, which is more constipating than barley or oatmeal, and give lots and lots of fruits. Prunes are a great source of fiber, as is barley cereal. Offer a few ounces of prune juice once or twice daily. If this doesn't do the trick, your doctor might recommend a stool softener. Maltsupex powder is a gentle natural stool softener for babies. You might want to give it a try.

Q: *I've heard that Gatorade is good to give for diarrhea. Is this true?*

A: Actually, drinking Gatorade, because of its very high sugar content, will often *increase* a child's diarrhea. Any too-sweet liquid tends to draw water into the intestines, thereby increasing loose stools. Electrolyte solutions like Pedialyte or Naturlyte have sugar for energy, but in a lower concentration, and don't cause diarrhea. They're a better choice for a child with diarrhea.

18

GERMS: WHY IS
HE ALWAYS SICK?

"Why is my baby always getting sick?" If I had a dime for every time I've had to answer that question! Babies do seem to get sick quite often. In this chapter we'll learn a little about all of those infections and the germs that cause them. We'll discuss the difference between viruses and bacteria, the two types of germs that are responsible for most childhood illnesses. Finally, we'll take a head-to-toe look at the most common childhood infections, what they look like, and how they're treated.

MYTH: If your baby is suddenly getting sick a lot, something must be wrong.
TRUTH: Nothing's wrong. It's his age.

For the most part, babies are pretty healthy for the first few months of life because they enjoy the benefits of **maternal immunity.** While he was inside of you, little Petie shared the antibodies your immune system produced to fight off germs. The problem with these inherited infection fighters is that they run out about five months after birth. Unfortunately, Petie hasn't yet learned how to make his own antibodies, so he's susceptible to infection from all sources. Sneeze on Petie and he may catch a cold. Hug him with a flu bug or a stomach virus and he may catch that, too. His low antibody supply also means that it will take Petie longer to get rid of his germs, which is why a baby's cold can last twice as long as Mom or Dad's cold.

MYTH: If you nurse, your baby won't become sick.
TRUTH: He may be sick a bit less often, but he's still going to catch his share of germs.

Breast-feeding supplies Petie with some extra antibodies, but even this noble effort is unlikely to totally prevent the slew of minor illnesses that you'll start to see around the fifth or sixth month of age. By the time his first birthday rolls around, however, Petie's own antibody supply will be pretty solid, and that run of colds, ear infections, stomach viruses, and other annoying germs will ease up for a while.

Now that we know *why* babies get sick so frequently, we can dispel three common misconceptions about illnesses in the first year of life.

MYTH: Your baby is getting sick because he's going out in cold weather.
TRUTH: Babies don't get sick from the cold.

MYTH: Your baby is getting sick because you're underdressing him.
TRUTH: Babies don't get sick from being underdressed.

MYTH: Your baby is getting sick because he needs more vitamin C.
TRUTH: Extra vitamin C is no shield against colds.

Children don't get sick from going out in cold weather, especially if they're comfortably dressed. They also don't get sick because you forgot their hats and gloves (sorry, grandmas). As far as vitamin C is concerned, the amount in the normal infant vitamin drops is plenty.

As we've said, your previously pristine baby is now getting sick a lot because he's susceptible to infection at this age. This is a temporary condition and a very normal one. About the only thing you can do to prevent a run of infections is to lock Petie up in his room with no visitors for most of his first year. Of course you, his parents, and any brothers and sisters would also have to stay away from germs. Most infections that plague babies come from you guys, not from strangers. Unless you all want to live in a bubble for several months, just accept these illnesses as a fact of life.

Don't let this depress you. You may be lucky. Not *all* babies are germ magnets. In fact, some babies hardly get sick at all. Perhaps some babies are better antibody makers than others. Maybe, in the lucky child's house, a sibling is having a good year healthwise and is not bringing home as many germs. For those of you who are not so lucky, think of all these little illnesses as inevitable. Imagine Petie carrying around a little scorecard with a list of germs. Every time he gets sick, he checks off the name of another bug that won't bother him in the future. If he catches lots of them now, think how many fewer bugs will be left to bother him later on, when each illness means another day or two of school missed. **Exposure to a germ is what helps us develop our own antibodies.** If he were in a bubble, Petie would never face these germs and would never have the chance to develop his own immunity.

VIRUSES AND BACTERIA

MYTH: Without medication, infections won't get better.
TRUTH: Most germs aren't affected by antibiotics at all.

Most infections that trouble humans can be divided into two categories: viral and bacterial. There are exceptions, of course. Athlete's foot and some diaper rashes, for example, are fungal infections. Mycoplasma and

Chlamydia, which are neither viruses nor bacteria but are classified as being in between the two, are responsible for many cases of pneumonia. These and a few other exceptions aside, though, the great majority of infections your baby will face in his first year are caused by either viruses or bacteria. So what's the difference?

Viral Infections

For the most part, viruses are self-limiting, which means that they get better by themselves. Although viral infections can be pesky and even serious, our bodies usually fight them off with little or no help from medication. Antibiotics are useless against viruses. Show a teaspoon of penicillin to a virus and he'll laugh in your face. Some **examples of viral infections include:**

- *Colds and most upper respiratory infections.* That's why antibiotics are useless against cold germs.

- *Stomach viruses.* Not only won't an antibiotic help rid you of your tummy ache, but it may even make your symptoms worse, since many antibiotics cause cramping and diarrhea.

- *Sore throats.* Other than strep throat, a problem babies rarely face in their first year, most throat infections are viral. That painful, fiery red throat will usually get better without medication.

- *Other exotic illnesses.* Roseola, fifth disease, and a slew of other illnesses are caused by viruses.

So, most of the infections that will annoy your baby and drive you crazy are viral, and thus get better by themselves. Nevertheless, when a baby gets a cold, there are some things we can do to make him feel better. Remember, however, that this treatment is directed at symptoms and is not curative. Cold medication may make your baby's nose run a *bit* less. Antidiarrheal medicine might make his bowel movements look a bit more formed. Tylenol may bring his fever down a point or two. But remember, we're not curing anything with such treatment. We're just treating symptoms to make a baby feel better.

Bacterial Infections

Bacterial infections, on the other hand, usually do not get better by themselves; they require treatment with antibiotics. Yes, our immune systems can fight off many bacterial infections naturally, but a great deal of damage is done while waiting for the immune system to do its job. Before the discovery of penicillin, for example, an ear infection might eventually clear by itself, but by that time there was often a permanent hearing loss. **Common bacterial infections** that usually need treatment with antibiotics include:

- Many ear infections
- Strep throat
- Many skin infections, such as impetigo
- Most urinary infections
- Many cases of pneumonia

Your pediatrician, after a careful examination, which may include such tests as a culture or a blood count, will determine whether or not your child's illness is bacterial. Keep in mind one important point: the fact that your child is running a high temperature is no indication that he has a bacterial infection. Many common childhood viruses are accompanied by a high fever.

ANTIBIOTICS

Does that mean we should avoid antibiotics altogether?

MYTH: Antibiotics ruin our immunity.
TRUTH: *Unnecessary* antibiotics impair immunity, but there are many times when antibiotics are essential.

Using antibiotics *unnecessarily* has caused problems in our communities. Bacteria, brainless though they may be, are smart enough to mutate, or change their genetic makeup, to develop resistance to a drug when it is overused. For example, when penicillin first came onto the scene in the 1940s, it was a true Terminator-like superdrug. Within a relatively few years, however, many bacteria developed resistance to penicillin. Drug companies were thus forced to develop stronger drugs to fight these tougher germs. Unfortunately, the more potent a drug is, the more likely it is to produce side effects, such as tummy ache and diarrhea.

On the other hand, avoiding all medications entirely can be dangerous as well. Before antibiotics, many people died from infections, such as pneumonia, that are now easily managed. Although many pediatricians are guilty of overprescribing, resist the temptation to treat nothing at all. Not all infections will get better by themselves. Allow your pediatrician to assist you in deciding whether or not to use antibiotics for your child's infection.

HOW TO GIVE MEDICATION TO A BABY: THE "PUCKER AND PUSH" TECHNIQUE

MYTH: If a baby refuses medicine, just put it in a bottle and he'll get it that way.
TRUTH: This isn't a reliable technique.

Medication that's hidden in a bottle will be of use only if the entire bottle is taken. Even if a baby drinks most of his bottle, there's no guarantee that he's getting the majority of the medicine. Some medications don't dissolve evenly in formula, pumped breast milk, or juice and just stick to the sides of the bottle, even after you shake it up. Finally, some medications aren't absorbed as well when taken with food as they are when taken alone.

There's no getting around it. You may have to learn, at some point, to force-feed medication to your stubborn little baby. Here's how to do it:

1 First of all, get a syringe from the druggist (or your doctor). A spoon is much too easy to spill, while a syringe holds on to the medication and provides easy measurement.

2 Next, lay your baby down. Put the end of
   the filled syringe into the back of his
   mouth, on the side, between his cheek and
   gums. This would be equivalent to where
   your lower bottom teeth end.

3 Pinch Petie's cheeks and lips into a pucker,
   like an exaggerated kiss position. This will stop him from spitting the
   medicine right back at you.

4 Push a little of the medication into your baby's mouth at a time—too
   much and it will overflow. If you have more than a teaspoon of medication to administer, you may have to give it in several increments.

5 Petie will cry and try to spit the medication out, but if you keep his
   cheeks and lips puckered, he will not be able to spit and will eventually swallow the medication.

6 If Petie gags, turn his head to the side
   for a second or two.

7 Repeat this until the full dosage is
   given, remembering to keep his lips
   and cheeks puckered. If he needs to
   catch his breath between portions,
   allow him to do this, but don't keep
   picking him up after each fraction and holding him; get all the medicine in before you pick him up.

   Does this sound like torture? It's really not. Remember that the
sooner Petie learns that he's going to have to take that medicine, one way
or another, the sooner he'll stop fighting and just open up and take it
like a trouper. If he doesn't learn now, you'll be bribing and pleading for
hours to get him to take his medication when he's older.

CONTAGION: WHEN CAN HE GO BACK TO DAY CARE?

The parent who is concerned about the spread of germs will often want
to know when a child is no longer contagious. Frequently, this concern

is phrased as "When can he go back to day care or to play group?" Each germ has its period of contagion, and some germs are spread for much longer periods of time than others. Most of the viruses that cause colds and stomach viruses, for example, are contagious primarily for the first two to three days of symptoms, whereas influenza is passed on for as long as a week after symptoms begin. Also, within a particular species of virus or bacterium there can be great variation. Thus, the child with recurrent herpes cold sores is contagious for only three or four days, but the infant with his very first such case of herpes can shed his virus to others for as long as eight weeks. What's a parent to do? Short of committing to memory a long list of contagious periods, along with an even longer list of exceptions, a good general rule is this: children with infections are most contagious for a day or two before they become sick and continue to pass on their germs to others primarily for the first two to three days of symptoms. Once a child's runny nose has slowed down, cough has eased, stools have become formed, or fever has dissipated, he can be deemed to be less contagious and therefore a candidate to once again join civilization. Sure, there is still a chance that he may be shedding some of his germs, but the amount of viral or bacterial shedding will be much less.

Let's take a head-to-toe look at some of the common infections your baby will be fighting in his first year. We'll start off with the nose, eyes, ears, and throat and then move down the body through the chest, intestines, and urinary tract. Infections with rashes will be described next, followed finally by the bloodstream.

INFECTIONS OF THE NOSE, EYES, EARS, AND THROAT

The Common Cold

• *What is it?* Colds are viral infections of the nose, throat, and upper airway.

• *What does it look like?* The baby with a cold will have a runny or stuffy nose, will likely have a cough, will often have watery eyes, and may or may not have fever. In other words, he will look a lot like his mom and dad when they have a cold, except that his cold will usually last long after Mom and Dad have recovered from theirs.

• *How did he get it?* As with any infection, you catch a cold virus from someone else who has that virus, not by going out in the cold without a hat. Someone who has the nerve to breathe, cough, or spray on you when he speaks is the culprit, not your bare head.

• *What do I do about it?* Although colds are caused by viruses and therefore get better by themselves, there are some things you can do to make Petie more comfortable while he waits out his cold.

• *Give fluids.* With any illness, babies use up lots of energy and fluids fighting the infection. So offer Petie the bottle or your breast more frequently than usual.

• *Let him eat if he's hungry.* Starve a cold? Feed a fever? Nope. If he's hungry, let him eat as usual, but don't be upset if he eats less when he's sick. Keep in mind that Petie's nose is full, and feeding him will block another airway, making it tough for him to breathe. Be patient. Allow him to take a few extra pauses to catch his breath. A nursing or bottle-feeding that might normally take fifteen to twenty minutes may now last twice as long, as little Petie takes breathing breaks between gulps. Some babies eat and drink just fine when they're sick, but others will eat and drink very little. Don't worry about it; just let him go at his own pace, making sure that you offer fluids more frequently.

• *Treat fever.* If your baby has fever, you can make him feel more comfortable with acetaminophen (Tylenol, etc.). It's a good idea, however, to let your pediatrician know when your baby has a fever, especially when he's under 4 months of age. (For more on fever, see Chapter 16.)

• *Cold medications.* Pharmacy shelves are loaded with decongestants, antihistamines, expectorants, and cough suppressants. None of these will shorten the duration of Petie's cold. Many cold medications also have side effects, such as irritability, wakefulness, drowsiness, or appetite suppression. The lesson to learn is simply this: if little Petie is handling his cold well and can drink a little and sleep a little, then leave him alone. His cold will get better by itself.

A warm-mist vaporizer will make him feel more comfortable, especially in the winter when the dry air that heats up your house makes him miserable. If his nose is particularly stuffy, ordinary normal saline (salt water) nose drops are the best treatment, since saline is a great nasal mucus loosener. Nevertheless, there will be times when your doctor will recommend a brief course of medication to help alleviate some of Petie's symptoms, if only in a minor way. To understand the choices you face as you stare at that dizzying display of cough-cold preparations on your pharmacy shelf, here is a brief primer on cold medications. Remember, the great majority of the time such medicines are neither necessary nor beneficial.

• *Decongestants.* Such products as pseudoephedrine and phenylephrine reduce stuffiness by narrowing the blood vessels in your child's nose. Unfortunately, they are also stimulants, and you'll need to balance the slight relief they afford with the sleeplessness that sometimes accompanies their usage. Some decongestants are administered by nasal spray, rather than orally. Although these are a bit more effective than the oral preparations, they also tend to have a "rebound effect": when you stop using them, little noses are often more stuffy than they were before you started.

• *Antihistamines.* Such compounds as chlorpheniramine and diphenhydramine are mostly used to treat nasal allergy. Although they slightly reduce sneezing in children with colds, they can cause dry mouth, sleepiness, or fussiness.

• *Expectorants.* Guaifenesin is the most common ingredient in expectorant medications, which are supposed to thin secretions to aid in their elimination from the throat and lungs. Do they truly have much effect? Not in little children.

• *Cough suppressants.* Codeine (a very strong narcotic cough suppressant) and dextromethorphan are two of the common cough suppressants. Although they can be effective (especially codeine) for some coughs, there are many times when we don't want to stop a child from coughing. It's the coughing that tends to remove harmful viruses and troublesome secretions from a child's respiratory tree, and allowing this removal is often a good thing. Also, codeine can cause sleepiness (or, conversely in some babies, irritability).

• **When do I call the doctor?** Most colds in babies take one to two weeks to go away. Occasionally, your baby may have a secondary infection from his cold, such as an ear infection, sinus infection, or lower respiratory infection (pneumonia or bronchiolitis). If your baby starts to get a bad cough, if he seems unusually fretful, or if the cold seems to be lasting longer than usual or is particularly severe, then give your pediatrician a call.

One last word about the common cold: sometimes it's not so common. Consider two examples wherein what seems to be the common cold is really something else.

Fake Cold #1: Allergic Rhinitis

Exposure to allergens in the air can make a baby's nose run clear, make his eyes itch and water, and cause a persistent cough. When your doctor examines a child with allergenic rhinitis, instead of seeing the usual red inside the baby's nose, the nasal lining is pale purple and boggy.

Most of the triggers of nasal allergy are airborne allergens. The main inhaled allergens, and the typical times they strike, include:

• *Tree pollen* (mid-March through May). A windy day or a car ride with the windows open can spell trouble for the allergic child.
• *Grass pollen* (mid-May through June). Crawling around on a freshly mowed lawn can cause the same respiratory symptoms as a cold.
• *Ragweed pollen* (August through September). This is what is known as hay fever. Your baby's symptoms may increase with the late summer pollen count.
• *Mold spores* (all year). Mold spores are present all year round but peak, along with ragweed, in August and September. Of course, a damp, moldy room or basement can cause indoor mold allergy symptoms at any time.

- *Dust mites* (all year). These mysterious little critters are the most common cause of year-round allergy. A thick shag rug, a less-than-clean heating system, or a room cluttered with stuffed animals and other dust-catchers can cause a child with dust mite allergy to be miserable.
- *Pet dander* (all year). Dogs, cats, guinea pigs, gerbils, and rabbits are no fun for the child with a pet allergy.

If your doctor suspects that allergies are making Petie's nose run, he might suggest an air purifier for his room, and he might advise you to get rid of shag carpeting and stuffed animals. Finally, he may suggest an antihistamine or immune modulator to allow Petie to breathe a little more easily.

Fake Cold #2: Foreign Body in the Nose

Babies just love to put things in their little noses. Unfortunately, an infection often develops when they do, characterized by a persistent runny nose that is one-sided, smelly, and bloody. Here are some of the things I've had to fish out of babies' noses in the past twenty-five years:

- Food (peas are the all-time nose champs)
- Small toys
- Pieces of tissue
- Small rocks
- Beads
- Bugs (yech!)

Conjunctivitis (Pinkeye)

- **What is it?** Newborns often get "gunk" in their eyes, especially in the first week of life. Frequently, a discharge is simply the result of the drops instilled in a baby's eyes in the delivery room to prevent eye infections passed on during the trip through the birth canal. A thin watery discharge that disappears by the time you come home from the hospital is usually such an expected chemical conjunctivitis. After the first week, a discharge may represent true conjunctivitis, an infection of the conjunctiva, the clear covering of the surface of the eye, and may require antibiotics.

• **What does it look like?** Conjunctivitis in babies can be recognized as redness in the white (sclera) of one or both eyes, usually accompanied by a yellow or green discharge.

• **How did he get it?** Conjunctivitis, as with ear infections, is usually a complication of a cold. When you consider that your baby is constantly putting his hands on his face, it's no wonder that a face full of "boogies" will quickly lead to an eye full of pus. At other times the cold germ to which your child is exposed when others breathe on him can jump right into his unsuspecting eye and cause conjunctivitis without a full-fledged cold.

One thing that will predispose a baby to develop conjunctivitis is a **blocked tear duct.** Babies' tear ducts are narrow little tubes which often have not opened fully by the time the baby is born. Your doctor will be able to diagnose a blocked tear duct and will demonstrate a technique of massage to open up the ducts. Rarely, and only when blockage persists past the first few months, an ophthalmologist will be needed to open up your baby's tear ducts surgically.

• **What do I do about it?** A trip to the doctor is usually a good idea. For one thing, conjunctivitis is often a bacterial infection, and an antibiotic drop, ointment, or oral medication might be needed to fight the infection. Also, eye infections in babies are caused by the same bacteria that cause ear infections. It's not uncommon, therefore, for a baby with oozing eyes to have an ear infection as well. Certainly any baby with a red or oozing eye who has fever, who is fussy, or who has a history of ear infections should see the pediatrician.

• **When do I call the doctor?** Any discharge that lasts more than a day or two or that is particularly severe should be seen by your pediatrician. Once you have started treatment, let the doctor know if the discharge has not lessened within a few days. It's also important to watch for a complication of conjunctivitis called **periorbital cellulitis,** a bacterial infection of the skin and underlying tissues around the eye. Suspect cellulitis when you see the skin around your baby's eye looking swollen and red or purple.

Ear Infection (Otitis Media)

• **What is it?** Known as otitis media, the ear infection that commonly follows a cold is an infection of the eardrum and the middle ear, located directly behind the drum.

• **What does it look like?** Recognizing an ear infection is a skill you will sharpen quite well if your child is prone to ear infections. Most commonly, this is the scenario: Petie has had a cold for a few days but has been eating fairly well, sleeping okay, and acting happy enough when awake. Today, however, he seems very fussy. Your little peekaboo trick isn't getting the laughs it usually does, his naps are shorter, and when you put him to bed at night, your normally great sleeper is getting up every two hours. Though not all babies follow this classic pattern, the **clues that will alert you to the possibility of an ear infection** in a baby include:
  • Fussiness, usually following a cold
  • Poor feeding
  • Poor sleep

Notice that I haven't mentioned fever yet. Many babies will get ear infections with no fever at all. Some get ear infections with raging fevers. If a fever *is* present, however, the temperature has nothing to do with the severity of the infection. Some very mild ear infections can be accompanied by a high fever, while some extremely red ears are seen with no fever at all. I also haven't talked about ear pulling, which is not a very reliable sign, at least not when it occurs without any other signs. A happy, healthy baby may start to pull his ears because he's just discovered that they're there.

• **How did he get it?** Contrary to popular belief, babies don't get ear infections from the cold wind blowing on a hatless head. An ear infection is a complication of a cold germ. Although the cold is viral, the ear infection is often bacterial. This pattern of a bacterial secondary infection on top of a viral infection is a common one in pediatrics, as the virus sets the stage for the bacteria. Ear infections are very common in the first year or two (the average child can be expected to have four or five ear infections in the first year of life) because the eustachian tube, which separates the nice clean eardrum from the dirty, mucus-filled nose and throat is very short and straight in babies, whereas later it gets longer and full of little kinks and turns. As is the case with many infections in children, ear infections are also common because of the reduced immunity seen between the ages of 4 months and 1 year.

Because the infection that you see in your baby is behind the eardrum, external things, like cold wind or water, do not affect it. When Petie has a cold, bathing will have no effect on his ear, and while going out without a hat may make him uncomfortable, it will also have no effect on his ear. This is also a complication that can't be prevented by using an antihistamine or a decongestant, so don't expect that well-advertised cold syrup to stop little Petie from getting ear infections.

• *What do I do about it?* The best treatment is prevention. You can reduce your child's chances of getting an ear infection in the following ways:
   • *Feed him upright.* Babies nursed or bottle-fed while lying flat get more ear infections than those who are fed at an angle.
   • *Don't smoke in the house.* Secondhand smoke increases the risk of ear infections, along with causing other respiratory problems.
   • *Don't use a pacifier.* For some reason, pacifier babies are more prone to ear infections.

Once your baby has been diagnosed with an ear infection, your doctor may prescribe an antibiotic. Ear drops can't penetrate the eardrum to get into the middle ear, where the infection is located, so the antibiotic is given orally. If the infection is particularly mild, your doctor may elect to postpone treatment—some ear infections are viral and thus resolve by themselves. Nevertheless, if your doctor feels that your baby's infection requires treatment, don't take it upon yourself to withhold medication; an untreated ear infection can lead to a much more serious complication, such as an infection in the bloodstream or even meningitis.

There are almost as many antibiotics out there for ear infections as there are cold medications. Your doctor will choose an antibiotic based upon such factors as:

- The severity of the infection
- The types of resistance to antibiotics he sees in your community
- The side effects of the antibiotic (tummyache, diarrhea)
- Any allergies to medication that your baby has shown in the past

In extreme circumstances—for example, in babies who seem to get ear infections on a weekly basis—prophylactic treatment may be tried. An antibiotic, administered for two or three months at a low dosage, may be the only way to keep a baby's ears clear.

What if the ear isn't clear at your child's follow-up appointment? Occasionally, a middle ear infection does not completely resolve after treatment with an antibiotic. Although little Petie may act fine, your doctor might still see some fluid behind his eardrum. In fact, a baby's ear can be checked with a simple and painless procedure called a **tympanogram** to see if the ear is now back to normal, with a perfectly functioning eardrum. Because persistent fluid can impair Petie's hearing, the pediatrician will want to make certain that it clears. If not, he may prescribe another course of antibiotics—either more of the same, if the ear looks somewhat better, or else a different medication altogether if the eardrum hasn't improved at all. If Petie's ear fluid persists longer than a few months, surgery is an alternative. **Tympanostomy** is a procedure whereby an incision is made surgically in your child's eardrum to drain persistent fluid or pus and a small plastic tube is fixed to the drum to prevent reaccumulation of the fluid. What are the **advantages of tympanostomy?**

- Children often hear better immediately after tubes have been placed.
- Draining fluid surgically can relieve discomfort.

The disadvantages of tympanostomy:

- The procedure requires anesthesia in young children.
- The body may reject tubes as foreign substances, and the tubes may fall out.

- Tubes can lead to leaking of fluid from behind the eardrum.
- If your child does get an ear infection with tubes, the infection is often worse.
- Recent studies suggest that tubes have no long-term benefit for hearing.

Usually, a good, conservative ear-nose-throat specialist will reserve tubes for the child whose ears are persistently infected for several months in a row. This means that a baby who has had three or four ear infections but whose ears are clear at his recheck exams will usually do fine without tubes.

Unfortunately, that's about it as far as treatment goes. Decongestants, antihistamines, and vitamins won't help. Some babies get lots of ear infections, while others get very few. The good news is that even those beleaguered by ear infections in the first year or two will usually outgrow them. So hang in there.

- **When do I call the doctor?** Call your pediatrician if your child has been seen for an ear infection and is still:
  - Fussy, eating poorly or still not sleeping after forty-eight hours
  - Running fever (if a fever was present to start) after forty-eight hours
  - Draining blood or pus from the ear—signs that the eardrum has perforated
  - Having troublesome side effects of medication—severe diarrhea, vomiting, rash
  - Just doesn't look right to your ever-sharpening parental eye

Finally, although we rarely see this in babies, a word about **swimmer's ear** (otitis externa). When a child spends a lot of time with his head in the water (and your baby should not), the water can wash away protective oils that keep the skin of the ear canal smooth and healthy. When theses oils are completely washed away, the ear canal skin becomes irritated, swollen, macerated, and eventually infected. A swimmer's ear is an infection, but not an infection of the middle ear, which we see after a cold. It is an infection of the outer ear, the skin of the ear canal, and is treated with prescription antibiotic ear drops and, if the infection is bad enough, with oral antibiotics. A clue that your baby may have a swimmer's ear is that gently pulling on his earlobe will make him cry.

The Flu (Influenza)

• **What is it?** Infuenza is a respiratory infection, occurring each year in epidemics, affecting the nose, throat, and bronchial passages. Although the term *flu* is used loosely ("He has a stomach flu"), there is a specific germ, the influenza virus, that is responsible for flu, and it is a respiratory illness, not an intestinal one.

• **What does it look like?** The typical case of flu in a baby will look just like a protracted bad cold, with runny nose, severe and often croupy cough, and usually a high fever. Babies with flu can't complain of achiness or headache, classic symptoms in older kids and adults, but their fussiness and irritability tell us that they feel the same way.

• **How did he get it?** The flu virus is transmitted by mucus and saliva and is extremely contagious, especially for the first several days of illness. Because there are several strains of flu, your child can catch the flu several times.

• **What do I do about it?** Although influenza is one of the few viral infections for which antiviral medication exists, flu medications that are currently available are not recommended for babies under a year of age. They also have only limited success in relieving symptoms, which makes flu another bug for which you push fluids and treat fever. Because of the similarity to cold viruses, it's sometimes difficult to tell if a child has the flu. The job is made easier, however, by the rapid flu test, a ten-minute procedure in which a swab of nasal mucus is tested chemically for flu. This is a valuable test, since flu medication is also useful as a preventative, and knowing that your child's bug is flu may save the rest of the family from suffering.

Another option in flu season, which runs from late October through February, is the **influenza virus vaccine,** which contains a mix of different strains of flu each year. The flu vaccine can be taken by anyone over 6 months of age and is recommended for all **high-risk kids** (those who are more likely to have complications from flu), including children with:

- Heart disease
- Chronic lung disease (asthma, cystic fibrosis)
- Chronic kidney disease
- Immune deficiencies, including HIV
- Sickle cell disease and other blood diseases
- Diabetes and other metabolic diseases

In addition, the flu vaccine is strongly recommended for children who are exposed to lots of other babies, including those in day care, and those whose parents are health-care workers. It makes good sense for *every* child over age 6 months to get a flu vaccine, since this is a bug that makes babies miserable and since little ones have a higher risk of complications than older kids and adults.

• *When do I call the doctor?* One of the complications of flu, which will make you bring your baby back to the pediatrician, is ear infections. Not uncommonly, a baby with flu will also have an ear infection. See your doctor if your baby is fussier than usual, has difficulty sleeping, is still running a fever after several days, or just doesn't look right to you.

Another complication is developing a secondary respiratory infection. Croup, bronchiolitis, and pneumonia are complications sometimes seen with the flu virus. If your baby's cough sounds particularly barky, or if he's running a protracted fever, feeding poorly, or acting more lethargic or more irritable, have your doctor take another look.

Pharyngitis (Sore Throat)

• *What is it?* Pharyngitis is an infection, usually viral, of your child's throat.

• **What does it look like?** Your best indication that your baby has a sore throat is that he will stop eating. He may also have fever, but, as with so many illnesses in babies, fever is not always there when you expect it.

• **How did he get it?** Petie picked up his sore throat from someone who had (or was incubating) a throat infection and had the nerve to breathe on him, cough on him, or slobber on his toys.

• **What do I do about it?** Because they're usually viral, most throat infections in babies get better by themselves, without antibiotics. One exception to the no-treat rule for sore throats, however, is **strep throat,** an infection caused by bacteria called streptococci. Strep throat is rare in babies, but if you have an older child around to share germs, you may be faced with strep. Of course, to be certain that this is not a strep throat, your doctor will want to do a throat culture or a rapid strep test (involving a swipe with a swab), and the results from these simple tests will determine if your child has strep.

• **When do I call the doctor?** If your child still seems uncomfortable or isn't eating after forty-eight hours, give your doctor a call. Even though that throat germ is viral, he may want to take another peek in your baby's ears, to make sure that an ear infection hasn't popped up.

Two special types of sore throat should also be discussed at this time: Coxsackie virus and herpes.

Special Sore Throat #1: Coxsackie Virus

• **What is it?** One particular virus that commonly causes a red throat in children, especially in the warmer months, is a nasty little bug called Coxsackie virus. A member of the enterovirus family, Coxsackie sets up camp in our intestinal tracts as well as our throats.

• **What does it look like?** When kids pick up Coxsackie, they usually end up with little blisters on the palate, gums, and throat and may experience fever, loose stools, and small red dots on the hands, feet, butt, and occasionally elsewhere (Coxsackie is also called "hand-foot-mouth disease").

There are many strains of Coxsackie virus, so your child can contract this annoying infection several times throughout childhood. The first such case is often the worst, since in future bouts he will have the benefit of antibodies developed from his initial exposure to the germ. Your child's first case of Coxsackie may last as long as a week, and the fever and blisters may be severe.

• *How did he get it?* Coxsackie virus is passed from person to person in saliva, in mucus, and also by the "fecal-oral" route. By fecal-oral we mean spreading germs from your baby's diaper area to another baby's mouth—wash your hands, guys! This tough little bugger can also survive on such surfaces as children's toys and even in a chlorinated pool, which is why we frequently see Coxsackie infections in children who play in kiddie pools.

• *What do I do about it?* After a few days, Coxsackie infections, like all viruses, resolve without antibiotics. Babies with Coxsackie infections will often refuse to eat and drink very much, since the blisters hurt their mouths. Acidic foods, such as orange juice, can be particularly irritating. Cold semisolids, such as ice cream, yogurt, and applesauce, are your best bet to keep your baby well hydrated. Tylenol or ibuprofen will help relieve fever and pain.

• *When do I call the doctor?* Assuming that your doctor has ruled out other causes of throat infections, such as strep, your job here is to watch for signs of dehydration, mentioned later in this chapter. Rarely, a child with a Coxsackie infection may need a little boost with intravenous fluids to supply him with enough liquids until his blisters resolve.

Special Sore Throat #2: Herpes

• *What is it?* Herpes simplex virus type 1, the same bug that causes recurrent cold sores in older kids and adults, can be a real nuisance for babies whose bodies are meeting this germ for the first time. This virus attacks the mouth and lips of babies, and less commonly the hands.

• **What does it look like?** The child with his first herpes infection (called primary herpes gingivostomatitis) can expect fever, irritability, and blisters on his mouth and lips. Because of their similar presentations, herpes is often confused with Coxsackie. The baby with herpes, however, is more likely to have blisters on the lips and less likely to have a rash on the hands, feet, and butt. Like Coxsackie, herpes tends to recur, but not because of different strains; herpes tends to come back because the virus, after pestering Petie for a week or so, "hibernates" on the nerve endings near Petie's mouth. When it reactivates (wakes up) it can start in with new blisters or the typical cold sores seen on or near the lips.

• **How did he get it?** Herpes is passed from person to person by touching herpes sores and by contact with saliva and mucus.

• **What do I do about it?** Since this is a viral infection, medication is usually not necessary. Particularly troublesome herpes infections, however, are sometimes treated with an antiviral drug such as acyclovir. Because Petie's painful blisters may interfere with eating and drinking, he is a good candidate for dehydration. Offer that bottle or breast frequently and, as with Coxsackie, stay away from orange juice. Ice cream, yogurt, and applesauce are your best bets. Tylenol or ibuprofen can help manage his pain and fever.

• **When do I call the doctor?** As with Coxsackie, the real concern with a primary herpes infection is dehydration, so watch for the signs that your baby is getting a bit dry, discussed later.

INFECTIONS OF THE CHEST

Bronchiolitis

• **What is it?** Bronchiolitis is an inflammation of the bronchioli, the tiny passages that lead air down into your baby's lungs.

• **What does it look like?** The child with bronchiolitis will start off with an innocent cold. After a few days, what was at first a mild, occasional cough is now harsher and more frequent. There may be fever, but often there is none. You might also hear wheezy noises when your child exhales, and his breathing may seem a bit more rapid than usual. If you're sharp, you might even observe that he is pulling in (retracting) the skin between his ribs when he breathes and that his diaphragm is drawing in as well. When you see these signs, it's a good idea to visit your pediatrician. Although most babies with this pesky infection do just fine, bronchiolitis can sometimes be more serious, especially in former small premies and in babies with heart disease.

• *How did he get it?* Bronchiolitis, common in the first two years of life, is caused by a virus, often respiratory syncytial virus (RSV), a fairly frequent cause of respiratory infections in kids and adults, transmitted from person to person by breathing and by touch.

• *What do I do about it?* Because it's caused by a virus, there is no need for antibiotics in bronchiolitis unless there is a secondary infection, such as an ear infection or pneumonia. Nevertheless, if you suspect bronchiolitis, pay a visit to the doctor. He will want to rule out any other respiratory problem. He will also, on occasion, prescribe medication designed to make Petie's breathing a little less labored. Medications that open up his airways (called bronchodilators) may help a bit to ease Petie's breathing. Also, all that rapid breathing means that Petie, who breathes out water vapor along with air, may need extra fluids. So offer the breast or bottle more often. In the winter, when your heating system has made your house as dry as a desert, a vaporizer may make him more comfortable. Although water droplets from a vaporizer are actually too large to get all the way down into Petie's bronchioli, his mouth and throat will welcome the extra moisture.

• *When do I call the doctor?* As I've mentioned, some babies with bronchiolitis, especially (but not exclusively) former premies and babies with heart disease, will get a more serious case. Their breathing may become particularly labored, with more rapid respirations and deeper retractions of the chest as they fight to get enough air through their narrowed bronchioles. The actual work of breathing may tire them out so much that they feed poorly. These babies will often need a day or two in the hospital for extra fluids and a whiff of oxygen. Occasionally, but fortunately not too often, bronchiolitis can lead to pneumonia. If your baby seems to be working too hard or is breathing rapidly or retracting deeply, pay another visit to your doctor.

While we're discussing wheezing, a word about asthma (discussed in more detail in Chapter 19) is in order, even though it's a condition more commonly diagnosed after a year of age. Asthma—or reactive airway disease, as it's also called—is another condition whereby the tiny air passages, the bronchioli, become squeezed down and inflamed. The result is the same cough and wheeze that we see with bronchiolitis. In asthma, however, the wheeze tends to recur frequently and can be brought on by a variety of factors, not just by infection. It can be difficult for you and your doctor to know whether a first bout of wheezing is simply an isolated case of bronchiolitis or if it is the beginning of a chronic pattern of wheezing, seen with asthma. If your baby has a chronic cough that lasts long past the week or two of his cold, if the cough seems worse when he gets excited or laughs, and especially if the cough and wheeze respond quickly to bronchodilators (these are less effective in bronchiolitis), then your baby may have asthma.

Croup and the Hoarse Baby
Babies frequently become hoarse with colds, and also simply from crying. Although Petie may sound raspy, such innocent hoarseness doesn't bother him at all. Babies also become hoarse when they develop croup.

• **What is it?** There are different types of croup, but for the most part, croup can be thought of as a viral inflammation in the area of the larynx (voice box) and trachea (windpipe).

• **What does it look like?** With croup, you can expect to hear a strange and frightening sound emanating from Petie's crib, like the bark of a dog or, more accurately, a seal. What's worse, he will seem to be gasping for air. Every time he inhales a breath, he will make a dry, raspy, painful-sounding noise (called stridor). This is croup. As frightening as these barks and rasps may be, they're usually quite harmless.

- *How did he get it?* Croup represents your child's overreaction to a cold virus. Petie's body is "surprised" by a cold germ, and his noisy breathing and barking cough are his body's way of saying, "Hey, I didn't expect this bug. What's going on here?"

- *What do I do about it?* Because it's a viral infection, croup will resolve without any antibiotics. There are, however, several things that you can do to make a crouper feel better and breathe more easily:
  - *Treat the fever.* If fever is present, Tylenol or ibuprofen can help make your child more comfortable.
  - *Steam therapy.* Steam up your bathroom by turning on the hot water in the sink and shower. Sit on the toilet or on the edge of the tub, plop little Petie on your lap, and sing him his favorite song to calm him (and yourself). After he's inhaled that nice steam for ten minutes, his breathing will usually be less labored. Even if he's still a bit raspy, once he feels well enough to fall back to sleep, let him go, and you do the same.
  - *The midnight ride.* Sometimes steam therapy doesn't do the trick and it's time to move on to plan B. This is a strange plan, but it works. Bundle little Petie up and take him out to the car (yes, even in the winter). Open the car window a few inches and take a nice ride for about five minutes. (We used to drive to the local Carvel—hey, why waste the trip?) This crazy trip to nowhere, in the cool night air, seems to break up the tight croupy cough like nothing else. Miraculously, it works most of the time.
  - *Vaporizer or humidifier.* When you get back home, put a vaporizer or humidifier in Petie's room to keep the air moist, and put him back to bed. In the morning he may have a cough, and there may even be a little bark to the cough, but he'll feel much better.

- *When do I call the doctor?* Sometimes croup can be more severe. Little Petie may not stop his barking and his labored respirations in spite of all your efforts. In this case, your doctor might want to examine him, or he may suggest that you take him to the emergency room. Steroids, administered by mouth, injection, or inhalation, shrink the swelling in the windpipe and voice box. Rarely, the severe crouper may have to spend a night in the hospital, either to get a little extra oxygen or for inhalation treatments. Again, these are extreme cases, and the great majority of little croupers do just fine at home. Nevertheless, if you don't like the way your child looks or sounds, and you don't feel comfortable trying to get him back to sleep, then by all means call your doctor or take your child to the local emergency room.

One final word about a croupy cough: not all that barks is croup. In rare cases, a child with the same noisy breathing and barky cough will have a more serious problem, such as:

• *Epiglottitis*. Caused by the germ Hemophilus and now seen much less commonly due to the HIB vaccine, epiglottitis is a sudden, severe inflammation of the flap of tissue just above the windpipe, called the epiglottis. When this tissue becomes inflamed, a child may have noisy breathing similar to that seen in croup, have a high fever, be extremely sick-looking, and even be unable to swallow his saliva (he'll be drooling). Steam and a midnight ride will have no effect on epiglottitis, and an immediate trip to the hospital is in order for medication and for help with breathing.

• *Aspirated foreign body*. A foreign body refers to something a child has put in his mouth and choked on. When such "contraband" as peanuts or pieces of meat find their way into a baby's windpipe, noisy breathing and a croupy cough may result. Again, the choking child will look much sicker than the usual crouper. Chapter 20 discusses such emergencies as foreign bodies.

• *Asthma*. Although the noisy breathing in asthma (wheeze) occurs when a child exhales and the noise in croup (stridor) occurs when a child inhales, that distinction is not always so easy to make. Also, some kids can have a combination of the two sounds. In any case, if your child's noisy breathing doesn't quickly respond to steam or a quick ride in the car, then think of the possibility of asthma.

Pneumonia

• **What is it?** Pneumonia is an infection of the small air sacs of the lungs (alveoli).

• *What does it look like?* Like bronchiolitis, pneumonia usually starts off as an innocent cold with a cough that becomes deeper and more frequent. Often, fever will be present. Petie's respirations may be rapid, and he may be retracting a bit as well. Sometimes the only clue that a cold has progressed to pneumonia is that little Petie just looks sicker. Maybe he's nursing or bottle-feeding less. Perhaps he just doesn't seem quite so active and peppy as usual.

• *How did he get it?* Pneumonia can be caused by bacteria (including two friends from our discussion on vaccines, Hemophilus and pneumococcus), by viruses, and by those germs classified as being between viruses and bacteria, Mycoplasma and Chlamydia. Regardless of the particular germ, your baby will usually develop pneumonia as a secondary infection following a milder respiratory problem, such as a cold, the flu, or bronchiolitis. Certain children are more prone to develop pneumonia, especially asthmatics, children with immune deficiencies, and former premies who had lung problems while in the hospital's neonatal unit.

• *What do I do about it?* When you see that Petie's cold is more than just a cold, make a trip to your doctor. He may diagnose pneumonia simply by listening to your baby's chest for crackling sounds, called rales, or he may need an X-ray. Ideally, once your doctor has made the diagnosis, he would want to determine if your baby's pneumonia is viral (in which case it will get better without medication) or if it is bacterial (which requires antibiotics). Compounding the problem are those two other bugs, Mycoplasma and Chlamydia, both of which respond to antibiotics. Unfortunately, short of an invasive test, he can only guess. For this reason, and for safety's sake, most doctors will treat all cases of pneumonia with an antibiotic.

You can help your baby by giving more frequent feedings. The extra fluids will help replace those lost in fighting off the infection. Tylenol or ibuprofen is also a good idea if there is fever. On occasion your doctor may recommend a bronchodilator to open up his airway.

• *When do I call the doctor?* If your child is already being treated for pneumonia, watch for signs that he might be tiring, such as:

- Poor feeding
- Rapid breathing or deeper chest retractions
- Markedly increased cough
- Poor color—if he looks a bit blue around the mouth
- Poor sleep
- Reduced activity or lethargy
- Irritability

If you see these signs, pay a return visit to your doctor. Occasionally, babies will need to spend a few days in the hospital for intravenous fluids, medication, and even for some extra oxygen to speed healing.

Pneumonia sounds scary. After all, until antibiotics became available, people with pneumonia were gravely ill. Nowadays, with the development of more powerful antibiotics, most cases of pneumonia can be handled quite well right at home. Of course, if your baby is having a tough time breathing or if you have a young baby under 6 months of age, hospitalization may be necessary. Even in these cases, he should do just fine.

INFECTIONS OF THE GI TRACT (STOMACH AND INTESTINES)

The Stomach Virus (Gastroenteritis)

• **What is it?** Rare is the baby who gets through the first year of life without a stomach virus or two. Gastroenteritis is a viral infection of the intestines. These nasty little bugs can occur at any time of the year, although babies under 1 year seem particularly prone to them in the winter months.

• **What does it look like?** Little Petie will be a bit more fussy than usual and will not have much of an appetite. His poops, perhaps just a bit softer to start, will develop into true diarrhea, meaning that they will be both frequent and loose. Stool color can be the usual brown, green, or even yellow, sometimes with strands of mucus or even some flecks of blood. Petie may also be vomiting. Sometimes there will be fever, although this is variable. Also, some babies will be as happy as can be while they're pooping their brains out, but others will be sleepy and lethargic. Still other babies may be fitful and whiny. Some stomach viruses last only one day, the so-called twenty-four-hour viruses. Other bugs can last a week or more.

• **How did he get it?** Babies pick up stomach viruses by something called the fecal-oral route, meaning that microscopic particles of baby feces are passed on to other babies by sharing food, toys, and bottles, or by caregivers who change one baby and then are less than meticulous in their hand washing. There are a slew of viruses responsible for gastroenteritis, but one of the most common in babies, seen most often in the winter, is called rotavirus.

• **What do I do about it?** Your child's stomach virus will go away without antibiotics, so your only real job, while waiting for him to recover from his virus, is to keep him comfortable and well hydrated, with plenty of fluids. Each year thousands of children end up in the hospital for intravenous fluids because they were dehydrated as a result of stomach viruses. In fact, in many underdeveloped parts of the world, **dehydration** is the number one cause of death in small children.

That said, here are a few tips on handling a stomach virus:
• *Push fluids.* First of all, if Petie is having diarrhea but is not vomiting, your job is easier. Continue nursing or giving him formula as usual. One change I would make, however, is to allow him to drink as frequently as he'd like. Don't forget, he needs his usual nutrition plus more to replace the fluids he's losing in diarrhea. So let his thirst guide you, and don't be afraid to offer the bottle or breast more frequently.
• *Let him eat if he's hungry.* As far as solid foods, Petie may not have much of an appetite. If he does, though, let him eat his usual favorites. He needs the extra energy, since he's losing calories continually in stool. If he refuses his favorites, try such easy-to-digest foods as rice, potato, overripe banana, or applesauce. If Petie has graduated to table foods, he may like toast with a little jelly or even some bland pasta. As long as he isn't vomiting, you can give most of these foods. Of primary importance, however, is replacing fluids. If Petie is not in-

terested in solids, that's fine. He's resting his sore, crampy little tummy. Just keep the liquids coming.

• *Stay away from foods that loosen stools.* Fruit (other than apples and bananas) and fruit juices increase diarrhea.

• *Formula change.* In rare instances, particularly after a very prolonged bout of diarrhea, your baby may develop what's known as a temporary lactose intolerance. A sudden relapse of frequent, watery stools may be a sign that his ravaged intestines cannot yet handle his normal lactose-containing formula. Your doctor may suggest one or two weeks of a substitute lactose-free formula, which is usually all that it takes for your baby's gut to heal itself and to allow him to return to his usual formula.

• *Electrolyte solutions.* If Petie is blessed with vomiting as well as diarrhea, he may not be able to retain formula or breast milk. In this case, you will need an alternative. Most pharmacies will have ready-to-feed electrolyte solutions available for just such an occasion. Such products as Pedialyte and Naturalyte differ slightly in their contents. Ask your pediatrician which one he feels would be best for your child. Regardless of which brand you choose, electrolyte solutions all contain some form of sugar, for energy, and various electrolytes, such as sodium, chloride, and potassium, to replace those lost in the diarrhea or vomiting.

• **When do I call the doctor?** Some babies, unfortunately, will feel too weak or nauseous, or just generally too sick, to drink anything when they get a bad stomach virus. If this does happen to little Petie, he may very well start to get dehydrated. It's important to know if this is happening, because dehydration is what takes an ordinary old stomach virus and turns it into something serious. So it's a good idea to have some feeling for the **signs of dehydration.** If he is becoming dehydrated, your baby will:

• *Urinate less often.* This can sometimes be difficult to determine if he has diarrhea, since the loose stool may be hard to distinguish from urine.

• *Stop crying tears.* Tears, like all body fluids, are mostly water, and if your baby's body is depleted of water, he will hold on to any water he can. While he may cry, there will be no tears.

• *Have a dry tongue.* Notice I've said tongue and not lips. In the winter, when the heat is on, your baby's lips may be dry and cracked most of the time. But it's the tongue, which should normally stay moist, that will tell you if your baby is drying out.

• *Lose some of the elasticity in his skin.* This sign is a bit more subtle, and it's also a sign of severe dehydration. Gently pinch a little of your baby's skin, over his chest or belly, between your thumb and forefinger, and then let it go. In babies who are properly hydrated, the skin will spring back quickly to its normal position. Those who are dry will have a much slower rebound of skin, much as would the skin of Grandma, who has lost some of her elasticity through aging.

• *Lose weight.* The first thing your doctor will do is weigh your baby. Weight that your child has recently lost is water weight, and some babies will lose as much as 15 percent of their total weight from a stomach bug.

If your baby shows any of these signs of dehydration, or if, in your ever-improving parental judgment, Petie just doesn't look right to you, then call your pediatrician, who will ask you to come in so that he can apply *his* judgment to evaluate your baby's condition. He may also recommend a blood test, which can give him an objective measure of how dry your baby is becoming.

If Petie is dehydrated, he may need to get fluids intravenously for a while. Your doctor may send him down to the local hospital for a quick fill-up at the emergency room, or even for a short inpatient stay in a pediatric ward. Intravenous hydration is a very benign procedure and your tough little guy, once the IV needle is quickly put in place, will be as comfortable as can be. Rest assured that a short stay for rehydration is a common and usually uncomplicated stay, and once little Petie has gotten some intravenous fluids, he'll be raring to go. Also, the added energy he'll have gotten from a few hours of fluids and sugar will usually perk him up enough so that he'll feel like eating and drinking again.

Even though we've used the word *virus* to describe your child's diarrhea and vomiting, not all of the bugs that cause these symptoms are really viruses. Sometimes, your baby's gastrointestinal infection will be caused by a bacterium, such as salmonella, shigella, *E. coli*, campylobacter, or yersinia. These exotic-sounding bugs tend to produce a more severe illness. Pay a trip to your doctor if you see the following signs that your baby's stomach bug may be more than a virus:

- There is blood or mucus in your baby's stool.
- Your child has a high fever or generally appears sicker.
- The diarrhea is particularly prolonged or severe.

To determine whether your baby's infection is just a virus and not one of these weird bacterial infections, your doctor will recommend a stool culture, in which a small specimen of your baby's poop is sent to the local lab for analysis. In a few days you'll know for sure if your baby's infection is a bacterial one or a virus. If your baby does have one of these bacterial bugs, don't fret. They are treatable with antibiotics, and in some cases they even resolve by themselves. Quite often, by the time the results of the stool culture come back from the lab the baby is all better and no treatment is necessary.

Finally, it's useful to be aware of one serious condition that sometimes follows a case of severe diarrhea, called **hemolytic uremic syndrome** (HUS). Although the exact cause of HUS is unknown, it usually follows infection with a particularly strong strain of *E. coli*, the normally harmless bacteria that lives in our intestines. The particular strain causing HUS comes from infected meats, dairy products, and even contaminated vegetables. After a bout of bloody diarrhea, a child with HUS will be weak, pale (from anemia), swollen (from kidney damage), and might even have such neurologic symptoms as irritability or seizures. Kidney damage can be quite severe, and these children become extremely ill. Again, this is a very serious but rare condition.

INFECTIONS OF THE URINARY TRACT

- **What is it?** A urinary tract infection (UTI) is an infection of the bladder, kidney, or any of the other structures that are involved in removing urine from the body.

- **What does it look like?** Some clues that your child has an infection in his bladder or kidneys include:

- Strong-smelling urine (although this isn't a very reliable sign in a baby)
- Fever
- Irritability, poor sleep, unenthusiastic feeding
- Vomiting or diarrhea
- Persistent poor weight gain (failure to thrive)

Doctors confirm a urinary tract infection by doing two tests on a urine specimen. One is a urinalysis, in which a specimen of urine is examined both chemically, with a special piece of test paper called a dipstick, and microscopically. The urinalysis will tell your doctor if there are any pus cells or red blood cells in the urine, or if a certain chemical, called a nitrite, is present. The second test, and the gold standard to make a diagnosis of UTI, is the urine culture, in which a cleanly obtained specimen of urine is incubated in a special urine culture medium. After a day or two, your doctor will know for certain if Petie has a urinary tract infection.

Urinary tract infections in babies can, at times, be a bit more serious than in older children and adults. Some babies with UTIs have what's known as urinary reflux, a condition in which urine from the bladder and urethra flows backward, toward the kidneys. When this happens, the kidneys are exposed to less-than-sterile urine, and if reflux persists, kidney damage may result. If your baby is diagnosed with a urinary infection, your doctor may suggest a renal sonogram (just as painless as your prenatal sonogram) to better examine his urinary "plumbing." In some cases, your pediatrician will want to schedule a voiding cystourethrogram (VCUG). The VCUG is a relatively painless and quick procedure wherein a small catheter is placed into your child's bladder and dye is injected to better visualize the kidneys with an X-ray.

If your child does have reflux, he may need to be kept on a low dosage of antibiotics, to keep his urine sterile, until the reflux resolves. In a few cases reflux doesn't clear spontaneously, and a surgical procedure must be performed to correct it.

- **How did he get it?** Urinary tract infections are usually caused by a child's own bacteria. Normally, bacteria in the intestinal tract are harmless; in fact, they help us digest our food. In some conditions, these normally tame germs invade the clean urinary tract, resulting in an infection. Little girls tend to have UTIs more frequently than boys, since the opening of the urinary tract in girls (called the urethra) is located just north of the rectum, and germs have a short distance to traverse to get from the stool to the urine. Boys are protected because the urethra is kept apart from the rectum due to the length of the penis.

• **What do I do about it?** Urinary tract infections are treated with antibiotics, usually given orally, but in severe infections or in very young babies, by injection into a muscle or vein.

• **When do I call the doctor?** Once the diagnosis of a UTI has been made, your child should begin to improve within a day or two of starting antibiotics. If there is no improvement, give your doctor a call. He may need to change the antibiotic or in some cases administer it by injection.

THE SKIN: INFECTIONS WITH RASHES

Thanks to the proliferation of effective vaccines, many of those pesky infections that cause rashes are rare visitors—I don't remember the last time I saw a case of German measles, for example. Nevertheless, there are many other infections that are accompanied by rashes. What follows are some of the "all-stars" of the rash world.

Cellulitis

• **What is it?** Cellulitis is a bacterial infection of the skin and the tissues directly under the skin (subcutaneous tissues).

• **What does it look like?** Typically the involved area of the skin is swollen, red, and warm. Fever may be present. The infection spreads along little vessels under your child's skin called lymphatic channels, which drain white blood cells from the periphery of the body toward the heart.

• **How did he get it?** Cellulitis can occur as a complication of an insect bite, a puncture wound, or even a simple scratch or cut. It may also appear after a bad cold, conjunctivitis, or sinus infection, in which case it is seen around the eye and is called periorbital cellulitis.

- **What do I do about it?** Cellulitis needs to be seen by your doctor and addressed quickly, since it spreads rapidly. Fortunately, it responds well to strong antibiotics.

- **When do I call the doctor?** Once your doctor has started your child on oral antibiotics, call him immediately if you see that warm red area of swelling enlarge. Cellulitis spreads rapidly in a linear pattern, from the area of the initial scratch or bite centrally in the direction of the heart. Thus, cellulitis of the hand will move up the arm; cellulitis on a toe will travel up the leg. If oral antibiotics aren't limiting the spread of infection, your doctor may suggest a short course of intravenous medication, especially for periorbital cellulitis, which, on rare occasions, can spread to the brain itself.

Chicken Pox (Varicella)

- **What is it?** With the introduction of the chicken pox vaccine, this is one pest we don't see too much anymore. Although it's often just a nuisance illness, chicken pox can have some nasty complications. Varicella is a viral infection, caused by a member of the herpes family, called the varicella-zoster virus.

- **What does it look like?** Typically following a two-week incubation, a baby with chicken pox will have a fever and an itchy rash that begins on the chest, face, or abdomen and spreads outward to cover the arms and legs. The pox appear as small red bumps but become little watery blisters over the course of a few days. The blisters start off clear, then turn yellow, and eventually become crusts and scabs. At any one time a child will have pox of all different "ages," young pox being solid and red, older ones blisters or crusts. Chicken pox infections are contagious until the lesions become crusts, usually by five days after they first appear.

- **How did he get it?** Varicella is spread from person to person by direct contact (touching) as well as by droplets (breathing).

• **What do I do about it?** Like any viral illness, chicken pox gets better by itself, but a child with pox can be made more comfortable with Tylenol and an oral antihistamine (such as Benadryl) to control the itch. Most topical remedies (Calamine, Benadryl cream) do little to lessen the itching of chicken pox. Keep your baby's nails short, so that scratching is less likely to lead to infection and scarring.

• **When do I call the doctor?** A small number of children with pox can get one of the following serious complications:
  • *Chicken pox encephalitis* is a serious infection of the tissues of the brain and spinal cord. Call your doctor if your child with chicken pox has a persistent high fever, is vomiting, if he is acting particularly lethargic and sleepy, or if he is more irritable than he has been for the first day or two of pox.
  • *Chicken pox skin infections* are secondary bacterial (usually strep or staph) infections of the pox. Call your doctor if your child's pox look particularly inflamed or if he is acting sicker than he was at the start of his pox. Rarely, a secondary varicella skin infection can be due to a particularly severe strain of strep, known as flesh-eating strep.
  • *Chicken pox hepatitis* is a secondary liver disease caused by the chicken pox virus. Call your doctor if your child is vomiting, if he appears a bit yellow (jaundiced), or if he is acting sicker than he has been.
  • *Reye's syndrome* is a severe liver and brain inflammation, usually precipitated by the use of aspirin during chicken pox or flu. The signs of Reye's syndrome are the same as those mentioned above for chicken pox encephalitis.

Fifth Disease

• **What is it?** Fifth disease, although much more common in school-age kids, can occur in babies as well. Once again, this is a viral infection—the particular offending bug is a parvovirus.

• **What does it look like?** Fifth disease results in what's known as a "slapped-cheek" rash due to its flat, lacy pink appearance on the cheeks. This rash can also involve the upper arms and thighs as well, and may last for as long as two weeks. It frequently looks worse when your child becomes overheated or takes a warm bath. Fifth disease isn't much of a disease; it is usually unaccompanied by fever or any other symptoms, although when older children or adults contract fifth disease, they commonly develop joint pains.

A less common illness caused by the same bug, parvovirus, is sock-and-glove syndrome. This little cutie, most often seen in older kids in spring and summer, causes a rash on the hands and feet with red dots that stop sharply at the wrists and ankles. Unlike fifth disease, a fever often accompanies this rash.

• *How did he get it?* Parvovirus is transmitted from person to person in droplets of mucus—another one of those breathe-on-me, sneeze-on-me bugs. It also can be transmitted from a pregnant mom to her developing fetus. Fetuses infected with parvovirus can have a rocky course, including severe anemia and even fetal death.

• *What do I do about it?* There is no definitive treatment for fifth disease, since it's caused by a virus. Also, since the rash is seldom itchy, no symptomatic treatment is necessary. Finally, fifth disease is only contagious *before* the rash emerges, so there is no need to isolate your baby from others. However, if your child does have fifth disease, let any pregnant moms who were around him recently know about his diagnosis.

• *When do I call the doctor?* Although usually a fairly distinct illness, some children with fifth disease have a less classic presentation. Many have a milder rash, a few have a slight fever, and some even have cold symptoms. If you are not sure that your child has fifth disease, let your doctor add his diagnostic acumen to yours.

Henoch-Schönlein Purpura (HSP)

• *What is it?* Henoch-Schönlein purpura, or HSP to anyone who isn't a linguist, is a vasculitis (inflammation of the blood vessels), affecting small vessels supplying the skin, kidneys, intestines and joints.

- *What does it look like?* Children with HSP typically get a red rash on the legs and buttocks that soon becomes purplish. Once the HSP rash becomes purple, it doesn't blanch; this means that if you press on the skin over an area of rash, the rash doesn't whiten, as it does in most other rashes. Pain in the joints and abdominal cramps may follow, sometimes with blood in the stool. Blood in the urine (usually only in microscopic amounts, so your doctor will make this determination by a urinalysis) is a consequence of kidney involvement.

- *How did he get it?* Although the exact cause is unknown, HSP usually follows a mild respiratory illness. It does not appear to be contagious, and it may be caused by more than one germ.

- *What do I do about it?* Most cases of HSP, although a bit frightening due to the many areas involved, resolve within a few weeks without treatment. More severe cases are treated with steroids.

- *When do I call the doctor?* Once he has been diagnosed with HSP by your doctor, if your child has severe abdominal pain, especially with blood in the stool, or if he has severe joint pain, give the doctor a call. He may elect to treat your baby with steroid medication.

Impetigo

- *What is it?* Impetigo is the most common bacterial skin infection in babies and young children and is caused by either strep germs or staph germs.

- *What does it look like?* Impetigo, most common in the summer months, begins as a bubble or yellow crust (this is often mistaken for chicken pox). As it spreads, other areas of the skin become involved, and little crusts can appear in any part of the body. Impetigo frequently starts inside or near the nose, since many baby noses are colonized by staph and strep germs.

- *How did he get it?* Impetigo usually starts off as a scratch, a bite, a patch of eczema, or anything that irritates the skin and makes it susceptible to infection. The damaged area is then invaded by the staph or strep germs that live on the skin.

   • **What do I do about it?** Like other bacterial infections, impetigo responds well to antibiotics, which can be given as an ointment if the area involved is small or orally if a larger area is affected. If your child has impetigo, be sure to use separate towels and washcloths, since these germs are contagious.

   • **When do I call the doctor?** After a few days of topical treatment, if you see no improvement, let your doctor know. He may prescribe an oral antibiotic.

Kawasaki Disease

   • **What is it?** Kawasaki disease is a vasculitis—an inflammation of the blood vessels—and is most common in young children under the age of 3.

   • **What does it look like?** Typically, babies with Kawasaki have the following symptoms:
   • Fever for several days (often more than a week)
   • A generalized rash anywhere on the body but often easiest to spot in the groin
   • Enlarged lymph nodes, especially in the neck
   • Red mouth and lips
   • Red eyes without discharge
   • Swelling and redness of the hands and feet
More significant is the fact that in about 20 percent of cases of Kawasaki, the blood vessels that nourish the heart, called the coronary arteries, become inflamed, develop bubbles (called aneurysms), and can even become blocked.

   • **How did he get it?** Although a particular germ has never been isolated, Kawasaki disease seems to be caused, at least in part, by an infection. So far, no bacteria, no virus, and no fungus has "stepped forward" to take credit for Kawasaki, and it doesn't appear to be contagious.

• **What do I do about it?** Although we don't know what causes Kawasaki, like many types of vasculitis it responds well to anti-inflammatory medications. Most of the time a combination of aspirin (this is one of the few remaining uses for aspirin in kids) and intravenous gamma globulin (sterilized pooled antibodies) is given. The response to these medications can be dramatic, and most children treated early do quite well.

• **When do I call the doctor?** Kawasaki is one illness that requires some diagnostic work. Blood tests and, frequently, a sonogram of the heart (called an echocardiogram) are needed to make the diagnosis, although your doctor will suspect Kawasaki disease in any young child with a week or more of fever, swollen lymph nodes, and a rash. Once the diagnosis has been made and the child treated, regular follow-up with a cardiologist is recommended to ensure that the coronary arteries have not become involved.

Roseola

• **What is it?** This can be a scary-seeming little sucker, but it's actually quite innocuous. Roseola is a viral infection, caused by a germ that's a member of the herpes family (herpes type 6). This is not the same herpes that causes cold sores and certainly not the germ that causes venereal herpes. Roseola affects mostly young children, from 6 months to 3 years of age.

• **What does it look like?** Roseola is the classic case of the really hot tot who's not all that sick. Typically, the baby with roseola will start right out with a nice high temperature, sometimes as high as 104 or 105 degrees. Besides the fever, there really doesn't seem to be much going on. There may be a loose stool, or perhaps a small swollen gland or two at the base of Petie's head. Then, after three to six days of a rising and falling fever, the temperature breaks, only to be replaced by a rash of tiny pink dots all over the body. After another day or two the rash is gone.

Since the classical fever-followed-by-rash scenario of roseola may vary, and because your doctor will not see an obvious focus for infection, he may want to reassure himself (and you) by doing a blood count. If this is indeed roseola, a viral infection, Petie should have a normal white blood cell count. If there is some more serious infection present, such as a urinary tract infection or a bacteremia (discussed a bit later), it will usually show up as a high white blood cell count. Viruses, in general, don't cause much of an elevation in a child's white blood cell count. Bacterial infections frequently do.

One of the consequences of the rapidly escalating temperature of roseola is that some babies may get a fever convulsion (febrile seizure). Yes, you heard me right: a convulsion. Before *you* convulse, however, read about fever convulsions in Chapter 16.

• *How did he get it?* The herpes type 6 virus that causes Roseola is passed from child to child through saliva and mucus.

• *What do I do about it?* Besides treating fever with Tylenol or ibuprofen and offering plenty of fluids, roseola is a wait-it-out type of illness.

• *When do I call the doctor?* It's frustrating and a bit frightening to have to wait out a viral infection with a high fever. Even if you have already made a trip to the doctor, and even if he has done a blood count to make certain that you are dealing with a viral infection, sometimes just having the pediatrician take another look can supply a parent with enough confidence to make it through another day of fever. If Petie is still percolating after a day or two, give your doctor a call; he may be able to reassure you on the phone, or he may even suggest that you come back in for a quick peek in the ears and throat to rule out a secondary infection.

Scarlet Fever (Scarlatina)

• *What is it?* The combination of a strep throat with a rash is called scarlet fever. In the days before antibiotics, kids with this pesky illness got pretty sick (this is a good illness not to mention to Grandma). Now it's no more annoying than any other strep throat.

- **What does it look like?** Typically the rash of scarlet fever looks like little red dots, anywhere on a child's body. This is one rash, however, that's more impressive to feel than to see—those dots actually feel like sandpaper when you rub your hand along a baby's belly or chest, two areas where they are particularly pronounced. Along with a red throat, fever, and those sandpapery dots, kids with scarlet fever often have tongues that look like strawberries—red with very pronounced taste buds and a white coating. As the rash fades it's not uncommon for the skin to peel. Severe scarlatina rashes may also produce thin red lines in the creases of babies' elbows, wrists, and knees, called Pastia's lines.

- **How did he get it?** As is the case with any strep infection, children pass the germ to each other through infected saliva and mucus.

- **What do I do about it?** Your doctor will suspect scarlet fever by the presence of the rash and red throat. He'll confirm his diagnosis with a test for strep, either a throat culture (results take one to two days) or a rapid strep test (less accurate but quicker). Scarlet fever, caused by a bacterium, responds quickly to antibiotics, and your doctor will prescribe a course of penicillin or some other strep-killer. It's important to continue the antibiotic for the full prescribed course, since strep can lead to complications, such as rheumatic fever, a serious disease of the heart and joints, when not treated fully.

- **When do I call the doctor?** Once your baby starts his antibiotic, he should quickly feel better. If he's not frisky and cool after a day or two, then perhaps that case of scarlet fever is really something else. **Conditions that mimic scarlet fever include:**
  - *Staph scarlet fever.* The staphylococcus germ, which may invade following a minor wound or skin infection, can spread through a child's bloodstream and cause a rash that looks very much like strep scarlet fever. In staph scarlet fever, which is treated with strong antibiotics, there may be fever but there will not be a red throat.
  - *Staph scalded skin syndrome.* This staph infection makes a child's skin appear burned—skin may actually peel off. Kids who have staph scalded skin syndrome tend to be quite sick, with high fever, fussiness, and tenderness of the skin even before the rash appears. Once the

rash does appear, it usually looks a lot like scarlet fever and may even be accompanied by a red throat. The skin becomes quite red and sensitive, especially in the folds of the elbows, in the armpits, and under the neck. Soon the rash progresses to big blisters. Like strep infections, staph infections usually respond quickly to antibiotics, so this is one serious and uncomfortable infection that can be treated.

• *Drug reactions.* Some antibiotics (sulfa and penicillin) and certain other drugs (such as seizure medications) can cause a rash that looks very similar to scarlet fever. These are serious reactions, often with extensive rashes and blisters, but usually respond well when the offending medication is stopped and drugs are used to halt the allergic reaction.

• *Viruses.* Some viruses that cause red throats also produce rashes that look very much like scarlet fever.

INFECTIONS OF THE BLOODSTREAM

Viremia and Bacteremia

• **What is it?** Viremia is a viral infection of the bloodstream; bacteremia a bacterial infection of the bloodstream.

• **What does it look like?** Have you heard the old saying that when a doctor can't find anything wrong, he calls it a virus? Actually, this isn't very far from the truth. Much like the infant with roseola, the baby with an infection of the bloodstream typically has fever, often 102 degrees or more, with few if any other symptoms. There may be a slight runny nose or cough, or else he may have spit up a bit. That's about it.

The pediatrician, faced with a febrile baby with no red throat, rash, or other symptoms to aid his diagnosis, will do a urinalysis and urine culture to rule out a urinary tract infection. If the urine is clear, then the most likely cause for fever is a hidden infection—an infection in the bloodstream. A complete blood count (CBC) will help him determine whether the germ circulating through the bloodstream is a virus (the white blood cell count will usually be normal or low) or a bacteria (elevated white cell count). If a child with persistent fever and no obvious findings on examination has an elevated white blood cell count, and if the urine tests show that the urinary tract is not responsible for this elevation, then your doctor will suspect bacteremia and do a blood culture. Like the urine culture, this will tell him definitively, in a day or two, if a bacterial infection in the bloodstream is present, and will also tell him which drug to use to treat the infection.

• *How did he get it?* Many different viruses and bacteria can cause these infections, and most of them are respiratory germs, transmitted from person to person in droplets, from coughing and from close contact.

• *What do I do about it?* As with most viral infections, viremia resolves without treatment, other than the usual fluids and fever medication. Bacteremia is treated with antibiotics, often intravenously for a few days and then orally, although older babies are sometimes treated exclusively with oral medication.

Very young babies (especially those under 4 months of age) with fever and without an obvious focus of infection often undergo a spinal tap or lumbar puncture to rule out a very serious infection of the spinal cord called **meningitis.** This test is done by quickly inserting a thin needle between the bones of your baby's lower spine and withdrawing a few drops of spinal fluid for analysis and culture (it is less painful than you would think). Meningitis is seen much less frequently now than it was before the HIB and pneumococcal vaccines, but it still occurs when those pesky viruses or even peskier bacteria pass through the bloodstream and invade the tissues of the meninges, protective membranes around the brain and spinal cord. Babies with meningitis become quite sick and often have a high fever, vomit, and feed poorly. If tests on the baby's spinal fluid suggest meningitis, then he will be admitted to the hospital to receive antibiotics intravenously. Like bacteremia, meningitis can be viral or bacterial, and if the spinal fluid culture shows that the meningitis is viral, antibiotics can be discontinued. A culture that is positive for bacteria means that an infant will need several days of intravenous treatment.

• **When do I call the doctor?** Although viremia requires no antibiotics, secondary infections may occur, such as an ear infection or pneumonia. If your baby has been diagnosed with viremia, be sure to make a return visit to the doctor if he develops any new symptoms, becomes increasingly fussy, begins to feed poorly, or if his fever persists for more than a couple of days.

KIDFIXER FREQUENTLY ASKED QUESTIONS

Q: *My baby has a cold. Should I stop giving her formula? I've heard that milk makes more mucus.*

A: There's no reason to stop giving formula or to stop nursing when a baby has a cold. Mucus is made by glands in the nose and throat, not by milk. We make more mucus when we're sick, regardless of what we eat and drink. If your baby is drinking formula, let her have it. If she's nursing, go for it. As we've said, the more fluids she takes, the better she'll feel.

Q: *Are all those ear recheck visits really necessary? If my child is acting well again, can't I assume that her ear is all better?*

A: On behalf of all the pediatricians and other ear specialists out there . . . sorry! Although your happy and peppy baby is once again her old self, her ear may not be completely healed. Frequently an examination by your doctor will reveal fluid behind the eardrum, which may suggest to him that the ear needs further treatment or just a little more observation. In fact, one-fourth of the ear infections that a doctor sees will require more than the usual five-to-ten-day course of treatment. So keep your follow-up appointments, which are your best way of ensuring that your baby's ear infection will not result in a hearing loss.

Q: When is it time to see an ear specialist?

A: There is no set formula for when it's appropriate to see an ear-nose-throat specialist. That decision is, of course, yours. Perhaps you're frustrated about all those ear infections. Maybe you're concerned that your pediatrician isn't doing enough. Or maybe you'd just like another opinion. Although your pediatrician is a specialist when it comes to ear infections in babies, he will gladly refer you to a good ENT doctor, who can test your baby's hearing more thoroughly. He may also suggest a different protocol of antibiotic treatment; for example, he may recommend prophylactic (preventative) treatment for your child.

Q: My daughter Mollie is nine months old. She has had a slew of ear infections already and has been treated with "tons" of antibiotics. Is it possible that she might be able to fight off an ear infection without resorting to medication?

A: Yes. We now know that some ear infections, especially if they are not too severe, resolve without antibiotic treatment. Sometimes this is because the germ responsible is a virus (not *all* ear infections are caused by bacteria). Even if an ear infection is bacterial, some children are able to fight off a mild bacterial infection simply by using their own natural infection fighters, those powerful antibodies and other substances that Mollie is beginning to develop. Many doctors will carefully follow a mild ear infection without resorting to antibiotics. The key here is to keep a close eye on Mollie and to bring her back to the doctor if she acts fussy, feeds or sleeps poorly, or in some other way acts generally sicker.

Q: Do diarrhea and vomiting always mean there is a germ, or can there be some other explanation for these symptoms?

A: As we discussed in Chapter 17, there are many reasons for vomiting and diarrhea besides a stomach virus. Babies can have allergies or intolerances to formula. They can get diarrhea from being overfed. After all, there's only so much fluid that your baby's little tummy can absorb before he's bound to get runoff. One of the most common causes for diarrhea in babies is the overfeeding of fruit juices. While fruit itself is healthy, supplying much-needed fiber to your child's diet, fruit juice is not. Once you remove the pulp and just serve the juice, most of what you're giving is water and sugar. So if your baby likes juice and you want to give him a little change from formula or breast milk, 4 to 6 ounces of juice a day is plenty. Much more than that and you'll "run" into a problem with diarrhea.

Q: *My baby has diarrhea. Should I stop her formula and switch to Pedialyte?*

A: This is a common misunderstanding. Drinking formula, breast milk, and (after a year of age) regular cow's milk does *not* increase the diarrhea of a stomach virus. Formula and breast milk are pretty tasty to a thirsty child and provide much-needed nutrition to fight off that bug. Of course, the baby who is having vomiting along with diarrhea may not be able to keep down her usual milk or formula. In such cases, an electrolyte solution will do just fine.

Q: *In spite of doing everything my doctor says for Max's stomach virus, he's still got the runs. What am I doing wrong? Isn't there medication to stop this diarrhea?*

A: Remember, a stomach virus is a virus; it will get better by itself. Neither you, your doctor, nor anything at the drugstore can kill off those little bugs inside your baby's gut. Only time will do the job. Just keep replacing all of that fluid, and Max's own natural defenses will help him knock out those little buggers. As long as he's still making tears, he's still urinating, and his tongue still looks moist, then he's probably not dehydrated and is doing fine. If you're not sure how he's doing, bring him over to the doctor and let his experienced eye reassure you. Again, your goal is not to stop the diarrhea, but just to replace the fluid that's lost.

Q: *How do I know that a croup attack is not an asthma attack? Can't asthma attacks start suddenly in the middle of the night?*

A: This is a good question. Asthma can indeed occur in the middle of the night. Here are a couple of **hints that tell you that this is croup and not asthma that you're dealing with:**

• First of all, asthma doesn't usually cause that characteristic barking cough that you get from croup.

• Although a steam treatment and a night ride may help a bit in loosening up an asthma attack, the effect is rarely as dramatic as it is with croup. If your child is strikingly better after steam or after a car ride, then you can be pretty sure that you're dealing with croup and not with asthma.

• Croup usually causes noisy breathing when a child *inhales* (breathes in). Asthma causes noisy breathing primarily when a child *exhales* (breathes out).

Q: *My older son, Joseph (3 years), has had a virus with a fever of almost 102 degrees for three days. I also have a newborn at home now (James, 4 days old) and I am extremely paranoid that he is going to get what his big brother has. Besides keeping the two of them apart and constantly washing my hands, is there anything I should be doing to ensure that James stays healthy?*

A: First, keep in mind that James still has lots of the same immunity that his mommy has, so if *you* don't catch anything from Joseph, James may be equally lucky. As far as precautions, keep in mind that Joseph was most contagious before you even knew he was sick. Other than hand washing and keeping the boys apart as much as possible, there's not too much you can do.

Q: *My daughter is recovering from pneumonia. Is she likely to get it again?*

A: Other than the child with asthma or with problems of immunity, one bout of pneumonia is just that—one bout. Lungs heal just fine, without damage, and there's no reason to expect that your child will get pneumonia again.

19

CHRONIC
ILLNESS

Babies are wonderfully resilient little critters, and they tend to bounce back from most problems. The child with a temperature of 106 degrees one day might be perfectly fine the next, enjoying her naps, her playtime, and her crib. Unfortunately, some conditions that affect babies are more long-lasting. This chapter will introduce some issues that don't resolve quickly.

Children with congenital malformations, cerebral palsy, muscular dystrophy, congenital heart disease, HIV, hearing and vision handicaps, and malignancies face, as do their families, challenges that require stamina and support. In addition to the concerned care provided by their pediatricians, these children often require the services of such specialists as pediatric nurses, physical therapists, occupational therapists, respiratory therapists, and social service workers. As much support as these children and their parents need, the siblings of chronically ill kids also need support. Watching a new baby sister undergo a procedure that is painful is often too much to ask of a child who must also deal with reduced parenting time.

Although these conditions are chronic, they are not hopeless. The increase in young children with chronic illnesses is due in large part to the many advances in medical diagnosis, immunization, and treatment over the last few decades. In the past, many children who are now enjoying happy childhoods would not have survived infancy.

CONGENITAL MALFORMATIONS

• *What is it?* Congenital malformations are any abnormalities that a baby is born with. Some have medical significance, like a cleft palate. Some are much less serious, like finger or toe malformation. Approximately 5 percent of newborns have one or more congenital abnormalities, and the great majority are minor.

• *How did she get it?* Here's a true story. When my first child was born, I was a fourth-year medical student working in the newborn intensive care unit of a major New York hospital. I felt as though every newborn was sick—of course that was because I was only seeing very sick little babies. As my wife's due date neared, I became increasingly concerned that our child would be born with something terrible. I didn't share my fears completely with my wife, who had enough on her mind, but did say this to her: "I hope the baby is born with an extra finger or an extra toe, or something simple like that. I can handle that as long as he is healthy throughout the rest of childhood." This was the deal I made with God or whoever listens to such foolish comments from paranoid medical students, doctors, and dads. Guess what? Our healthy baby boy was born with a cute little eleventh toe! Thank God, the deal I made "took." My son had a healthy childhood, extra toe and all.

There are many reasons for such abnormalities (besides foolish deals bartered by prospective parents). Congenital malformations result from genetic factors (such as an extra chromosome, as in the case of Down syndrome) and from environmental factors (the drug thalidomide is the best-known example—it caused major limb abnormalities before its use during pregnancy was discontinued). Many abnormalities, such as heart defects, are caused by a combination of genetic and environmental factors, and many congenital anomalies have no known cause at all.

Some relatively **common minor congenital abnormalities** seen in newborns include:

• *Preauricular sinus and skin tag.* This tiny pinhole or nubbin of skin in front of an ear reminds us that we were once fish—or at least our ancestors were. Other than needing to be kept clean, they pose no problem. Such skin tags and holes can be surgically closed in a simple cosmetic procedure.

• *Extra nipple*. This bit of darkened tissue along the same line as the regular nipple is not a fully functioning nipple, not even in girls. Again, its only significance is cosmetic.

• *Clinodactyly*. The incurved pinky is one of the most common minor malformations. Few people even notice it, since the curve is so slight, but if you look at all the people you work with, there are probably one or two who have clinodactyly (and probably never noticed it themselves).

• *Syndactyly*. Webbed toes aren't just for ducks. They're caused by a small web of tissue, usually between the second and third toe. Once again, the condition is of no significance.

• *Polydactyly*. What, you thought my son was the only one with an extra toe? An extra digit can be just a thin piece of tissue or it can have a bone as well (he had the works). Removing extra fingers or toes is a simple surgical procedure.

CEREBRAL PALSY (CP)

• **What is it?** Although there is no single cause for cerebral palsy (CP), we know that it is a motor disease (it affects motion) resulting from brain damage in a newborn or young child.

• **How did she get it?** A specific cause for CP has not been defined. For years it was felt that CP most often resulted from complications during labor and delivery. Recent studies suggest that obstetrical problems are not a major cause of CP. Cerebral palsy is seen most often in:

• Babies who were extremely premature.

• Babies or young children who have had asphyxia (lack of oxygen to the brain). Thus a history of a low five-minute Apgar score (the rating system that grades a newborn's color, reflex activity, muscle tone, heart rate, and respirations), a sure sign of lack of oxygen, is not uncommon in babies with CP. Similarly, a young child who has had a near-drowning episode also might develop CP.

- Babies who had bleeding into the brain as newborns—as may be seen with very small premies.
- Babies with congenital malformations of the brain, heart, and spine.
- Young children who have had severe infections of the brain (meningitis or encephalitis) or who have had severe brain trauma.

There is no way to predict whether such high-risk infants will go on to develop CP. Many babies are born very early or have multiple malformations but develop normally.

- ***What does it look like?*** Diagnosing CP in a baby can be difficult because signs of CP usually don't appear until after two years of age. Nevertheless, doctors become suspicious about the possibility of cerebral palsy when a child has:
  - *Extremely late motor development.* The baby who sits a month late and walks a month or two late would not be of concern, as opposed to the child who sits six months late and who cannot walk by age 3.
  - *Persistence of newborn reflexes.* When the startle and rooting reflexes persist well past the usual 6 months of age, CP may be the cause.
  - *Markedly increased muscle tone.* When a child is lying on his back and you move his arm or leg, there is always some resistance. Resistance to passive movement is what doctors mean by muscle tone. In a child with CP, moving an arm or leg actually can be difficult. Less commonly, CP may also show up as reduced tone—a "floppy baby."
  - *Abnormal movements.* In certain types of cerebral palsy, children may have random writhing or twisting movements.
  - *Overactive reflexes.* The knee-jerk reflex, for example, is often much too strong in kids with CP. Others with CP have reflexes that are much stronger on one side of the body than the other.

There are also many types of cerebral palsy. Hemiplegia involves one side of the body, diplegia affects only the lower half, and involvement of both arms and both legs is called quadriplegia. Athetoid CP is marked by abnormal writhing movements of arms or legs. These classifications may also be combined, and a child may be said to have athetoid hemiplegia. There is also great variation in the severity of CP. Some affected children have only a slight limp; others require a wheelchair. Finally, children with CP may also have other neurologic problems such as seizure disorders and learning disabilities.

• *What can we do?* A parent's goal should be to **treat each aspect of a child's disability.** If a young child has difficulty walking, he should receive physical therapy. The child with seizures might need anticonvulsant medication. The parent whose child has CP can often feel as though he or she faces a long and impossible journey on a bumpy road. Fortunately, your pediatrician, neurologist, social service worker, and physical therapist can all help. Also, two excellent Web sites for families dealing with CP are:

The Children with Disabilities Web site for CP
www.childrensdisabilities.info/cerebral_palsy/resources.html

Cerebral Palsy: A Guide for Care
gait.aidi.udel.edu/res695/homepage/pd_ortho/clinics/c_palsy/
   cpweb.htm

MUSCULAR DYSTROPHY

• *What is it?* The muscular dystrophies are inherited diseases characterized by progressive weakness and degeneration of muscles. Although most forms of muscular dystrophy are diagnosed after a year of age, I will mention this condition briefly because these days doctors are able to diagnose it earlier and earlier.

• *How did she get it?* Specific genes that affect muscle fibers cause muscular dystrophy. The most common type, called Duchenne muscular dystrophy, is passed on through sex-linked inheritance, which means moms who carry the defective gene may (in 50 percent of cases) pass the gene on to their newborns. This also explains why muscular dystrophy is much more common in boys, since a girl gets two X chromosomes from her parents and would need an abnormal gene on both X chromosomes to be affected, whereas boys only have one X chromosome and need only this one chromosome to be affected.

• *What does it look like?* Diagnosing muscular dystrophy used to require a muscle biopsy, but blood tests are now being done that can make this diagnosis easier. The symptoms that will alert your doctor to the need for such tests include:

• *Severe muscle weakness.* Different types of muscular dystrophies involve different muscle groups. Thus, one type of muscular dystrophy involves mostly shoulder muscles, while another affects primarily arm and leg muscles.

• *Delayed motor development.* Infants with muscular dystrophy often sit and crawl much later than expected. Getting up from a sitting position is especially difficult for these children, as is pushing a toy or climbing stairs. When children with muscular dystrophy do walk, it is often with a waddling gait or a toe walk.

• *Pseudohypertrophy.* Many infants with muscular dystrophy go on to develop large calves. This isn't extra muscle, but actually abnormal tissue that has replaced normal calf muscle.

• *Progression.* In time, many children with muscular dystrophy are unable to sit properly, walk, or even breathe easily, since muscles that affect respiration can also be affected.

It should be kept in mind that many children with muscular dystrophy have much less severe illnesses, with only minor disabilities beginning much later in life. Unfortunately the most severe type of muscular dystrophy, Duchenne muscular dystrophy, is also a relatively common one, affecting about 1 in 3,000 boys. Finally, although some children with muscular dystrophy have an increased incidence of learning problems, the great majority have normal intelligence.

• *What can we do?* Treatment for kids with muscular dystrophy involves recruiting the assistance of many specialists, including:

• Physical therapists, for exercises to improve movement and lessen muscle spasm and to provide bracing
• Neurologists, to diagnose complications and to prescribe steroids, which can slow the progression of muscle weakness

- Surgeons, who may need to perform spinal surgery to treat possible scoliosis (spinal curvature)
- Respiratory therapists, who watch for such complications as pneumonia, brought about by weakened breathing muscles

The future of muscular dystrophy is a hopeful one. Advances in computer technology can assist a child or adult with muscular dystrophy to lead a more productive life. Eventually, a cure for muscular dystrophy will be possible through gene therapy.

A good place to begin looking for more information about muscular dystrophy is the National Institutes of Health muscular dystrophy Web site: *www.nlm.nih.gov/medlineplus/musculardystrophy.html#generaloverviews*.

CONGENITAL HEART DISEASE

- *What is it?* Any heart condition present at birth is called congenital heart disease. In all types of heart disease, the heart, or the large blood vessels entering and leaving the heart, are not functioning properly to supply the body with oxygen and nourishment. Congenital heart disease is the most common significant congenital malformation, occurring in about 1 percent of all newborns.

- *How did she get it?* Heart disease in a newborn can occur for many reasons. We know that heredity is involved, since parents with one child with heart disease are slightly more likely to have another child with heart disease. Rarely, an infection during pregnancy (German measles is the best-known example) can predispose an infant to heart disease. Moms who take certain drugs during pregnancy are also putting their babies at risk for congenital heart disease.

- *What does it look like?* Some common signs of congenital heart disease include:
  - *Cyanosis.* Although it's quite normal for a baby to have cold blue hands and feet, it's not common for a baby to be blue all over. Cyanosis is usually most visible around the lips of a crying baby.

- *Heart murmur.* Your doctor, instead of just hearing the normal *lub-dub, lub-dub* of a heartbeat, will hear an extra sound, called a murmur. Although some murmurs are present at birth, many are not heard until 3 to 4 months of age. Many babies have innocent heart murmurs. These are extra sounds with no abnormality of the heart itself. The infant with an innocent murmur will be found to have a completely normal electrocardiogram and echocardiogram and requires no treatment.
- *Breathing difficulties.* The baby who has a severe heart malformation can have a back-up of blood from the weakened heart into the lungs, called heart failure, which can result in rapid, labored breathing.
- *Edema.* Swelling is another result of failure, but here blood backs up into the tissues of the body rather than into the lungs. Babies may become swollen over the back, arms, and legs.
- *Failure to thrive.* Heart disease is one of the causes of failure to adequately gain weight.

Although some congenital heart conditions can be diagnosed with reasonable confidence by just the character of a heart murmur, you will usually be asked to have certain tests done to ascertain exactly where the problem lies. An electrocardiogram (EKG) measures electrical impulses and can identify abnormalities in cardiac rhythm or enlargement of one of the chambers of the heart. The echocardiogram is the same painless sonogram that you probably had done during pregnancy, only here the little microphone is placed over your baby's chest. Sound waves bounce back to the sensors on the machine to get an actual picture of the heart.

Congenital heart disease may take many forms based on the location of the defect in the heart and large blood vessels. Although this book will not attempt to describe all **types of congenital heart disease,** a few of the relatively more common types that a doctor will see are:

- *Septal defects.* A tiny pinhole in the tissue that separates either the two atria (smaller chambers) or the two ventricles (larger chambers) is one of the most common heart defects. Usually diagnosed in children under 6 months of age, a septal defect is seldom very serious and often closes by itself. If the hole is large, it may have to be closed or patched surgically, usually when a baby is older.

- *Patent ductus arteriosus* (PDA). This mouthful is another very common occurrence in newborns, especially in premies, in which the two major blood vessels leaving the heart (aorta and pulmonary artery) are abnormally connected. A murmur is heard as blood flows from one vessel to the other. This defect usually closes all by itself shortly after birth. When it remains open, it can be closed either medically or surgically.

- *Stenosis.* Stenosis is a narrowing of one of the valves of the heart or of a heart chamber itself. A mild stenosis might require no treatment at all, while a severe narrowing can lead to cyanosis or heart failure.

- **What can we do?** Thanks to early diagnosis, effective medications to prevent heart failure, and new noninvasive surgical techniques, children with most types of congenital heart disease can have full lives, including participation in all types of recreation and sports.

Regardless of the type of congenital heart defect, even a mild abnormality brings with it an increased risk of infection. For some reason, germs like to lodge on abnormal heart valves and on tiny heart pinholes. Even such a minor source of germs as routine dental work can cause an infection in the heart. An infection of the heart lining, **bacterial endocarditis,** can be a difficult one to diagnose, since the only initial sign might be a prolonged fever. To prevent endocarditis, many children (and adults) with congenital heart disease take prophylactic antibiotics before undergoing dental work or minor surgery. Your doctor will tell you if such a precaution is required for your child.

ASTHMA (REACTIVE AIRWAY DISEASE)

- **What is it?** As the name might imply, reactive airway disease, known also as asthma, is an overresponsiveness of the tiny air passages (bronchioles) to a variety of stimuli. Although most commonly diagnosed after 1 year of age, I'll discuss asthma briefly, since it is the most common chronic condition in kids, present in 5 percent of all children.

- **How did she get it?** Although a single specific cause has not been found, asthma tends to run in families; when parents have either asthma or allergies, their children are more likely to have asthma as well.

• **What does it look like?** The hallmark of asthma is the wheeze, a whistling sound made on expiration as air passes through the narrowed air passages in your child's chest. Children with asthma typically cough and wheeze in response to the following stimuli:

- Viruses
- Bacterial infections, such as sinusitis
- Change in weather
- Exercise (even laughter)
- Exposure to such allergens as pet dander, dust mites, mold spores, and pollen
- Stress (usually in older kids and teens)

The child with reactive airway, after exposure to one of these factors, will have inflammation and constriction (squeezing) of her bronchioles. When bronchioles narrow, it becomes difficult for air to pass further along into the lung, but even more difficult for it to pass out of the lung, since exhaling is a weaker force than inhaling. Thus, kids with asthma have difficulty getting air out of the lungs, and whistle or wheeze when they exhale. Sometimes, especially in babies, a parent will hear a cough but not a wheeze—it may take a doctor with a stethoscope to actually hear that sound. Nevertheless, if your child has a persistent cough, especially with laughing or exertion, have your doctor take a listen.

• **What can we do?** Asthma is treated in several ways:

• *Avoidance.* If your child has asthma, make his room as allergen-free as possible.

- Keep Scoobie the dog out of his room.
- Put away all but his very favorite stuffed animal.
- Pull up that thick dust-catching carpet.
- Replace heavy drapes with a simple shade.
- Get an air purifier for his room.

• *Bronchodilators.* Part of the narrowing seen in asthma occurs because the bronchial passages are actually squeezed into narrow channels by the muscles in the bronchial walls. Bronchodilators such as albuterol relax those muscles, allowing the bronchioles to become wider. Dilators can be given as liquids but work better and with fewer side effects when inhaled, either from a hand-operated inhaler or from a small electric nebulizer.

• *Anti-inflammatory medications.* Another component of the bronchial narrowing we see with asthma is inflammation. The walls of the bronchioles become inflamed and filled with mucus. The most commonly used anti-inflammatory medications are steroids, given either through an inhaler, with a nebulizer, or orally. Oral steroids are restricted to short-term use, however, because they can adversely affect a baby's growth. Used judiciously, however, they are not only safe but often essential in comforting an asthmatic baby. Other anti-inflammatory medications (called immune modulators) are available as chewable pills and granules.

Although an asthmatic baby makes more trips to the doctor's office than many of her friends, she can still have a terrific quality of life. With her wheeze and cough controlled, she will be able to take the same dip in the pool in the summer, make a snowman in the winter, and play in the park with the rest of the kids. The great news here is that she can expect to outgrow her asthma later on in childhood; most babies do just that.

CYSTIC FIBROSIS (CF)

• **What is it?** Cystic fibrosis, one of the most common inherited diseases in white children, affecting about 1 in 2,000 to 3,000 births, is a disease that affects primarily the digestive tract and the respiratory system.

• **How did she get it?** CF is inherited as a recessive trait, which means that if both parents are carriers of the same CF gene, their child has about a 1 in 4 chance of being born with cystic fibrosis. The underlying problem is an abnormality of cells lining the lungs, intestines, pancreas, and other organs, resulting in abnormally thick mucus. The thickened mucus:

   • Prevents the pancreas from releasing enzymes to digest food, especially fat
   • Blocks air passages, resulting in repeated infections and wheezing
   • Blocks the intestinal tract, resulting in constipation and bowel obstruction

• **What does it look like?** Many cases of CF are not diagnosed until later in childhood, but even under a year of age doctors will suspect cystic fibrosis in a baby who has:

  • *Recurrent lower respiratory tract infections.* Any child can have a bout or two of bronchiolitis and even a case of pneumonia in the first year of life, but the child who has *repeated* bouts of severe bronchiolitis and pneumonia warrants testing for CF. Keep in mind that even these kids may very well not have CF, but a test is probably indicated to rule out this possibility.

  • *Abnormally greasy or bulky stools.* Stools vary a great deal, but the baby with very large and very fatty stools might be tested for CF, since fat malabsorption is one of the problems for CF kids.

  • *Failure to thrive.* Because much of the fat from formula, breast milk, and solid food is not absorbed by kids with CF, they are usually poor weight gainers.

  • *Bowel obstruction.* Infants with CF can have different types of bowel obstruction. At birth there can be a total blockage of newborn stool in the bowel, called meconium ileus. Later on CF kids can be plagued with severe constipation. Intussusception (a telescoping of one part of the bowel into another) is also much more common in kids with CF.

  • *Liver disease.* Cells of the liver can be affected as well, and some kids with CF can have jaundice or other signs of liver disease.

  • *Salty sweat.* Sweat glands are also affected in CF, and parents report that their CF babies actually taste salty when kissed.

These days doctors screen for CF with that little sample of blood taken from a baby's heel in the hospital. There is even a test that parents can take to determine if they are carriers. Ultimately, the definitive test for CF is the sweat test, in which a small sample of sweat is produced from a baby's arm through electrical stimulation (it doesn't hurt) and the sweat is analyzed for its level of chloride, which is high in CF.

• **What can we do?** Because of the many systems of the body affected by cystic fibrosis, treatment is usually supervised in a cystic fibrosis center. Treatment of CF consists, in part, of:

  • *Respiratory care.* Parents are taught to watch for signs of lung infection and administer medications that control wheezing. They are also taught to do postural drainage—a technique involving gentle pounding of the child's chest to promote drainage of mucus. Respiratory therapy can be given right at home, including nebulizer treatments and, if needed, oxygen.

• *Nutrition.* Because the pancreas is unable to supply enough digestive enzymes, supplemental enzymes are needed for these children, as are high-calorie formulas and supplements.

• *Monitoring for and treating complications.* These can include heart disease (which may result secondarily from lung damage) and diabetes (which can occur because of damage to the pancreas, which produces insulin—the hormone that regulates blood sugar).

Kids with CF and their parents face a tough road, but the picture becomes more optimistic each year. Whereas in the past few CF kids could be expected to live past adolescence, with early diagnosis and improved treatment many now live well into adulthood. More important, the quality of their lives has greatly improved. Ultimately, there will be a cure through genetic engineering—we already know just where the abnormal gene for CF lies—so the outlook is hopeful.

THE HIV-POSITIVE CHILD AND AIDS

• **What is it?** AIDS stands for acquired immune deficiency syndrome, a weakness in the body's natural defenses against germs and malignancies brought about by the human immunodeficiency virus (HIV).

• **How did she get it?** Almost all cases of AIDS in children occur from transmission of HIV through the placenta from mother to child. Fortunately, anti-HIV drugs can reduce the chances that an HIV-infected mom will pass her virus on to her baby. Administering such drugs during pregnancy, during labor, and during the first several weeks after birth can often reduce the rate of transmission to as low as 10 percent. Moms who are positive for HIV should bottle-feed their babies, since HIV can be passed through breast milk to a child. Fortunately, such ordinary activities as bathing and kissing do not put babies at risk for catching HIV from their moms.

• **What does it look like?** As is the case with cystic fibrosis, many hospitals now screen both pregnant moms and newborns for the presence of HIV. If a mother is HIV-positive, her antibodies will be passed on to her newborn, so a very early positive screening test on a baby will not necessarily mean that the infant has acquired the virus — she may just be showing Mom's antibodies. A definitive diagnosis is therefore frequently delayed until a child is several months old. Though symptoms may not show up for months to years, children who develop AIDS in the first year of life may exhibit any or all of the following signs:

- Rashes
- Swollen lymph nodes
- Recurrent infections of all types, some mild, some severe
- Chronic diarrhea
- Abnormalities of the blood
- Fevers
- Malignancies
- Failure to thrive

• **What can we do?** In addition to routine well-care visits with the pediatrician, HIV-positive children are treated with antiviral medications and often require preventative treatment for a particularly pesky germ called *Pneumocystis*, a frequent cause of pneumonia.

There are also many things a parent can do **preventatively** to keep a child with AIDS healthy:

- A healthy diet is the best way to beef up a child's immunity and fight infection.
- Good hygiene, especially of the mouth, emerging teeth, and gums, is important to prevent yeast infections, common in babies with AIDS.
- Give all medications as directed.
- Keep all routine checkup appointments and make sure your child is properly immunized. Children with AIDS can receive most vaccines. Your doctor will tell you which immunizations she can and cannot have.
- Watch carefully for signs of infection; prompt attention to the many infections that plague children with AIDS is vital.

With new medications, reduced transmission from mother to fetus and, one day soon, with a vaccine, there is hope for the future in the fight against AIDS.

THE CHILD WITH CANCER

It's certainly *not* fair, but kids do get cancer. Luckily, this is less common than in adults, and is especially rare under a year of age. Between the ages of 1 and 18, however, cancer is the number one cause of death.

• **What is it?** Some of the more common malignancies in children include:

   • *Leukemia.* A cancer involving the white blood cells of the bone marrow.

   • *Brain tumor.* A relatively common malignancy in children.

   • *Retinoblastoma.* A malignancy of the retina of the eye, which may show up in the first few months of life as a squint or as a whitish reflection in one eye.

   • *Neuroblastoma.* The most common tumor in babies under a year of age is a malignancy of nerve tissue, and can show up as a mass in the belly, chest, or neck.

Kids also get tumors of the kidneys, lymph nodes, bones, genitals, digestive tract, and other areas. Again, most of these tumors are extremely rare in babies.

• **How did she get it?** There is no single cause for cancer, whether in an adult or a child, but both genetic factors and, in some cases, environmental factors are involved (for example, HIV predisposes children to cancer).

• **What does it look like?** The warning signs for cancer in adults don't apply to children; kids have their own warning signs, as provided by Dr. C. Philip Steuber. Taken individually, none of these signs is particularly ominous. Nevertheless, if there is no other explanation, then cancer should be considered in children with:

   • Persistent fever, without any obvious cause

- Persistent headache (this symptom requires an older, more verbal child)
- Persistent pain in one location or an unexplained limp
- A mass that cannot be explained
- Changes in gait and balance—a good walker suddenly becomes extremely shaky
- A change in appearance of the eyes
- Extreme pallor (pale) or unusual bleeding or bruising

Once again, noticing any of these things does not mean your child has cancer. In the majority of cases, there will be a much more common—and much less upsetting—explanation. One good example of this is bruising. As young children learn to walk they also learn to fall. The baby with bruises up and down the legs is seldom a cause for concern. On the other hand, there is less likely to be an explanation for a child with multiple bruises over the belly or back.

- **What can we do?** Fortunately, tumors in children tend to respond much better to treatment than tumors in adults. The overall cure rate for all childhood malignancies, taken together, is around 70 percent— a huge improvement in the last thirty years brought about by advances in detection and treatment. The thought of aggressive treatment, including the possibility of surgery, radiation, and chemotherapy, can be a frightening prospect for a young child and his family. Yet current advances have made even these difficult modes of treatment more tolerable. Babies are resilient and wonderful little critters, and we are amazed to see them go through chemotherapy sessions more interested in the toy they were just given than in the needle they have to tolerate.

Before leaving the topic of malignancies, a word about skin cancer is in order. I mention this not because it is a common occurrence in babies—it isn't—but because skin cancer prevention begins in infancy. Because a child's skin is more sensitive, sunburns during childhood are even more dangerous than during adulthood. Even though it's extremely rare for a child to get skin cancer, baby sunburn can make skin cancer more likely years later. Some **steps to prevent sunburn in kids,** as provided by Dr. Barton Schmitt, professor of pediatrics at the University of Colorado School of Medicine, include:

- Choose a sunscreen for your baby with an SPF of 15 or more. Higher SPFs don't add significantly more protection.
- Make sure you apply the sunscreen frequently (at least every three hours) — even the ones that claim to be water-resistant will wash off in a pool or with perspiration.
- Apply sunscreen 20 to 30 minutes before going out, so that the lotion can penetrate the skin.
- Put on lots of sunscreen in areas that are more likely to burn: nose, ears, cheeks, and shoulders. Fifty percent of skin cancers occur on the face.
- In babies, sunscreen without PABA is least likely to cause an allergic reaction.
- Use a hat when your baby is going to be spending time outside.
- Try to keep your baby out of the direct sun. If you're at the beach or a park, use a sun umbrella.
- Try to limit exposure at times when the sun's rays are most direct: 10 a.m. to 3 p.m.
- Cloudy days can fool you; so can sunny winter days. Seventy percent of the sun's rays make it through the clouds. Surprised? You can see the light on these days, can't you?
- If your child is particularly fair-skinned or has had burns despite using sunscreen, consider using a heavy layer of zinc oxide, which blocks the sun physically, rather than chemically.

THYROID DISEASE

- **What is it?** The thyroid is an endocrine gland (that means it makes hormones) located in the front of the neck. When the thyroid produces too little hormone, the condition is called hypothyroidism; too much thyroid hormone is seen in hyperthyroidism.

- **How did she get it?** Thyroid disease runs in families and, in children, can occur at birth or can be acquired later on.

• *Congenital hypothyroidism.* Babies born with an underactive thyroid gland can have growth problems and even learning problems if the diagnosis is delayed. Fortunately, the routine metabolic screen done at the hospital checks for hypothyroidism.

• *Acquired hypothyroidism.* Rarely, a thyroid gland can appear to function normally at birth but then begin to undersecrete thyroid hormone after a number of months.

• *Transient hyperthyroidism.* Less common is the overactive thyroid, usually a temporary condition whereby a mom with an overactive thyroid gland passes some of her thyroid stimulators through the placenta to her baby. Most of the time such babies' symptoms are only temporary; after Mom's thyroid stimulators are no longer being passed along, the baby will do fine.

• **What does it look like?**
Signs of hypothyroidism in babies include:
  • Poor feeding
  • Constipation
  • Cool, dry skin; dry hair
  • Slow pulse
  • Prolonged jaundice
  • Poor growth and development
  • Large tongue
  • Hoarseness
  • Reduced muscle tone
  • Generalized puffiness
  • Umbilical hernia

Signs of hyperthyroidism in babies include:
  • Rapid pulse
  • Reddened moist skin
  • Failure to gain weight despite a good appetite
  • Irritability

• **What can we do?** As with so many medical conditions in children, any one or two of these signs can be common in healthy babies; when several are present, however, then your doctor will do a blood test to determine the level of thyroid hormone in your baby's blood. If an underactive or overactive thyroid gland is found, the condition can be treated with thyroid medication.

CONGENITAL ADRENAL HYPERPLASIA (CAH)

• *What is it?* Another chronic health issue that may affect newborns is called congenital adrenal hyperplasia. CAH is a defect in functioning of the adrenal glands, endocrine glands located just above each kidney. Adrenal hormones have three functions: they affect the sodium (salt) balance in the body, help to regulate male sex hormone production, and are involved in metabolism of sugars, fats, and proteins.

• *How did she get it?* Congenital adrenal hyperplasia is an inherited deficiency of an adrenal gland enzyme. Different enzyme deficiencies exist, but all affect the functions mentioned above.

• *What does it look like?* Some of the adrenal functions are overactive, whereas others are underactive. Babies who have congenital adrenal hyperplasia can have one or more of the following serious health problems:
  • *Loss of body salt.* Dehydration, low blood pressure, weakness, and vomiting can be severe and even life-threatening in some babies.
  • *Increased male sex hormone.* Girls can have ambiguous genitalia; although they are genetically girls, with the same two X chromosomes as other girls, the extra sex hormone can make their labia appear like a scrotum and their clitoris appear like a small penis. Boys so affected will either have no change in their genitalia or will have precocious (too mature) genitals.

• *What can we do?* Hormone replacement therapy can reverse the virilization effects and prevent the severe salt loss seen in this disease. The key is to make the diagnosis early.

KIDFIXER FREQUENTLY ASKED QUESTIONS

Q: *My year-old son has CP. Is there any medication that can help his muscles relax?*

A: In some cases, children with spastic CP can benefit from a muscle relaxant. Physical therapy can also be a big help in loosening the muscles of a child with CP.

Q: *I have one child with CP. Does that mean my next child is at risk, too?*

A: Not usually. Unless your child with CP has some malformation of the heart, spinal cord, or brain, there is little chance that your next baby will have CP.

Q: *My husband has a cousin with muscular dystrophy. Is there a test we can take to see if we are carriers?*

A: Yes, there is. Blood tests can be done to determine, with some certainty, whether you and your husband are carriers of the most common types of muscular dystrophy.

Q: *I've heard about a new blood test for muscular dystrophy. What is it?*

A: A recently perfected blood test for muscular dystrophy, called single condition amplification/internal primer (SCAIP) sequencing, tests for the most common type of muscular dystrophy, the Duchenne type.

Q: *My 4-month-old son was found to have an innocent heart murmur. What is that? Does he have heart disease? He seems very healthy.*

A: That extra sound, called a murmur, that doctors listen for as a sign of heart disease can also be quite innocent—in other words, it can occur with no heart disease at all. Sometimes doctors hear this extra sound just from the blood rushing past a normal heart valve. Often such an innocent murmur (it's also called a functional murmur) can be differentiated from a more significant murmur just by listening through the stethoscope. Other times a diagnostic test, such as an electrocardiogram or an echocardiogram, can make that determination. If it has been determined that your baby's murmur is an innocent one, then he needs no special treatment or care.

Q: *What's the difference between asthma and reactive airway? Is there a difference?*

A: Although the two terms are often used interchangeably, some doctors reserve the term *asthma* for kids who are chronic wheezers for a long period of time and use the friendlier term *reactive airway disease* when we don't yet know how long or chronic a child's wheezing will be.

Q: *My year-old daughter, Marcia, has just been diagnosed with asthma. The specialist we saw has her on two different medications, albuterol and budesonide. I'm afraid to give her all this medication.*

A: There are some conditions where treating is actually *more* conservative than not treating. Reactive airway is one of those conditions. When a child with asthma coughs, she's probably wheezing, and wheezing means her airways are narrowed from inflammation and constriction. A child who wheezes is saying, "Open up my airways, please," a message we should heed. The medications that Marcia takes are safe. The best proof that she *needs* these medications is that she coughs (and wheezes) without them. When used conservatively, asthma medications won't retard Marcia's growth or affect her adversely in any way.

Q: *My obstetrician suggested that my husband and I be tested for cystic fibrosis. Is this really necessary? How common is CF?*

A: It may be a good idea. CF is particularly common in whites of European descent and in Ashkenazi Jews. One out of every 30 people from these groups carries the CF gene, and if two such people have a child, their baby would have almost a 1 in 4 chance of inheriting the disease. CF is much less common in African Americans, Asians, and Hispanics.

Q: *My 10-month-old daughter never burns—she only tans. Is it safe for her to be in the sun without sunscreen?*

A: No, it's not. Although red or blond hair, freckles, and blue or green eyes are risk factors for sunburn, that golden tan is no guarantee that skin is not being damaged. Use the same precautions for your "golden girl" that you would for a fairer baby.

20

CALL 911:

SAFETY AND EMERGENCIES

No matter how careful we try to be with our children, emergencies do happen. In this chapter we'll cover some common emergencies and some rare ones. You'll learn how to handle them and how to prevent them whenever possible.

KEEPING YOUR BABY SAFE

It's a dangerous world out there, and it can be just as dangerous right in your home. How dangerous? *The leading cause of death in babies, after the first month of life, is accidental injury.*

The safety precautions you should follow depend upon the age of your baby. Obviously, 4-month-old Joshie will not be able to get your prescription drugs down from the shelf or crawl into the street chasing a ball. He may, however, surprise you by rolling right off his changing table onto the cold hard floor. We pediatricians have an old saying: "The first time a baby rolls over, he rolls onto the floor."

Safety Tips
The American Academy of Pediatrics provides age-appropriate safety tips to keep in mind as Joshie gets older, faster, and becomes more of a daredevil.

In the First 6 Months

• *Scalds and burns.* Babies have sensitive mouths. Check the food or formula that you warmed up before feeding it to your child—especially if you used a microwave oven. Stir it well and test it on your skin. *Warning: A cool bottle may contain very hot liquid.* Babies also have sensitive skin. Before placing a baby in the bath, check the water temperature. To ensure that the bath water cannot become too hot, keep your home hot water heater set at 120 to 125 degrees. The hotter your water, the quicker your baby can be scalded. In fact, look at how easy it is for a scalding burn to occur when your water heater is set too high:

> **If your water heater is set** at **150 degrees**, it takes **2 seconds** of exposure for a bad burn
> at **140 degrees**, it takes **6 seconds**
> at **125 degrees**, it takes **2 minutes**
> at **120 degrees**, it takes **10 minutes**

• *Falls.* The only safe places to leave a baby alone are the crib and playpen. Don't leave Joshie alone on a bed, even in the middle of a king-size bed. Never leave your baby alone, even for a second, on a changing table. Remember, the first time a baby turns over always seems to be when he's falling.

• *Chokes and pokes.* Keep any small toys away from your baby. Only give him toys that are too big to swallow, that are too tough to break, and that have no sharp edges or dangerous parts that might come loose.

• *Back to sleep.* Always put your baby to sleep on his back. Crib death is more common when babies sleep on their sides, and is *much* more common when they sleep on their bellies.

• *Strangulation.* Hazards include plastic bags, long cords, soft pillows, blankets or pajamas with ragged ends, necklaces, and pacifier cords. Keep these items away from baby—and out of his crib.

• **Safe travel.** Make every trip, no matter how brief, in a properly secured, size-appropriate car seat. Remember, not even Superman could restrain a baby in his arms in a car crash. If you need to know just what type of car seat is best for your baby, check out the American Academy of Pediatrics car seat Web site: www.aap.org/family/carseatguide.htm.

• **Water hazards.** Don't leave your baby alone in a bath, no matter how little water there is in the tub. It only takes 2 inches of water for a child to drown. Never let go of your baby in a pool, even for a second. Stay away from any tot swim instruction that is not one-on-one. Babies cannot float, and they do not have any special reflex that allows them to bounce up to the top of a pool when you dunk them. Babies sink, like a rock, right to the bottom of the pool.

From 6 Months to 1 Year

• **Kitchen care.** Hot irons, stoves, toasters, coffeepots, and electrical appliances are all dangerous for your inquisitive creeper. Long tablecloths are dangerous too, since they allow him to pull all these hot and heavy objects down to his level.

• **Poisoning.** Keep all drugs, alcohol bottles, and cleaning materials locked away from your baby. Have the phone number of the local poison control center handy and keep an up-to-date bottle of activated charcoal (to prevent the absorption of any poison) nearby. Don't give this without first speaking to your doctor or the local poison control experts.

• **Stair safety.** Babies love stairs, but stairs don't always feel the same way about babies. Use sturdy gates for stairways and stay away from child walkers; these baby hot rods give Joshie enough momentum to push right through a gate.

• **Shocks.** Cover all electrical outlets with safety plugs. Electrical cords look just like toys to a crawling child, so keep these out of reach.

• **Falls.** When Joshie begins to stand up, he also begins to fall down. Lower the crib mattress, remove toys from cribs, use safety locks for all doors that lead to stairs, and put guards on windows above the first floor.

• *Pet safety.* Keep Joshie away from your pet's food bowl. Dogs are particularly protective, and the sweetest family pooch becomes vicious when he sees a baby crawling over to his Alpo.

EMERGENCIES

Now that we've made you aware, let's take a look at some of the emergencies that might arise in spite of all your efforts to keep little Joshie safe.

Dog or Cat Bites

• *Emergency plan.* If your child is bitten by your own dog (this is especially common if little Joshie is trying to get at Fido's food bowl) or by a neighbor's dog, wash the area well for ten minutes with soap and water. Apply a thin layer of Bacitracin ointment and cover the wound with a Band-Aid. If your child isn't up to date on his DTaP, he may need this vaccine now.

• **When to call your doctor.**
  • If you don't know which dog or cat bit your child or if the animal was a stray.
  • If the bite was on a hand, foot, the face, or the genitals. These areas are most likely to become infected, and your doctor may want to treat the bite with an oral antibiotic.
  • If the wound looks infected. Signs of infection include swelling, increasing redness, and draining pus.

• *Prevention tip.* Keep your baby away from the dog's food bowl.

Tick Bites

MYTH: Burn a tick with a hot match or suffocate it with Vaseline before removing.

TRUTH: The match is more dangerous than the tick. The Vaseline is a waste of time.

• *Emergency plan.* If you see a tick embedded in your child's skin, remove it by grasping it with tweezers as close to the skin as possible and firmly pulling it straight out. If the head stays attached to your child's skin, try to remove it using a sterile needle. That's it; no hot match and no Vaseline.

• *When to call your doctor.* If you can't get the whole tick out by yourself, let your doctor have a crack at it. There is no rush to do this, since it usually takes at least twenty-four hours for a tick that's carrying Lyme disease to transmit the bacteria responsible for this disease to your child. Also, keep in mind that most ticks are harmless. Only a small percentage, even in areas where Lyme disease is common, carry illness. Nevertheless, if you're not sure how long a tick was attached, or if your child develops a fever or rash within two weeks of a tick bite, visit your doctor.

• *Prevention tip.* To reduce your child's chances of being bitten by a tick, use an insect repellent and keep his arms and legs covered, with pants tucked into socks, before going outside in tick-infested areas.

Spider Bites

Although most of the twenty thousand species of spiders produce some

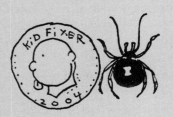

form of poison or venom, only the black widow and the brown recluse spider produce venom strong enough to cause significant illnesses.

The **black widow spider** female (only the females are dangerous) is about the size of a quarter and black with a red hourglass-shaped mark on the underside of her belly. Black widow spiders can be found all over the United States but are most common in the South and Southwest, on the West Coast, and in the Ohio Valley. After the bite, which may be mildly painful or even painless, a hivelike red mark develops, with a pale halo around it. Thirty to ninety minutes after the bite, the venom of the black widow causes painful cramping in a child's arms, legs, and belly, as well as irritability or agitation. Breathing difficulties may follow, as may flushing, vomiting and sweating. Symptoms may last as long as three days.

The bite of the **brown recluse spider** is often painless, and it's not until the typical blister forms that its venom is suspected. This one-fourth- to one-half-inch brown pest is also called a fiddleback spider because of the yellow or brown violin-shaped marking on its back. Within twelve to seventy-two hours of the bite, fever, irritability, a  generalized fine red sandpapery rash, and vomiting may occur. The blister at the site of the bite may widen and develop into a large crater.

- *Emergency plan.* If you suspect that your child was bitten by a black widow or brown recluse spider, ice the bite and bring him to an emergency room for further treatment.

- *Prevention tip.* Avoid areas where these venomous spiders are known to be common such as firewood, old tree limbs, and rock piles.

Snakebites
Rattlesnakes, cottonmouths, and copperheads account for the great majority of the seven thousand or so venomous snakebites in the United States each year, usually in the South. Within a half hour or so of a snakebite, the area bitten typically becomes red or bruised and swollen and then may become blistery. Children can develop vomiting, muscle twitching, and in severe cases even shock.

- *Emergency plan.* Go to the nearest hospital for wound treatment and antivenin.

• *Prevention tip.* Avoid areas these venomous snakes are known to inhabit.

Bee Stings

Other than an annoying swelling and the small risk of infection, the main problem with bee stings is the possibility of allergy.

• *Emergency plan.* Those who are not allergic to a particular bee (whether it is a honeybee, wasp, or hornet) need only apply ice and take an antihistamine, such as Benadryl, to limit the size of the bite.

• **When to call your doctor.** If little Joshie is one of the 4 percent of people with an allergy to bee stings, then he may develop such symptoms as a very large swelling at the bite ("local allergic reaction"), flushing of his skin, hives, or even difficulty in breathing from swelling in the throat or bronchial passages. Such symptoms can occur anywhere from a few minutes to several hours after a sting. Treatment for any severe reaction involves a quick dose of antihistamine, if one is handy, and an even quicker trip to the emergency room.

• *Prevention tip.* Once a child has had such an allergic reaction, he should always have an **EpiPen** nearby. This easy-to-use and potentially lifesaving injection contains epinephrine (adrenaline) to counteract a severe allergy. Your doctor will prescribe an EpiPen for you and will show you how to use it.

Foreign Bodies and Choking

When a child chokes on food or on a foreign body (something other than food), it can either pass along the digestive tract, lodge in the esophagus, or else become trapped in the respiratory passages. An object in the esophagus can be a prickly problem, but a foreign body in the respiratory tract—we call this aspiration—is the number one accidental cause of death in preschool kids in the United States. The majority of cases of aspiration occur in children younger than 3 years of age.

What might hungry little Joshie choke on? The items most often fished out of little ones' windpipes and esophaguses are:

Peanuts and other nuts
Hard vegetables
Metal or plastic toys
Bones
Toy balloons
Hot dogs
Hard candy
Grapes
Coins
Marbles
Buttons
Batteries

While most objects, amazingly, pass right through the intestines with little or no problem, some don't make it into the stomach but become **lodged in the esophagus.** When this happens, you will see two signs: drooling and the inability to swallow.

• *Emergency plan.* If your child is drooling and unable to swallow, then he'll need to make a quick trip to the emergency room. If the object doesn't pass quickly into the stomach, it will have to be removed.

When a swallowed object passes the narrow esophagus and makes it into the stomach, you can wait for it to pass out of the body as long as there are no signs of intestinal obstruction (vomiting, abdominal pain, blood in the stool). An exception to this wait-and-watch-the-poops approach is with a button battery—the kind used in many cameras and small electronic devices. If an X-ray shows that this hasn't immediately passed into the stomach, even if there are no symptoms, it should be removed, since its alkaline contents can damage the esophagus.

Sometimes food and foreign objects don't enter the esophagus but pass into the trachea (windpipe) instead. Such **aspirated foreign bodies** will show up in one of two ways:

• If the object **lodges lower down in the respiratory tree,** in a bronchial passage, then your baby may develop a persistent cough or wheeze. When your doctor finally sees Joshie, because his cough just won't go away, he will notice a big difference in what he hears on the two sides of the chest. An X-ray will confirm that something was aspirated into his bronchial passages. The foreign body can then be removed, usually by a surgeon or ear-nose-throat specialist.

• If the object becomes **trapped in the windpipe** (trachea), your child will choke, cough, have trouble breathing, have difficulty speaking, and may look pale or even cyanotic (blue). This is a true emergency and requires rapid first aid.

The steps to take to **give first aid for a choking baby** are:

• If he is coughing, crying, or speaking, then he is getting some air past the obstruction, and you should let him continue to cough to relieve the blockage.

• If you can't hear him speak, cough, or breathe, or if he's blue, limp, or unconscious, then it's time to take action.

• First, breathe three or four times directly into his mouth. Then dial 911.

• Hold him facedown, resting on your forearm. Support his head by firmly holding the jaw. Rest your forearm on your own thigh. His head should be lower than his trunk.

• Forcefully give five back blows between his shoulder blades, using the heel of your hand.

• After giving the back blows, if he's still choking, place your free hand on his back, holding his head so that he is sandwiched between your two hands. One hand supports the neck, jaw, and chest, while the other rests on the back.

• Flip him over, supporting his head and neck carefully, and position him face up across your thigh. His head should remain lower than his trunk.

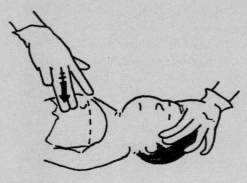

• Make five quick downward chest thrusts with your hand to the lower half of his chest, approximately one finger's width below the nipple line. Breathe three or four times directly into his mouth. If the airway remains obstructed, go back to the facedown back blows and repeat the process.

• *Prevention tip.* Keep all those problematic foods and other dangerous small objects out of your infant's reach. Also, babies frequently choke when moving around with food. When a baby falls while eating, he makes a sudden deep cry, and presto—the object is inhaled. To prevent this, try not to let your baby move around while he's eating.

Head Injuries

Rare is the child who doesn't fall and hit his head, especially once he begins taking those first toddler steps. Being close to the ground has its advantages, of course. The toddler who falls usually doesn't have very far to go, and therefore most head injuries in little ones are pretty mild. Of course, if your little explorer has managed to climb up on a chair or table, then he may have to pay for his boldness with a bigger bump. Also, a child approaching a year of age, who is just beginning to cruise or walk, is at the perfect height to bump his head into a table.

Because the blood supply to the scalp is so very rich, an innocent little bump can result in a pretty scary-size bruise. This rich blood supply also means that a head injury that cuts the skin can be a messy little problem. Fortunately, even these big bruises and scary gashes are usually harmless.

MYTH: A concussion means that a child has brain damage.
TRUTH: A concussion just means that your child has passed out or become confused.

After we've examined a child who's had head trauma, parents frequently ask if there was a concussion. Actually, a concussion is not something that a doctor sees when he performs an examination; it's something he hears about when he asks a parent or other witnesses what happened. The term *concussion* means simply that someone has had a head injury and has either lost consciousness or has become temporarily confused.

• ***Emergency plan.*** When a head injury results in a significant break in the skin, one that doesn't stop bleeding within a few minutes, then the cut will need the same treatment as any other laceration (discussed a bit later in this chapter). If not, then your concern is to make sure that no injury occurred to that adorable little brain that sits inside Joshie's adorable little skull. Make a visit to your doctor (or the ER) immediately for any head injury that:

• Results in a loss of consciousness (your child bumped his head and "blacked out")
• Results in your child vomiting (this can be a sign of pressure in the head)
• Makes your child seem "not like himself"

If, to your eye, Joshie is just not acting like Joshie, then that's enough to warrant a doctor visit as well. If your child seems groggy, if he isn't walking or crawling the way he normally walks, if he seems confused, or if his speech is slurred, it's always better to be safe than sorry. Any pediatrician would rather have a young child make an extra visit to his office or to an emergency room than find out later that a visit should have been made but wasn't.

Assuming that your baby did not lose consciousness, has not vomited, and is acting okay, what do you do to keep an eye on him?

• Give no medication stronger than Tylenol; you don't want to give something that might make Joshie sleepy while you're watching his behavior.

• For the first two hours after a blow to the head, give your child only liquids to drink, no solids. If he does vomit, liquids are less likely to make him choke.

• If your child is due for a nap, keep him up for one hour before the nap. If he's acting okay after that, it's fine to let him nap, but not longer than two hours.

• If your child is due to sleep for the night, again keep him up for an hour. Then, once he does go to sleep, awaken him before you go to sleep, making sure he is alert and responsive. Then let him go back to sleep again. Awaken him once more in three hours to make sure he is easily arousable and responsive. Then let him go back to sleep. If his behavior at these awakenings seems not to be typical for him (or at least not typical of his middle-of-the-night behavior), then it's time for a doctor visit again.

Nosebleeds

Nosebleeds are common at any age. Kids get nosebleeds because:

• They just love to pick their noses.
• They frequently get colds, which irritate nasal passages.
• Winter heating dries out their nasal linings.

MYTH: If a child gets a nosebleed, have him lean back and put ice over his nose.
TRUTH: Not a great idea—the ice is useless and lying back causes choking.

• *Emergency plan.* If your child has a nosebleed:

• Sit him up straight, or even leaning slightly forward, to prevent choking.

• Have him breathe through his mouth and, with a clean dry handkerchief or washcloth, pinch the soft part of his nose. Look at a clock and don't let go of the cloth for fifteen minutes. Letting go of the cloth to see if the bleeding has stopped will only cause the bleeding to start up again.

• After fifteen minutes, gently remove the cloth to see if the bleeding has stopped. If it hasn't stopped, repeat for another fifteen minutes.

• **When to call your doctor.** If your child's nose is still bleeding after all that, then you need to see your doctor or go to an emergency room to have a doctor pack the nose to stop the bleeding.

If your child is one of those kids who gets lots of nosebleeds, let your doctor see him to make sure he has no bleeding disorder. Although isolated nosebleeds are an uncommon sign of a bleeding problem, your doctor may want to do a blood count to ensure that your child has no problem with his ability to heal wounds.

• **Prevention tip.** Assuming that all is well with the blood count, you can often prevent future nosebleeds by taking the following steps:

• Use a clean warm-mist vaporizer in your child's room when the heat is on.

• Apply saline gel inside your child's nose at bedtime.

Cuts (lacerations)

MYTH: If a cut is less than ½ inch, it doesn't need stitches.

TRUTH: It's not just the length, it's the width and depth.

• **Emergency plan.** A small cut may be very deep and need sutures (stitches) to close it. Also, even with a small one, the sides of the cut can be widely separated. In this case, sutures may be needed as well. Finally, some long but very thin cuts, especially if they're not on the face, can be closed without stitches. So how do you know if a cut needs stitches? In general, **the following cuts will need some type of skin closure** (of course, there are exceptions):

• Any cut over ¼ inch on the face; any deep cut elsewhere over ½ inch

- Any cut where the skin is obviously separated
- Any cut where bleeding can't be stopped by applying pressure for fifteen minutes

Notice that I said "skin closure." Not all wounds that need closure have to be closed with stitches. Nowadays some wounds, like scalp lacerations, are actually stapled. Also, skin "glue" can now be used to repair many lacerations.

If your child has a **small cut** and you don't feel it needs stitches or some other type of skin closure, then here's what to do:

- Stop the bleeding by applying firm pressure with a clean cloth.
- Clean the wound well with soap and water or with hydrogen peroxide or Betadine.
- Apply a small amount of an antibiotic ointment such as Bacitracin.
- Cover the cut with a Band-Aid, sterile gauze pad, or liquid bandage.
- With cuts that aren't clean, make sure your child's tetanus is up to date (DTaP).
- Don't remove scabs; let them fall off naturally.

As far as scarring is concerned, the main **causes of scarring** are the **depth** of the wound and whether or not the wound becomes **infected.** Keeping a wound clean is your best way to prevent scarring.

- **When to call your doctor.** If you see any sign of infection (excessive redness, swelling, or drainage), visit your pediatrician.

Bruises (Contusions)

MYTH: If a child gets a bruise, apply heat to promote healing.
TRUTH: For the first forty-eight hours the best treatment is ice.

- **Emergency plan.** Ice brings down swelling, and to minimize little Joshie's pain we want to keep his swelling down. Most little ones aren't crazy about ice; it tends to sting, and a baby who is already crying because of a fall will usually cry even more if forced to sit with an ice pack for any period of time. Apply ice for just a minute, then remove it before it starts to sting. Wait a minute or two and do it again. If you manage to get in ten minutes of ice time, spread out over an hour, you're doing well. Repeat this, if you can, every four hours while he's awake.

After forty-eight hours, if the bruised area is still swollen, apply wet heat (a warm washcloth or small towel is fine) for ten minutes a few times a day. The heat will increase blood supply to the bruised area and promote healing.

• **When to call your doctor.** If you call the doctor for every bruise, you'll probably spend half your waking hours on the phone. Babies, especially the brave ones who are just learning to cruise around furniture and take their first steps, get lots of bruises, especially on the legs. If, on the other hand, your child gets a bruise and is not using the bruised arm or not putting any weight on a leg, then it's time to contact your doctor.

Nursemaid's elbow

A common cause of a screaming child is nursemaid's elbow. In this very common scenario a child is pulled by the arm, often after a fall, and suddenly begins to scream. Eventually the parents notice that he is reaching up with only one arm, holding the other gingerly at his side. A brief visit to the pediatrician will confirm that the elbow has been pulled out of its socket, and a quick manipulation by the doctor will pop the elbow back into place.

• **Emergency plan.** If your baby, after a fall, refuses to move one arm, bring him to the pediatrician or emergency department. Since some babies are actually prone to recurrences of nursemaid's elbow, your doctor can even show you how to pop the elbow back yourself.

• **Prevention tip:** Don't pull your child, or drag him along behind you, by the arm.

Scratched Cornea (Corneal Abrasion)

Another common cause of inconsolable baby is the corneal abrasion or scratched cornea. All it takes is one wild swipe with a sharp baby fingernail or even an accidental scrape by Mom or Dad to cause this very sensitive transparent covering over the colored part of the eye to become injured.

• *Emergency plan.* A baby with a corneal abrasion will often have a red eye and more tearing from the scratched eye than from the other eye. If you see these signs in little Joshie, then take him to your doctor or to an emergency room, where the scratched cornea can be diagnosed and treated. Simply patching the scratched eye for a day is usually enough to rest the area and allow the cornea to heal.

• **When to call your doctor.** If, after a corneal abrasion has been patched, pain recurs or a discharge results, then it's time for another trip to the doctor.

Tourniquet Injuries

A loose thread from a child's pajamas or an old blanket, or even a long hair can become wrapped around a little finger or toe. This is called a tourniquet injury and is one good reason to check your howling baby's fingers and toes if he awakens at night and won't stop crying.

• *Emergency plan.* If your infant's finger or toe is swollen and either red or blue—signs that circulation has been cut off—it's time for the doctor's office or ER.

• *Prevention tip.* Make sure there are no loose or frayed strands of cloth on your child's clothing, pajamas, or on any toys, dolls, or blankets.

Poisoning

• *Emergency plan.* Even a childproofed home can, unfortunately, fail to keep an inquisitive and resourceful child out of harm's way. Accidents happen, and accidental poisonings are a very real threat to the health of your baby. If your child swallows something he shouldn't have, here are some **general poisoning first aid principles:**
  • Keep the number of your poison control center near the phone. Call poison control or your doctor immediately if you suspect that your child has ingested anything dangerous or if he has spilled something dangerous on his skin, on his clothing, or in his eyes.
  • Keep activated charcoal (to prevent absorption of a poison into the bloodstream) in the house. However, don't use it without first speaking to a poison control expert or to your doctor.

• If your child has gotten a dangerous chemical on his clothing or hands, remove all clothing and thoroughly wash him all over with soap and water for ten minutes.

• If your child has gotten something dangerous in his eyes, thoroughly rinse out his eyes with water for ten minutes and then call your doctor.

• If you go to the hospital or to your doctor's office, bring any bottle or container from which your child may have taken medication.

Although anything a child eats or touches *can* be a potential poison, some **notorious poisons** for little children include:

• *House plants.* Some of these are very caustic and can burn a child's mouth and esophagus. Others cause vomiting and diarrhea. Still others have more severe effects, including causing an irregular heartbeat. Make sure you give poison control a call if your child gets into any of these:

Philodendron	Daffodil	Poinsettia
Elephant's ear	Lily-of-the-valley	Snow-on-the-mountain
Dumb cane	Foxglove	Anemone
Caladium	Oleander	Iris
Peace lily	Monkshood	Jerusalem cherry
Pothos	Larkspur	Aloe
Narcissus	Autumn crocus	Christmas pepper
Amaryllis	Glory lily	Chrysanthemum

• *Wildflowers and weeds.* Watch out for:
   Nightshade
   Jimson weed
   Henbane

• *Acetaminophen (Tylenol).* This is a great drug for fever and pain, but a child who gets too much can end up with vomiting, drowsiness, and even liver damage. Get in touch with poison control to determine if your child has taken enough Tylenol to necessitate treatment with activated charcoal or a specific antidote (there is one for Tylenol).

• *Antibiotics.* These helpful germ fighters can be little people fighters as well if taken in very large doses. Many different adverse effects, from a plain old bellyache to kidney damage, may result. If your child has gotten into Mommy's penicillin or if he has decided that his amoxicillin really does taste like bubble gum, then get in touch with poison control immediately to determine whether or not to use activated charcoal or induce vomiting.

• *Antidepressants.* This class of drugs can be particularly dangerous for tots, causing severe heart and nervous system toxicity. Keep them out of reach, and if Joshie ingests even a small amount, call poison control stat.

• *Acid.* Toilet cleaners, car batteries, and swimming pool chemicals all contain strong acids that can burn a child's mouth and esophagus. If your child puts any of these acids in his mouth, make sure you *don't* try to make him vomit—they're even worse coming back up. Give water or milk and head for the hospital ASAP.

• *Alkali.* Drain cleaners are notorious caustic solutions. Milk or water to dilute the alkali is essential, as is a superfast trip to the ER.

• *Stimulants.* Speed, STP, MDA, DMT, and MDMA (Ecstasy) are street drugs that overstimulate kids' hearts and nervous systems. Call poison control to see if you should "speed" down to the hospital.

• *Petroleum products.* Such garage regulars as turpentine, motor oil, gasoline, paint thinner, kerosene, moth balls, and furniture polish can all be extremely toxic—some even more so when vomited. Call poison control, since most ingestions of petroleum products require treatment or observation in an ER.

• *Vitamins.* That's right, even vitamins can be dangerous, especially those with extra iron. Give poison control a call to see if your child needs treatment.

• **Prevention tip.** Let's look at all the rooms in your home and see if we can poisonproof them.

The kitchen

• Don't store any cleaning products under the sink, or use safety locks.

- Remove all medications from the counters.
- Use safety locks on all low cabinets.

The bathroom

- Get rid of outdated medications in the medicine cabinet.
- Store all medications in their original, marked, safety-capped bottles.
- Keep all perfumes, mouthwashes, and other cosmetics out of reach.
- Use safety locks on all low bathroom cabinets.

The bedroom

- Remove medications from night tables.
- Keep all cosmetics out of reach (if it smells good, it must be candy).

The laundry room

- Store all detergents, bleaches, and softeners out of reach or keep them safety-locked.
- Keep all washing products in their original containers.

The garage and basement

- Keep all garden and insect sprays out of reach.
- Store all paints and thinners out of reach or locked up—these are killers!
- Gasoline and motor oil are killers too—lock them up.
- Store everything in original containers.

Other areas in the house

- Make sure that all wine, liquor, and beer are out of reach or locked.
- Keep all dangerous plants out of reach.
- Don't take your medications in front of your children; kids copy their parents.

Burns

Here are three popular burn myths:

MYTH: If my child has a burn with a blister, it will scar.

TRUTH: Unless a burn is third-degree or infected, it usually won't scar.

MYTH: If a blister forms after a burn, break it.

TRUTH: Leave blisters alone. They protect the skin underneath.

MYTH: Apply butter to a burn.

TRUTH: Butter is for bagels.

First of all, what do doctors mean when they talk about the "degree" of a burn?

- *First-degree* means that a burn is only red, without blisters. Keep this clean and there will be no scarring.
- *Second-degree* means that a burn forms blisters. These usually don't scar unless infected.
- *Third-degree* burns are the full thickness of the skin and usually need skin grafting to heal fully without a scar.

- *Emergency plan.* Here are some tips for burn first aid:
  - Immediately cover the burned area with cold running water for ten minutes, either by holding it under the tap or by repeatedly pouring cold water over it.
  - Wash the burned area well but gently with soapy water two to three times daily.
  - If blisters form, try not to open them. The wall of the blister protects the skin underneath it. Breaking blisters intentionally is a good way to infect a burn.
  - If a blister does break, clean the skin as above two to three times daily and apply a thin layer of Bacitracin ointment. Then cover the burn with a piece of sterile gauze.

• For pain, use the dosage of ibuprofen (Advil, Motrin) recommended on the bottle.

• **When to call your doctor.** Visit the ER or call your doctor if the burn:
   • Is more than 2 inches in diameter.
   • Is on the hands, feet, face, or genitals.
   • Is an electrical burn.
   • Looks infected (increased swelling, more redness than originally, pus).
   • Just seems worse, or your child is acting sick.

• **Prevention tip.** It only takes two seconds of exposure to water heated to 150 degrees for a bad burn to develop. It takes ten minutes of exposure to water set at 120 degrees. So turn your water heater down to 120 to 125 degrees.

The Baby Who Is Not Breathing:
CPR (Cardiopulmonary Resuscitation)

The ultimate emergency is the child who has stopped breathing. First of all, let me say that reading this section will *not* make you certified to successfully perform CPR. It takes a course, with a trained CPR professional, to do this. If you would like to take such a course, your local hospital or local Red Cross branch will offer one. This is a good idea for a group of friends to take together. Such training may enable you to save a life.

• **Emergency plan.** Nevertheless, let me present to you the basics of CPR for a young baby. Keep in mind that techniques are different for older children and, certainly, for adults. With this in mind, here are the basics of infant (up to 1 year) CPR for a baby who appears not to be breathing:
   • Have someone call 911.
   • Lay your baby flat on his back.

• Tilt your baby's head back and his chin forward to open up his airway.

• Put your ear next to your baby's mouth to listen and feel for breathing for five to ten seconds. Look at his chest to see if it's moving. If you don't see, hear, or feel breaths, then you will have to breathe for your baby.

• To breathe for your baby, cover his mouth and nose with your mouth and breathe out into his mouth and nose. Breathe forcefully enough to make his chest rise. This will not take a very full breath, since his lungs are smaller than yours; usually a mouthful of air is all that is needed. Give one slow breath every three seconds. If you can't get the chest to rise, then your child's breathing may be obstructed. Make sure his head is extended enough and his chin is forward enough so that his tongue isn't flopping back and blocking his breathing. Look and feel in his mouth to make sure that nothing is there. If you see a foreign body in his mouth, sweep it out with your finger. If you believe that he may have aspirated something into his windpipe, quickly attempt to dislodge it, using the back and chest blows described in the section on choking.

• Feel for a pulse for five to ten seconds by lifting your baby's arm over his head and placing your index and middle fingers on the inside of his arm, halfway between the shoulder and elbow.

• If there is no pulse and no breathing, then you will have to do chest compressions and breathe for your baby. If he has a pulse but is not breathing, then skip the chest compressions and just breathe for him.

• To do chest compressions for your baby, locate his breast bone by drawing an imaginary line between his nipples and measuring one finger's width down from the middle of that line. Place your index and middle fingers on that spot and depress the chest about ½ to 1 inch with your fingers. Repeat five times within about three seconds. Then breathe for him. You will be doing five chest compressions for every one breath; in other words, press-press-press-press-press-breath, press-press-press-press-press-breath. Your rate should be 100 compressions per minute and 20 breaths per minute.

• Check for a pulse and a breath every minute.

• Continue until help arrives or your baby has a pulse and is breathing.

Practice this on a doll, several times. Once again, this is *not* a substitute for a CPR course. I provide this information simply as a way of stimulating your interest in taking such a course.

KIDFIXER FREQUENTLY ASKED QUESTIONS

Q: *Is swim class a good idea to get babies used to the water right away so that they won't fear water?*

A: Swim class is fine for babies after 6 months of age, but make certain that there is always one instructor or one parent for each child. Also, don't feel that your child needs to be submerged to get used to the water. Babies tend to drink the water they're submerged in, and drinking large quantities of pool water is not a great idea for a baby's sensitive body chemistry.

Q: We're a family of pet lovers. I think that turtles are adorable and safe pets, but my husband thinks they're dirty. Who's correct?

A: Sorry, but your hubby wins this argument. Reptiles, including snakes, lizards, and turtles, can carry a bacterium called salmonella, which causes severe diarrhea and vomiting.

Q: We have a dog, Terry, whom we love dearly. Terry seems to love our new baby daughter and is very protective of her. Is it safe to leave Terry in the baby's room while we're in another room?

A: As sweet as Terry is, it's not safe to leave your daughter in the same room with your dog when you're not there. Smart, affectionate Terry may become startled by your baby's cry or sudden motion and harm her.

Q: How can I pick a safe toy for my very bright daughter's first birthday?

A: Most toys will carry age suggestions on the package. Even if your child is much smarter than the average year-old child, don't get a 2-year-old's toy for a 1-year-old. Despite her intelligence, she's still subject to the same safety risks as other 1-year-olds. Avoid the following **unsafe toys:**
- Dolls and stuffed animals with removable eyes, noses, and other parts.
- Any toys with sharp edges and surfaces.
- Toys with long strings or cords; these can become wrapped around a finger, toe, or neck.
- Toys with small parts that can be removed; these are choking hazards.
- Balloons and batteries are choking hazards.
- Bean bag toys can be dangerous if the beans leak out.

Q: My year-old child has bruises all up and down her legs. Does this mean that she has a blood problem?

A: Not at all. Bruises up and down a young child's legs are common—the result of all those attempts at walking. When a child has a bleeding or clotting problem, you will see bruises all over the body, not just on the legs.

Q: *If my child is allergic to wasp stings, will she also be allergic to honeybee stings?*

A: Not necessarily. Each type of insect is a different family, and allergy to one does not mean allergy to another.

Q: *What if my baby swallows something sharp, like a jagged piece of plastic or a pin? Shouldn't that be removed right away?*

A: Not always. Although you will want to let your doctor know about such an episode, it won't always be necessary to remove it. The body tends to coat ingested foreign bodies with mucus, which usually helps these objects pass right through the intestines.

Q: *My 9-month-old daughter, Jennie, swallowed a dime a few days ago. She seems fine, but I think my nanny may have missed seeing it in her diaper. What can I do?*

A: First of all, dimes almost always pass through the digestive tract easily, as do most coins. If Jennie is acting fine, it's okay to wait a week. If you still don't find the dime, your doctor may elect to send her for an X-ray, to make sure that it's gone.

Q: *I've heard that injuring one part of the head is most dangerous. Which part is that?*

A: Any head injury can be dangerous. Doctors do get a bit more concerned when an injury occurs just above the ear. That's because this is an area above a prominent artery, and if a child has a bad blow to the head in this area, there will occasionally be more swelling. That doesn't change the fact that the same precautions should be observed for *any* head injury. It also doesn't mean that *every* injury to this part of the head will be dangerous.

Q: *My son Jay, age 8 months, needed stitches to close a cut on his forehead. Is there anything I can do to reduce his chances of getting a scar?*

A: The best way to ensure that Jay's laceration has a minimum of scarring is to keep it clean. The most common reason for a cut to leave a scar is infection. Some doctors feel that applying vitamin E oil once daily after sutures have been removed promotes healing. It's worth a try.

Q: If I turn the hot water heater setting down to 120 degrees, won't I have trouble getting my dishes and clothes clean?

A: Actually, dish and clothing detergents work best in water that's between 120°F and 125°F.

Q: Shouldn't all burns be covered, to keep them clean?

A: Not really. Unless a burn covers a large area, unless blisters have opened, or unless your child is about to play in the sandbox or the yard, a burn can be left exposed to the air. In general, injured skin, whether burned or scarred, does best when left uncovered. Germs just love warm dark places, and covering every little wound is just what bacteria enjoy.

PART VI

SPECIAL ISSUES FOR SPECIAL MOMS, DADS, AND KIDS

Children thrive in a variety of family forms; they develop normally with single parents, with unmarried parents, with multiple caretakers in a communal setting, and with traditional two-parent families. What children require is loving and attentive adults, not a particular family type.

— SANDRA SCARR,
DEVELOPMENTAL PSYCHOLOGIST

21

SPECIAL
PARENTS

THE MYTH OF THE NUCLEAR FAMILY

Children of the sixties and seventies were often raised in families with a full-time working dad, a stay-at-home mom, and two or more children. In truth, such families are now in the minority. Census studies show that such traditional nuclear families now make up only 11 percent of all families in America. For many reasons, including a changing economic climate and improved respect for women in the workplace, family structure has changed. Dads work, moms work, dads take care of babies, and moms take care of babies. Also, in many cases, children are raised by one parent instead of two.

FINDING TIME

Whether you are a working mom, a single parent who has never been married, or a divorced parent, one important issue will be finding time for your baby and even an occasional hour or two for yourself—you're still entitled to that. Some suggestions to help you budget your time include:

• **Combine tasks.** Why not tell that evening story while you bathe your child or prepare dinner?

• **Lunch together.** If you work full time and have your baby in day care, choosing a day care center close to work will allow you to spend part of your lunch hour with your baby.

• **Flex time.** Some parent-friendly corporations allow their employees to make a flexible schedule. That forty-hour work week might be better divided up with a midweek day off or with an early start time and early leave time.

• **Telecommute.** With the help of e-mail and the Internet, perhaps some of the work that you are now doing in your office could be done from home.

• **Delegate.** Learn to assign some of your work to others. Not all tasks require your personal attention; your baby does.

• **Prioritize.** Who says a child needs a home-cooked meal every night? There are plenty of healthy take-out options, and your baby will appreciate mommy time much more than stove time. Do you really need to vacuum that carpet every day? We won't tell.

• **Get some help.** As we will see in Chapter 24, there are many different options for child care, from the hour or two afforded by a friend, grandparent, or babysitter to such formal options as an au pair, nanny, or day care center. Don't be too proud to ask for help.

WORKING MOTHERS

Many working moms express concern that their children's mental health will be jeopardized if the moms have a job outside the house. To answer such concerns, I usually point to scientific studies that have shown that children of working mothers show no signs of emotional deficit. In fact, about the only psychological difference found in these kids is that they often score higher on tests of independence. To me this sounds like a pretty good thing. When a child sees Mom leave and is forced to survive for a good part of the day without her constant attention, that child will quickly realize that he can make it on his own. Such a realization goes a long way toward helping a child establish a sense of independence and self-confidence.

I have found that a mother who would like to work but doesn't because she mistakenly feels that she is depriving her child of attention will only be unhappy, and may even resent the child for whom she is staying home. In the end, Junior gets less quality time from his unhappy mom than he would if she happily went off to work and then returned in the evening, eager to play with her baby.

Years ago, working moms were the exception. Now, most of the mothers in our practice work, if not full time, then at least part time. Most work because they enjoy their careers and do not want to risk giving up their seniority by staying home with a baby. Other moms really have no choice but to work, either because they need the money or because their inflexible bosses will not allow them more than a few weeks of maternity leave.

One positive side effect of having a working mom is that the dad *must* share the family load and get involved in baby care right away. Paternal involvement is a good thing, not only for a grateful mom, but for the baby and for Poppa as well.

Not only is it okay to work, but you are expected to play as well. Although you may have to sacrifice some of your former-life activities, a working parent is not expected to give up living. If several hours at the gym followed by a two-glasses-of-wine lunch is no longer practical, surely a quick workout and a bite with a friend at the diner are reasonable.

There are many child care options to consider when both Mom and Dad are working. Keep in mind that the people you choose to care for Rasheed while you work will play a significant role in his early development, and they are responsible for his safety for a major part of the day. It does little good to be the world's best parent only to leave Rasheed with someone who does not share your views on child care or who cannot be trusted in case of an emergency. *You must assume that an emergency will occur, and your child's caregiver must know whom to call and what to do.* I'm often amazed to return a call to the house of a very responsible mom and dad only to have the phone picked up by a babysitter or housekeeper who has no idea what is wrong with the baby or who is unable to communicate the problem to me. Remember, just because someone can be trusted to clean your house or cook your meals, there is no guarantee that she or he can be trusted to care for your child in an emergency. For more on child care, see Chapter 24.

Working moms can find more information online at www.working woman.com and www.familyeducation.com/topic/front/0,1156,2-3208,00.html?relinks.

SINGLE PARENTS

Single-parent families, now making up approximately 30 percent of all families in the United States, can come about in one of three ways:

- *By chance.* An unexpected pregnancy occurs after intercourse between two single people, one of whom wishes to raise the child alone.

- *By choice.* A single man or woman decides to either adopt a child or have a child with a surrogate parent.

- *By split.* Divorce or separation will result in a one-parent home, although the parent who has moved out will usually continue to share some parental responsibility. Children of divorce and separation will be covered a bit later in this chapter.

The single mom or dad who has decided to raise a child without a spouse (or who has been thrust into the role of parent by an unexpected pregnancy) has a tough but by no means insurmountable job. The absence of a spouse does not mean that the single parent is alone. Friends and relatives can pitch in and help, and there are plenty of support groups now for all types of single parents. Certainly there is no reason to deprive a single parent of the joy of raising a child, just as there is no reason to deprive a child of the opportunity of being raised by a loving single parent.

Unfortunately, there is still a stigma attached, unfairly, to many single-parent families. Single moms and dads are often deemed inadequate, especially if never married. Because many children in impoverished areas are raised with one parent, single parents are often assumed to be poor. Finally, some people even consider single parents to be psychologically unfit or immoral. Being a successful parent does not necessarily require a partner. It does, however, require a caring, responsible, and committed adult. When it comes to parenting, it's quality that counts; not quantity. So **how can you be the best single parent possible?** As Shellee Darnell, MFCC, a family therapist with experience supporting single moms, relates, the steps to take include:

- *Be positive.* Being a single parent, whether by choice or not, isn't a sign of failure, but a viable option for raising a child. Keep in mind that, as a single parent, you can apply your own views and attitudes without having to compromise; you can be exactly the kind of parent you want to be.

- *Be in charge.* As your baby matures, remember that you are running the show. Many single parents feel the need to be more lenient with their children, especially after a separation or divorce. Your child needs guidance and constancy, not a buddy.

- *Don't be afraid to show affection.* Children need a nurturing environment, which means lots of love, along with the limits. For more on "love, limits, and leave them alone," see Chapter 12.

- *Manage your time.* As was discussed earlier, it's important to prioritize and free up more time for your baby and for yourself.

- *Take care of yourself.* If you're sick, overtired, underfed, or depressed, you can't be a good parent. Allow some time for reasonably healthy meals, exercise, your regular checkup, and, if possible, a nap. As is the case with working parents, the fact that you are a single parent does not mean that you are no longer entitled to have a personal life. You should take time for your own leisure. If you spend all your time either working or caring for your baby, you will not be a very fulfilled person, and Rasheed will get shortchanged in the happy-parent department. Remember, an hour of play with a fit, happy, and rested mom or dad is worth a lot more than several hours with a depressed, impatient, and crabby one.

- *Forgive yourself.* Your job is a tough one, and you're doing your best. There are no perfect parents out there, even in two-parent homes. Accept that you will have your good days as well as your bad days, as we all do. Your child will forgive you—forgive yourself.

- *Get help.* As we have said, don't be afraid to ask (beg?) for help from Grandma, your favorite aunt, a good friend, or a babysitter. Make safe, reliable child care a priority. If you feel that all of this is too much for you, ask your doctor for the name of a good therapist to help you handle things.

- *Make to-do lists; make schedules.* These days, it's difficult enough making sure that you are where *you're* supposed to be throughout the day. Now you have another person to organize. Make weekly lists and refine them before bed each night or at breakfast each morning.

The following Web sites are useful resources for single parents:

www.kidshealth.org/kid/feeling/home_family/single_parents.html
singleparentsnetwork.com
www.parentswithoutpartners.org
www.singleparentcentral.com
www.fathers.com
www.singlerose.com

DIVORCE AND SEPARATION

The issue of being a single parent also arises when a marriage ends, as happens in nearly half of today's marriages. Although child care will be divided, evenly or not, both parents now have a tougher job than in the family with two parents living together.

Children whose parents divorce face different problems, depending upon the age of the child and the relationship between the two parents. **The way a child reacts to separation or divorce** depends upon:

• *The child's age.* Infants under a year of age often react to stress in the home by having eating problems. Rasheed may seem to have less of an appetite now than he did before the divorce. He may also develop sleeping problems. That good sleeper may now be tougher to get into the crib and may awaken several times at night. He may act irritable more often. He may even show some regression in his behavior.

• *The way the parents handle the separation.* In general, the more trouble parents have before their divorce, the more problems they can expect to see in their babies when the separation occurs. Also, the more conflict that persists after the split, the more difficult it will be for little Rasheed to cope. **Studies show that the best way to ensure that your child will be able to handle divorce or separation is to have his parents act in a civil way toward each other.** He needs all the support he can get, and now he may have to get it from a daddy who is seldom around and from a mom who has emotional issues of her own to deal with. One thing is for sure: when young Rasheed is dragged into the conflicts between his parents, his adjustment will be more difficult.

To best help him cope with the staggering changes in his life, try to keep things as stable as possible. Any routines, whether they be bedtime rituals or meals, should be kept as constant as possible. If you normally read Rasheed to sleep, continue to do so. If this was Daddy's job and it now falls to Mom, try to read the usual stories for a while. If dinner time was 6 p.m., attempt as often as possible to eat at 6. Don't feel that you will cushion the blow of a divorce by being more lax with rituals or with discipline. What Rasheed needs now is constancy, not treats. He needs his parents, not buddies. When things change, a child has a tendency to assume that *everything* will change. If Daddy has left home, perhaps Mommy will be next. The more you keep his routines the same, the more confident Rasheed will be that things will stay safe.

Try these Web sites for more information:

www.kidshealth.org/parent/positive/talk/divorce.html
www.kidshealth.org/parent/positive/family/help_child_divorce.html
www.ivillage.com/topics/relation/0,,166906,00.html

GAY PARENTS

MYTH: Gay parents make for kids with severe psychological problems.
TRUTH: Studies say no; as long as the home is stable, the child will be fine.

Recent studies suggest that somewhere between 6 million and 10 million children in the United States are raised by one or more gay parents. In some cases, heterosexual couples may separate or divorce, and a gay partner may join one parent in a new household. In others, primary homosexual couples choose to raise children, either by adopting or with the help of a surrogate biological parent. Although prejudice and ignorance may make the childhood of such children difficult, studies show that **the best predictor of normal psychosocial development for children of gay parents is the stability of the household.** Regardless of sex-

ual orientation, a peaceful, loving, stable home is the best environment
for a child.

Psychological studies also assure us that same-sex couples are just as
capable of caring for a child as heterosexual parents. Similarly, studies of
children raised by homosexual couples have failed to find any deficits in
learning or in psychological development. Finally, there is no evidence
to suggest that kids raised in homosexual homes are significantly more
likely to have gender-identity or self-esteem problems than children
from heterosexual households.

Web sites that provide support for gay parents include:

archive.aclu.org/issues/gay/parent.html
www.proudparenting.com

KIDFIXER FREQUENTLY ASKED QUESTIONS

Q: *I'm a working single mom. I love my career (I'm a paralegal) but I
worry about the impact working will have on my 9-month-old son,
Dougie. Will my long hours away cause emotional problems for
him?*

A: Dougie will actually benefit in two ways from his successful single
mom's career. First, he will learn independence, as he must separate
from his loving mom. Second, as he grows up watching his proud
and confident mom do so well, your success and pride will boost his
own self-esteem. You are his primary role model, and if he sees that
you are confident and successful, these traits are more likely to be
passed on to him. As long as the time you *do* have to spend with
Dougie is quality time, then he will be fine. To that end, try to spend
as much of your home time as possible interacting with Dougie

(read to him, sing to him while you bathe him, speak to him while you prepare his dinner).

Q: *I'm a single mom, raising a baby boy (Manolo is now 6 months old). Will he suffer from not having a male role model at home?*

A: Little Manolo will be exposed to many male role models in his life. If you have any close male friends, their visits to your home will provide an opportunity for him to interact with males. An uncle or grandfather can also help in this respect. Later on, teachers, coaches, and older male friends (try a male babysitter) make good male role models for your son.

Q: *My husband and I are thinking of separating. What's the best time for us to do this so that our 6-month-old daughter will not be affected too badly?*

A: There is no good or bad time for a separation. The way a child reacts depends on how stressful things are in the home and on the age of the child. Babies tend to react to separation by changing their sleeping and eating patterns, by regressing, or by showing increased irritability. Older children may react by having difficulties at school or by turning inward and playing less with friends. Although there is no good or bad time, the best thing you can do to ease the transition is to act courteously and caringly toward your spouse and to keep your baby's routine as normal as possible.

Q: *I've read that children from divorced families have severe psychological problems. Is this true? What can we do to prevent these problems?*

A: Recent studies show that although the incidence of emotional or school-related problems is higher in families with divorce, the majority of children from such families do *not* have major problems. What can minimize the risk of such problems? The mental health of a separating or divorced parent is of major importance in determining how a child handles the change. Children whose parents are more emotionally stable are less likely to have psychological problems. Also, the more conflict a child sees surrounding the separation, the more likely he is to suffer. So, taking care of your own mental health needs and minimizing fighting would be a great start.

Q: *Isn't a gay father less likely to be a proper paternal role model for a child?*

A: Actually, studies show that gay dads are at least as adept at instilling traditional patterns of discipline, structure, and support as heterosexual fathers. Lesbian moms also test perfectly in measures of traditional mothering behavior. Keep in mind that children find role models in relatives, friends, and teachers as well as parents. Finally, children raised by gay parents have not been found to be predisposed to homosexuality significantly more than those raised in strictly heterosexual families. If any difference has been found, it is that children raised in households with gay parents grow up to be more tolerant of differences in the people they see—a very positive trait to develop.

22

SPECIAL KIDS:

TWINS, TRIPLETS, AND PREMIES

TWINS AND TRIPLETS

Well, you've really done it now! If you're bringing home more than one baby, expect to work more, but don't panic.

MYTH: It's twice as hard to raise twins, and three times as hard to raise triplets.
TRUTH: In some ways, having twins is easier than having two children of different ages.

Many people look upon twins as double the work. I prefer to think of them as an instant two-child family in half the time! Time management takes some work, and a little help from a nearby grandma, aunt, or friend is a big help, but twins and triplets can be managed. In addition, your two (or three) newcomers will have the wonderful support of a handy playmate. As they get older, you will not have to be relied upon as the only buddy. Of course, one additional problem faced by twins is the fact that they are often premature. As such, they can be expected to have all the problems of premies, discussed later on.

Some general tips about **making those difficult first few weeks manageable** include:

• **Rest when you can.** When Rachel and Jennie doze off, try to do the same. For the first few weeks, until your twins or triplets get on a schedule, sleep will be very precious to you. Learn to catnap when you can and eat when you can. You need your strength to be the great mom you want to be. Take care of yourself; if you're overtired or underfed, your babies won't benefit.

• **Get some help.** Whether it's Grandma, an aunt, a close friend, or that responsible teenager down the block, ask for help and accept it. Don't be afraid to recruit your spouse, either.

• **Get organized.** Before you feed, have everything ready. Before you have to change your babies, make sure all your supplies are nearby. Make sure the soap, towels, and shampoo are handy before you begin baths.

• **Feeding frenzy.** Feeding can be a chore, of course. If breast-feeding, some moms prefer to feed two at once, a baby to a breast, holding each baby in an arm, football-style. Other moms prefer to line them up at the pump, nursing and burping one after the other. This will usually be the more manageable option, and it has the added benefit of affording you a few precious minutes to enjoy one child at a time. In either case, you may well have to add some extra calories if you're nursing two babies. Plan on eating an additional 800 to 1,000 calories on top of your maintenance, and make sure you drink at least eight to ten glasses of water each day. In addition, take a look at the tips for managing your time in Chapter 21.

Many moms of multiples ease the burden of breast-feeding more than one baby by supplementing with formula. This may be a good idea, especially if caring for triplets. Supplementation is also a good way for Dad to help out. A mom who is completely worn out from exclusively breast-feeding her twins or triplets isn't likely to be interacting with her new babies when she's not nursing; in fact, she may be too tired to do anything besides nurse. Nevertheless, many moms want to exclusively breast-feed their babies, and do so quite successfully. Keep in mind that more sucking means more milk production, so nursing two babies means more milk will be produced than would be from nursing just one.

Twin-Specific Development Issues

Your twins (or triplets) will go through the same stages as singleton babies, but with a few important differences:

- **Birth to 2 months.** Things are wild and woolly for Rachel and Jennie for a while, as they consume seemingly every hour of their parents' day. The usual 1 to 1½ hours that most babies spend crying feels like many times that amount with the effect of "twin stereo." Fortunately for their harried parents, Rachel and Jennie also seem to calm each other down quite a bit.

- **2 to 6 months.** The twins begin to differ in personality. One may be calm, the other fussy; one bold, the other shy. Parents often express guilt during this stage, since they find themselves favoring the "easy baby" over the "hard baby," or the small and "vulnerable" baby over the bigger, "rugged" baby. Such feelings are normal, but there's no reason for guilt. Those labels will shift back and forth many times over the first few years, and today's "favorite" will soon be tomorrow's "burden."

- **6 to 8 months.** Babies often become attached to transitional objects (stuffed animal, doll) at this age. For Rachel, the best transitional object is her sister, Jennie. While singletons outgrow their objects, twins continue to be comforted by theirs.

- **8 to 10 months.** Your twins will console each other more actively at this stage; when Jennie cries, Rachel may bang a toy or babble as a distraction for her sister.

- **10 to 12 months.** While many singletons are beginning to use words by their first birthdays, twins often substitute nonsense words that, remarkably, mean something only to each other. This idioglossia, or special language, is seen in 40 percent of all twins, and accounts for the slight lag in normal speech development seen in many multiples. Have no fear; they'll soon catch up.

As your twins or trips grow and mature, other issues arise. Keep these thoughts in mind as your twins get a bit older:

• *Praise their strengths.* Many twins seem to be mirror images of each other. The bigger twin, Jennie, may be very advanced in motor skills, sitting, crawling, and walking before little Rachel. At the same time, Rachel may seem more in tune with her environment. Perhaps she smiled at an earlier age than her sib, and now speaks real words while Jennie only babbles. Often these differences can promote rivalries as the twins get older. Jennie the jock may boss around her puny sister, who responds by teasing Jennie about being "stupid." Such competition, seldom a real problem in the first year, can be lessened as the twins grow by encouraging and praising their strengths. Let Jennie feel good about her athletic prowess. Praise Rachel for her beautiful recitation of the alphabet. Again, these are issues more germane to a book about older children than they are to this baby manual. Nevertheless, keep in mind that their different levels of development may lead to minor problems as they get older. Remembering to praise their strengths will make any such problems easier to face in the future.

• *Make other friends for your kids.* Often, when twins are only exposed to each other, they tend to communicate in nonverbal ways, seeming to sense each other's needs without using words. This isolation may also make them less likely to socialize willingly with others as they get older. To minimize these potential problems, encourage your twins to play with others. As they get a bit older and your social secretary functions increase, try to arrange separate play dates so that they can get used to playing with others and so that they can be stimulated by, and learn from, others as well.

For more support, check out the following Web site: www.nomotc.org.

PREMIES

Babies who are born prematurely—that is, three weeks or more before their due date—often have added premie issues.

• *More time in the hospital.* For one thing, premies usually require a longer stay in the hospital, so you will have to go home without them. Although this can be a bit depressing, don't fret. You'll be visiting daily, and before you know it, your new buddy will be coming home. Rest assured that today's high-tech neonatal units not only provide great medical care, but are staffed by some of the most wonderful, caring nurses and doctors in the hospital. It takes a special breed of doctor and nurse to work in such a busy and critical facility as a hospital's neonatal ward, and I am always impressed by the dedication and warmth of these professionals. Your mini-bundle will probably get more hugs, kisses, and attention there than even you, a caring parent, could provide.

• *Premies are used to lots of action.* Often this high level of attention and monitoring becomes so reassuring to your premie that he will miss all the action when he finally comes home to your relatively calm and quiet house. Gone are all the fawning and motherly nurses, constantly touching, checking, and holding him. Gone are the beeps, lights, and conversation that he has heard for the past days or weeks. Don't fret. Even the peppiest of newborns will soon become acclimated to conditions in his new and permanent home. Although he may need a few extra rocks in the rocker or a few extra reassurances that you are still there, within a few days he'll be comfortable in his new and quieter surroundings.

• *Don't compare your premie to full-term babies.* Your premature baby is developmentally younger than your friend's full-term baby. Don't try to compare Juan at 6 months, either in terms of size or in terms of development, to 6-month full-term Pedro down the block. If Juan was born one month early, then compare him to little Julio, the neighborhood 5-month-old. If Juan was two months early, then look at little 4-month-old Manuel. Of course there's no need to compare your wonderful Juan to anybody, anyway. Each baby is special and, as has been stated several times, each baby develops at his own rate. When you visit your pediatrician, ask him to show you how six-month-old Juan's weight and length compare to a four-month-old's on the growth chart. Of course, little Juan will not be the neighborhood runt forever. He may still make the middle school basketball team and the high school chess team. Just give him some time.

• **Premie good looks.** Since he wasn't in your womb for a full nine-month stay, Juan may be a bit fragile-looking when you first see him in the hospital. His skin may be thinner, with less fat than you'd expect, since he only got "womb service" for seven or eight months, and you may see his veins more easily through the skin. He will probably be kept in a warmer or incubator for some time, since it's hard for him to regulate his temperature.

• **Premie lungs.** Juan's lungs also didn't have a full nine months to develop, so he may be having a bit of trouble breathing on his own. Some premies, due to lung immaturity, have a condition known as respiratory distress syndrome, wherein their little air sacs (alveoli) collapse. To help them breathe they often need extra oxygen, and even the help of a respirator.

• **Premies may be floppy.** If you gently tug on your premie's arm, it will not resist your gentle traction, but will seem limp. Similarly, his neck will seem floppier than you might expect. He may tremble a bit more as well. These are all signs of immaturity of the nervous system and are quite normal in babies born prematurely.

• **The premie diet.** No, this isn't the latest fad diet from Beverly Hills. (Hmmm, maybe I've hit on something!) Some premies are actually born so early that they are unable to drink from a bottle or to breast-feed. Such very small premies get plenty of nutrition from intravenous fluids and from feeding tubes that can be passed by the nurse through the baby's mouth or nose into the stomach.

• **High-tech terror.** Between IVs, feeding tubes, monitors, and respirators, poor little Juan may be a real fright when you visit him in the premie unit. Amazingly, none of these inconveniences are particularly troublesome to him. Once the purpose of all the wires and tubes are explained, you will actually feel comfortable visiting Juan in his temporary digs. You will also be allowed to pick him up, hold him, and do all the things you would if he were home. Before you know it, he'll recognize his mom, and your visits will pep him up and help speed his hospital course.

MYTH: You can't nurse a premie.
TRUTH: They can really use the many wonderful benefits of breast milk.

• *Feel free to nurse.* Breast milk to a premie is like spinach to Popeye. It has just the right amount of nutrients and lots of antibodies to help fight off infection. If your baby is extremely premature, you may not be able to nurse right away. Just keep pumping your breasts and saving the breast milk. Eventually Juan will get to drink this pumped milk in the hospital, and the pumping will keep up your milk supply so that you can nurse him when he comes home.

• *Vaccines are fine.* Contrary to popular belief, once they come home from the hospital, most premies can be immunized right on schedule. Once Juan returns from his long stay in the neonatal unit, he's raring to go. Unless he has an ongoing health issue that compromises his immunity, he can receive his vaccines at the usual time. In addition to the regular immunization series, small premies and infants who have had lung problems need the RSV (Respiratory Syncytial Virus) vaccine. Because of their immature lungs, premies are more susceptible to RSV bronchiolitis, a disease of the tiny air tubes inside a baby's chest. To protect against this virus, such babies are given the RSV vaccine monthly throughout the RSV season (from October through April) in the first year or two of life. Premies should also receive a flu vaccine each fall after 6 months of age. For more on RSV, see Chapter 18.

• *Vitamins.* Many premature infants require supplemental vitamins earlier than their full-term buddies. Some also need added iron. The doctors and nurses in the neonatal unit will let you know if Juan requires such supplementation.

• *Premie formula.* Special formulas such as NeoSure have more calories, protein, calcium, and phosphorus than regular formulas, all of which help premies catch up in size more quickly.

• *Vision screening.* Premies who have had respiratory difficulties requiring extra oxygen are more likely to have a visual problem called retinopathy of prematurity. This should be screened for once the baby comes home, and regularly in the first three months of life.

• *Hearing screening.* Hearing screening is now done routinely in many hospitals once before discharge. Your doctor will tell you if your baby's neonatal course requires further testing.

• *Neurologic evaluation.* Particularly small premies are at risk for later neurologic problems. If a premie had a particularly rocky course in the hospital, he may be more likely to have learning problems or muscular problems later on. Within a few months of discharge from the hospital, your pediatrician may ask you to have Juan visit a pediatric neurologist or early intervention center to monitor his neurologic status.

 **MYTH:** Babies who were born prematurely are bound to have lower IQs.
TRUTH: This is no longer the case.

Recent studies show that except for extremely tiny premies, the majority of babies born prematurely do not have significant developmental handicaps. This is due largely to the amazing technological advances in the care of premies and the dedication of the wonderful nurses and doctors who care for them in neonatal departments.

KIDFIXER FREQUENTLY ASKED QUESTIONS

Q: Will my premature son always be behind in size, or will he catch up?

A: Most premies do catch up in size. Assuming that he didn't have too many complications in the neonatal unit of the hospital, and assuming that he wasn't smaller than expected for his gestational age, your baby can be expected to catch up before his second birthday; many catch up even earlier.

Q: I've got month-old twins and I'm sooooo tired. When will this get better?

A: Hang in there. Usually by 3 to 4 months twins get into a good rhythm of sleeping and eating, and you'll have a decent night's sleep and even a few minutes for yourself. Keep your strength up by napping when you can and eating well, and you'll survive. Accept help from your well-meaning friends and family and get out of the house when you can. Your life will soon get better, I promise.

Q: My premature baby girl, born six weeks early, is due to come home from the hospital this week. Can you give me some advice about a car seat that won't be too big for her?

A: First of all, stay away from car seats with trays or shields; they can hit your baby's head if you stop short. Try to pick a seat with a short distance from seat back to crotch strap and from seat bottom to harness slots. If your baby still seems lost in her car seat, use some rolled-up receiving blankets to fill in the gaps. Some extremely small premies who have had respiratory problems in the hospital have difficulty breathing in any car seat. For these babies, car beds are the right choice. Ask the doctors in the neonatal unit of the hospital if your daughter requires a car bed.

Q: *My baby Mayer was born a month premature. I love him to death, but I'm a little frightened by the prospect of bringing him home from the hospital. Is there anything I can do to prepare myself for that happy (but scary) day?*

A: It helps a lot to get your feet wet at the hospital. Ask the nurses to let you change Mayer several times, feed him when possible, and even wash him. You'll see that he's not quite so fragile as you may have feared, and you'll become much more confident and ready for his homecoming.

23

ADOPTION: LOOKING FOR LOVE

Congratulations! You've decided to adopt.

There are many reliable agencies and attorneys to help would-be parents adopt a child. Your doctor will also be able to provide references, and there are numerous support groups, books, help lines, and Web sites. This chapter is no substitute for these sources, but is an attempt to introduce some of the issues adoptive parents face.

HOW TO BEGIN THE ADOPTION PROCESS

A good place to start is by getting in touch with your state's chapter of the American Bar Association or the American Academy of Adoption Attorneys. In addition, Adoptive Families of America can help you begin your search.

TYPES OF ADOPTION

There are three types of adoption situations:

• *Closed adoption.* In a closed adoption, birth parents are anonymous, and there is no contact between the sets of parents, either before birth or afterward. Medical information in closed adoptions is usually not supplied. On occasion, an arrangement is made whereby adopted children can meet their biological parents later on, although this is not always the case.

• *Partially open adoption.* In this scenario, adopting parents will have contact with the biological parents before birth, but there is no contact afterward. Adopted children are usually allowed to contact their natural parents at some point.

• *Open adoption.* In an open adoption, all information is exchanged and there is continued contact bewteen all parties after birth. Such a situation often resembles an extended family.

QUESTIONS TO ASK ABOUT A BABY YOU MIGHT ADOPT

Once you have made the decision to adopt, you will want as much information as possible about your new baby. It would be wonderful to have some idea about the birth parents' medical histories. Unfortunately, in many adoption scenarios this information is not available. Though you may not get every answer, here are some questions to ask:

• Is either parent HIV-positive?

• Is either parent positive for the hepatitis B virus?

• If the child is African American, does either parent have sickle cell disease or is either a carrier of the sickle cell trait?

• What were the details of the biological mother's pregnancy? Did she have any prolonged illnesses? Did she have the usual visits with an obstetrician? How was her nutrition? Did she use any prescription medication? Did she take any illegal drugs?

• Are there any significant diseases in the family history of either biological parent? Inquire about such conditions as childhood-onset diabetes, kidney disease, sickle cell disease, Down syndrome, mental retardation, seizures, heart disease, and cystic fibrosis.

• How did the baby do during labor and delivery? Were there any complications of the birth process? Was a cesarean section required, and if so, why was it necessary? Did the baby require a stay in the hospital's neonatal unit? What was the Apgar score (a rating given in the first five minutes of life to evaluate a baby's fitness right after birth)? Was the baby released from the hospital at the same time as the biological mother, or did the baby require an extended stay? Were any health problems noted on the initial examination by the pediatrician who examined the baby in the hospital?

Your new pediatrician will help you evaluate all the information you have been given. Most will even give an opinion about the difficulties you can expect from any problem that you discover. Quite often, for example, I am called upon by a prospective adoptive parent to make a judgment about the fitness of a baby that the parent is considering adopting. What can the adoptive parents expect with a newborn who has a heart murmur? What can they look forward to with a premature baby? If a newborn had a prolonged stay in a neonatal intensive care unit, will he or she have problems once at home?

Many of these questions are difficult to answer. Some are not. The baby who is born with a significant birth defect will be a high-risk child. The baby who has an extra finger or toe will not. Another confounding issue is the willingness of the adoptive parents to take on the added responsibilities of a child with a handicap or high-risk problem. Some parents will elect to pass on such a baby. Others will accept this child in spite of the hardships involved. Such a decision belongs only to the adoptive parents. The job of your baby's future doctor is to give you all the information so that your decision will be an informed one.

ADOPTING FROM UNDERDEVELOPED COUNTRIES

Once you take your wonderful adopted baby home, you will want to make an appointment with your new pediatrician as soon as possible. A visit in the first few days is a good idea, even if you have been in contact by phone during the adoption process, especially for babies who have been adopted from underdeveloped countries. Such infants are more likely to have certain significant health issues, related to limited access to health care, poor nutrition, and less than optimal sanitation. Your pediatrician will want to look for signs of malnutrition, including poor weight gain and small head circumference. He may also elect to do certain **screening tests,** including:

- Newborn metabolic screening panel (done on all U.S. newborns)
- Blood count for anemia
- Blood lead level
- Urinalysis to rule out urinary infection
- Stool examination to rule out an intestinal parasite
- Blood tests for hepatitis B, hepatitis C, syphilis, and HIV
- Skin test for tuberculosis
- Hearing and vision screening

Finally, immunization records from underdeveloped countries are notoriously sketchy, and your doctor may have to give your adopted infant a catch-up vaccine schedule.

ALL YOU NEED IS LOVE . . .

Babies are tough little critters, and the vast majority of adopted babies, even those adopted from less than ideal circumstances, do great once they are taken into homes with lots of love and care. Also, rest assured that your affection for this little stranger will surely grow, just as will the feelings that biological parents have for their children. As you hold your shiny new little baby, feed her formula, and comfort her when she cries, your affection for her will grow, as will hers for you. Love is not something that requires a genetic link to get it started. After all, you love your spouse (I hope) and you two aren't biologically related.

NURSING AN ADOPTED BABY?

It is possible to nurse an adopted newborn using a device called a nursing trainer, which is a tubelike structure that attaches to a mother's breast. Using such a device, a baby can suck formula from Mom's breast. In time, this stimulation may even result in some milk production in the adoptive mom.

"WHERE DID I COME FROM?" THE "SPECIAL CHILD" FABLE

MYTH: Tell your adopted baby nothing until age 6. Then tell her she's a "special child."

TRUTH: This is way too late, and the "special child" story won't fly for long.

Most qualified experts agree that informing a child about adoption is something that should happen naturally and gradually. As the subject comes up, and as your child asks questions about birth, answer the questions she asks. For example, if you happen to be reading a book to her and there is a picture of a pregnant mother with a baby in her belly, little Carrie may ask if she came from your belly. The appropriate answer at this time may be nothing more than a simple "No, you came from another mommy's tummy." Perhaps in a few months, when Carrie sees another pregnant mom, or a pregnant animal giving birth on TV, she may now ask for more details. Answer these questions as she asks them, in as simple, direct, and honest a way as you can, using words that she will understand. In this way, she will gradually and comfortably become aware of her adoption and will be better able to handle this information. It's also important to be positive about the adoptive experience. A good idea is to say that although her biological parents loved Carrie very much, they felt that an adoption was best for her. No magic story about a "special chosen baby," picked out over all other babies, will do the same for her; especially once she learns that her adoption did not take place in this way at all. Face it, adoption is a huge pill for a child to swallow. When the information is withheld until she is several years old, this news will be a shock, made even more upsetting by your delay in telling her. The best advice I can give is this: **tell your child that she is adopted** gradually, naturally, and honestly, and do so by answering her questions in the same limited framework in which she asks them.

For more on medical aspects of adoption, try the following Web site: *www.comeunity.com/adoption/health/clinics.html.*

KIDFIXER FREQUENTLY ASKED QUESTIONS

Q: Are adopted children more likely to have psychological problems?

A: With a lot of love and an open, natural approach to adoption, these wonderful and fortunate children usually do very well. The exception to the rule is the adopted child who has behavioral problems relating to adoption. Such children may have what is known as adopted child syndrome. These children, the theory says, feel abandoned by their biological parents. Fearing that their adoptive parents may abandon them as well, they act in socially unacceptable ways to precipitate this abandonment on their own terms. In other words, they misbehave to *force* their adoptive parents to abandon them, before this can be done to them without their control. This is, of course, just a theory, and if it applies at all, it certainly applies to the minority of adopted children. Nevertheless, some adopted children show the following antisocial behaviors, described by Joni Bosch in *Contemporary Pediatrics:*

- Refusal to accept affection from their parents
- Poor peer relationships
- Poor impulse control (many appear hyperactive or inattentive)
- Low frustration tolerance
- Lying
- Preoccupation with fire, blood, and gore

Psychologists tell us that an open, honest, age-appropriate discussion about a child's adoption goes a long way toward preventing antisocial behavior. If your adopted child shows such signs, ask your pediatrician for the name of a good child psychologist with experience in caring for adopted children.

Q: *I just brought home my wonderful adopted baby girl—she's beautiful. She's also very small for her age. Will she catch up or will she always be small?*

A: Children who have been adopted from abroad can lose as much as one month of growth for every two to three months in their previous home, but most do catch up. Expect your daughter to lag a bit behind for a while, but with a good diet she very well may be caught up within a year.

Q: *My adopted baby came to us, at age 9 months, with no immunization record at all. How will she receive all of her immunizations?*

A: Fear not—the American Academy of Pediatrics has a catch-up immunization schedule perfect for just such a situation. Your doctor can obtain a copy of this schedule and use it to quickly get your baby right on course.

Q: *My newly adopted 8-month-old son doesn't seem quite as advanced as some of my friends' babies. Is this because he was adopted? Will this change, or will he always be behind?*

A: Babies who have spent significant time in an orphanage (especially those who have spent more than six months in such an institution) may not receive the stimulation that is so essential for normal development. Many will be a bit developmentally delayed when they arrive in the homes of their adoptive parents. Many are also unaccustomed to the attention they are about to receive and for the first few months find holding and touching threatening. More than one-third of such babies will quickly catch up developmentally, and another third usually do so with some professional intervention.

Q: *I recently adopted a 2-month-old baby girl from Russia. I'm afraid that since she didn't have me with her for her first two months,*

we've lost out on the bonding that parents do with newborn babies.
What can I do to make up for this?

A: There's nothing you need do other than care for her each day. Bonding is not an all-or-none instant reaction; it occurs over time. Adoptive parents who have previously had biological children tell us that the feelings they have for their adopted babies grow in just the same way as the affection for their biological children. Your feelings for your little Russian beauty will grow, as will hers for you.

24

CHILD CARE:

A LITTLE HELP, PLEASE!

After you've used up all your favors by imposing on little Homer's grandma, you will probably realize that you now need some formal arrangement for child care. Whether you choose a babysitter for an hour or two a week, an au pair, a nanny, or some type of day care, finding a good caregiver is no easy task. After all, you've grown kind of fond of Homer and you want to keep him in good health. Even if it's only for an hour a week, you want to feel completely safe leaving your baby in the care of someone else. It doesn't take very long for Homer to be hurt or mistreated. We're all too familiar with the horror stories of evil babysitters and crazed nannies. Although these tabloid favorites are the exception, it makes no sense to care for your child fastidiously all day and then leave him with an unknown caregiver for even one hour. I'm sometimes amazed to see some really great parents leave their kids with truly irresponsible people. *Just because you trust someone to clean your house and make your meals, that is no assurance that you can trust that person to care for your child.* How can you be confident that a particular caregiver is right for your baby? Well, just as we discussed the three important questions to ask when interviewing your baby's pediatrician (see Chapter 2), there are **six issues to consider in choosing a caregiver:**

• *How does the caregiver interact with your child?* Is she affectionate with your child? Does she seem comfortable picking him up? Does your baby seem comfortable with the sitter? During the interview, watch for signs that the caregiver is affectionate and patient. Does she seem rattled because Homer is squirming? Is she able to concentrate and speak while Homer is vocalizing?

• **Ask the caregiver about her experience.** Has she cared for many other children? Has she cared for infants? If you have an older child as well, does she mind caring for two or three kids? Ask a sitter how she handles a cranky baby, a child with a temper tantrum, and specific emergencies.

• **Make sure she is mature and composed.** You don't want an immature high school student to care for your child. I remember the first time my wife and I left our two sons with a sitter instead of with Grandma or an aunt. Arriving home from a very nervous and quick dinner out, we found our boys watching TV on the couch but our babysitter, a 15-year-old boy, hiding under the couch. Why was the sitter hiding? According to our sons, "He thought he heard someone trying to get in and he got scared."

• **Check references.** It's not enough to look at a list of references and say, "Well, she certainly has a lot of experience; she seems perfect." Call those references. Ask them how the sitter got along with their children, how mature and responsible she seemed, and how she handled emergencies. Why isn't she still working for them?

• **Watch her work.** The first time that you use the caregiver, stay there with her. Hire her for two or three hours some afternoon when you can be around, or at least in and out. This will give you another opportunity to see how she interacts with your child.

• **Keep her in contact.** Make sure she has all the proper emergency phone numbers, including those of the doctor, poison control, and a trusted neighbor or nearby relative. If you have a beeper or cellular phone, have it with you whenever you leave your baby, and make sure the caregiver has that number as well.

THE BABYSITTER

Advantages

- A babysitter is a perfect choice for the parent who needs a few hours off one or two days a week, whether to work or for recreation.
- Using a sitter is your most economical solution.
- The babysitter is a flexible choice, especially if you have two or three people whom you trust, so that a last-minute meeting or activity is possible.
- Your baby gets one-on-one care.
- Your baby is usually cared for right in your home, although some sitters take babies into their own homes.

Disadvantages

- Many sitters are young and inexperienced.
- You are often at the mercy of your sitter's schedule, unless you are blessed with two or three trusted sitters.

How Do I Find One?

Finding a good babysitter can be difficult, but it's not impossible.

- Begin by asking a friend for a recommendation.
- If you're new to an area, try the local high school.
- Your pediatrician may know an experienced teen, young adult, or senior citizen.

THE AU PAIR

The au pair (the term means "equal" or "on par") plays a big part in child care. Usually a young woman from another country or another state, the au pair spends a year in your home and helps care for your child. In exchange you will be asked to pay a significant fee to the au pair's agency, pay for her travel to your home, for her classes if she is attending a local school, and a small salary for living expenses as well.

Advantages
- One great advantage of an au pair is the fact that your child will be cared for in your own home.
- You reap the benefits of your au pair's international experience.
- The au pair can also travel with you on family trips or outings.

Disadvantages
- The biggest disadvantage is, certainly, the cost. Expenses for the year can total several thousand dollars.
- The au pair is usually young and may have limited experience, especially when compared to a professional nanny, who may have been caring for children for many years.
- The au pair will almost always leave after one or two years, just when your kids have developed a good relationship with her. Many au pairs find themselves homesick and leave even earlier.
- Having a stranger in the house is not everyone's cup of tea, although I have found that most people quickly come to see an au pair as a member of the family.

How Do I Find One?
If you choose to hire an au pair, or you need some more information to help decide, a good place to start is by looking up "child care services" in the yellow pages. If you're a Web surfer, there are several good au pair Web sites, but remember to check references. Once you feel that you've found one, make sure you cover the six main issues again.

For more information on au pairs, try the following sites: www.au pairsearch.com and www.aupairinamerica.com.

THE NANNY

A good experienced nanny can be worth her or his weight in gold, and hiring one is much like hiring any full-time employee. Because she is an experienced professional, it's important to know how the nanny's philosophy of child rearing compares to yours. Does the nanny believe in being strict with children? Does she feel that showing affection is proper? Does she see herself as an educator who will read to a child and explain things she sees on the daily walk?

Advantages

- A nanny is a professional; hiring one means you are employing someone whose career is taking care of children.
- A nanny will usually have more training in child care than a sitter or au pair.
- One-on-one care is a great advantage for your baby.
- Your child will usually be cared for in your own home.

Disadvantages

- Hiring a nanny can be a very expensive proposition.
- Once you have hired a nanny, you will be expected to pay her salary for the full term of employment, even if you come to feel that she is not a good match for your family.
- Again, you now have a stranger in the house.

How Do I Find One?

Just as with the au pair, many agencies will help you find an experienced nanny. Hiring a nanny is similar to hiring any important employee. Make sure you have decided upon the terms of employment: When will she be expected to start? When will she have days off? How much vacation will you provide? What are you prepared to pay? In addition, when you hire someone who will, no doubt, have strong views of her own about child care, it's important that your views are compatible with those of the nanny. How do you both feel about discipline? Does the nanny feel the way you do about spending time with your child, or can you expect your baby to now spend hour after hour alone in her crib or playpen? Finally, cover the same six issues that were mentioned earlier.

More nanny information is available on the Internet at www.4nanny. com/parentspage.htm.

DAY CARE

Advantages

- You are not inconvenienced by the presence of a newcomer to your house.

- Day care is much less expensive than in-home child care.
- Whereas hiring an au pair or a nanny means you are entrusting your child, for a significant portion of the day, to one particular person, most day care centers have several people involved. The responsibilities and personalities of those involved are therefore divided.
- If you only work two or three days a week, and therefore only need care for those days, you will have no problem with a day care center. With an au pair, and often with a nanny, you are paying for a full week, every week.

Disadvantages

- The biggest disadvantage in day care is the fact that you are exposing your baby to several other babies, and therefore several other sources of germs, when you drop him off at the day care center. There is no question that you can expect your day care baby to have more colds, stomach viruses, and other annoying little infections. Keep in mind, however, that exposure to germs is not a terrible thing. By exposing your baby to bugs earlier, he may build up his immunity and be bothered less by these pesky infections when he reaches school age.
- Because they are well aware of the spread of infection, the day care center will usually exclude babies with colds and other minor illnesses, making it necessary for you to make other arrangements for that day.
- With day care, your child will not receive the one-on-one attention that he would get with a nanny, sitter, or au pair.

How Do I Find One?

If you do choose to put little Homer in a day care center, consider the following:

- Visit the center more than once. What is your overall impression? Are there enough toys and are they safe, clean, and well maintained? In general, is this a happy place?
- Are there enough caregivers for the number of children? For children under 1 year of age there should not be more than three or

four babies per caregiver. Do they seem to be playing with the children, or are the babies just placed in playpens?

- Do the caregivers seem responsible, mature, enthusiastic, and cheerful?
- Do the children seem happy? If there are crying babies (and this is inevitable), are they ignored, or is someone comforting them?
- Get references. Does anyone have special training in child care? Are there any teachers? Is the center approved by the National Association for the Education of Young Children (NAEYC) or the National Association for Family Child Care (NAFCC)?
- What do they do with the kids? If it's a nice day, do they go outside? How often are babies changed? Are there adequate hand-washing facilities?
- How careful are they about handling sick kids? Are babies allowed to attend when they have fevers? Are they kept home if they have a stomach virus?
- What is the policy if there is an injury, illness, or some other emergency? Is there an arrangement whereby a doctor is called? Which doctor do they call? Is there a policy about trips to an emergency room? Is anyone there trained in CPR and first aid?

Another option in the realm of day care is the **family care center.** This is usually a private residence where an experienced mother, often assisted by one or more helpers, adds your baby to her own kids and watches him for part or all of a day. If you know the person involved *well*, this can be a good alternative. Of course, since there is rarely any licensing involved, there is some risk involved without good references. At its best, however, a family care center is often a nice compromise between the personal touch of care in your own home and the less personal (and usually more expensive) choice of a day care center.

Finally, some corporations have child care facilities right in the workplace (for a quick pop-in visit from Mom or Dad) or employee-managed child care co-ops, in which parents share responsibility for child care.

Exclusion from Child Care
Sick infants are most contagious *before* they develop any signs or symptoms of infection. By the time a child appears ill, he has usually done

most of the germ spreading that he's going to do. For this reason, most babies need not be excluded from day care very often. Nevertheless, there are times when it's appropriate to exclude a child from a care group. As provided by the American Academy of Pediatrics Committee on Infectious Diseases, children should be excluded from child care for:

- Any illness that prevents a child from comfortably participating in activities
- Illness that requires more care than the staff can supply
- Fever, irritability, lethargy, persistent crying, difficulty breathing
- Diarrhea, stools with blood or mucus, or proven *E. coli* or shigella infection
- Vomiting twice in twenty-four hours, unless due to a noninfectious cause
- Mouth sores causing drooling
- Rash with fever or change in behavior, unless not contagious (as per physician)
- Conjunctivitis with a yellow or green discharge
- Infectious tuberculosis
- Impetigo, until twenty-four hours after treatment is begun
- Strep throat, until twenty-four hours after treatment is begun
- Head lice or scabies (a mite infestation), until after one treatment
- Chicken pox, until lesions are crusted and dry
- Pertussis (whooping cough), until after five days of treatment
- Mumps, until nine days after first swelling
- Measles, until four days after appearance of rash
- Hepatitis A, until one week after onset of illness

A FINAL WORD ABOUT CHILD CARE

The choice of help is, of course, a personal one. Your own finances and lifestyle are important determinants. Whichever choice you make, however, make sure that your precious child is cared for by someone you trust. Also, make certain that in case of an emergency, your sitter, au pair, nanny, or day care center knows exactly what to do, and knows precisely how to get in touch with you and a doctor.

KIDFIXER FREQUENTLY ASKED QUESTIONS

Q: *My year-old daughter seems happy around everyone except my nanny. The nanny seems very nice, but my daughter seems terrified of her. Is it just stranger anxiety?*

A: It may be nothing more than stranger anxiety, but if your child really has stranger anxiety, why is she happy around everyone else? Nannies, since they're around children so much, are often relatively exempt from stranger anxiety. How well do you know your nanny? Although stories of such nannies are far less common than you would think from watching movies and afternoon TV, there are enough true stories of abusive nannies to warrant further investigation. Spend a couple of days with your baby and the nanny. Make sure the nanny's behavior seems appropriate. Does she have a quick temper? What does she say about discipline? If you have *any doubt* at all, then you have only two alternatives: either consider a "nanny cam" company or let your nanny go. You can't afford to make a mistake.

Q: *What can I do to keep my child safe with the sitter?*

A: First of all, don't allow deliveries while you're away. This is one way to make sure that your sitter will not be allowing a stranger into the house while you're gone. Also, if your sitter has to prepare a meal, make it a simple one. Discourage a young gourmet cook from having several hot pots and pans bubbling. Snacks should be premade; there's no reason for a sitter to start baking cookies. Finally, make sure that you know about any friend who will be keeping your sitter "company" while she is caring for your child.

Q: *How much will I have to pay an au pair? Do I give the au pair a day off?*

A: The au pair agency will usually suggest a salary, but most au pairs currently are paid between $120 and $150 a week. It is also customary to give an au pair one day off per week.

Q: *Can I interview an au pair in person?*

A: Because they usually come from out of state or even out of the country, most au pair interviews are conducted by telephone. Some agencies permit you to interview an au pair in person, but you will be expected to pay for travel expenses. Personal references are supplied by the au pair agency.

Q: *How much will hiring a nanny cost? Does a nanny get a day off? How about a vacation?*

A: The salary you pay a nanny depends in large part on her age and level of experience. Expect to pay anywhere from $300 per week for a young new nanny and up to $1,000 a week for an experienced and mature nanny. Most nannies work a five-day week and get one to two weeks off per year with pay. You may also have to pay for medical insurance.

Q: *Can I ask a nanny to do housework?*

A: In general, nannies (and au pairs) will only do housework involving your children, such as preparing a meal for a child or cleaning up after a child. Major housework is not usually a nanny function. Some agencies will suggest that a nanny provide further housework duties for higher pay.

Q: *When is it proper to send a child with a cold back to day care? It seems that everywhere I look there is a runny nose!*

A: It really isn't feasible to exclude babies with nothing more than a cold from day care. First of all, in any large day care group you can expect that there will be a few children who, though looking perfectly healthy, are incubating a cold and are therefore contagious. Second, your baby is bound to catch plenty of cold germs in the first couple of years no matter how hard you try to isolate him from

sneezes and coughs. Most day care facilities understand the futility
of keeping babies with common colds or other minor infections at
home and will only exclude children with serious illnesses.

On the other hand, there are certain basic steps that a day care
center can and should take to **limit the spread of germs,** including:
- Frequent hand washing, with soap, especially after diaper changes
  and before feeding
- Keeping disposable diapers covered at all times
- Proper food preparation and storage
- Frequent cleaning of toys
- The use of tissues (rather than handkerchiefs)

A FINAL THOUGHT

For a parent, it's hard to recognize the significance of your work when you're immersed in the mundane details. Few of us, as we run the bath water or spread the peanut butter on the bread, proclaim proudly, "I'm making my contribution to the future of the planet." But with the exception of global hunger, few jobs in the world of paychecks and promotions compare in significance to the job of parent.

— JOYCE MAYNARD

This book is an attempt to share with you, dear parents, some of the experience I have accumulated in over twenty years as a pediatrician. Of course, much of this wisdom came from parents just like you and from children just like Juan or Clarisse. It is a sincere attempt to help you handle your new "package" that seemed, miraculously, to appear out of nowhere.

I have tried to stress that common sense and a good heart are more important than a genius-level IQ in caring for a new baby. Raising a child may be a bit more difficult than setting up a new stereo, but it's not impossible. It's certainly easier than programming a VCR. Many of the decisions you make during your baby's first year of life and later, whether they are decisions about nutrition, discipline, education, or illness, are important ones. You will be guided by the experiences of others: family, friends, your pediatrician, and, I hope, this book. Ultimately, however, the decisions will be yours to make. Make them wisely.

As far as what to do once your baby is older than 1 year of age, I can only say this. Each year gets easier. As Sammy and Joshie get older, they will take up less of your time. True, there will be plenty to worry about, but you will find that parenting is no longer a twenty-four-hour-a-day job. You will be more confident in your parenting skills and better able to face all the unexpected emergencies that each day will bring. You also will be better able to relax and appreciate all the amazing things that your now verbal and mobile child can say and do. Remarkably, as you find that you are no longer caring for a baby, you will see that you have made a wonderful new friend.

Until then, good luck and enjoy your new baby as much as I have enjoyed my own.

APPENDIX 1

TROUBLESHOOTING GUIDE

The next few pages will help you find solutions to some common "glitches" with your brand-new baby.

Spots, Dots, and Bumps

If your baby has . . .	He may have	Try this . . .	See Chapter . . .
Little red and white pimples on face	Baby acne	Nothing; will clear up on own in few weeks to months	8
Little white pimples on nose in first weeks	Milia	Nothing; will clear up on own in few weeks to months	8
Red pimples all over in first few days	Erythema toxicum	Nothing; will clear up on own in few weeks to months	8
Itchy, red, scaly skin	Eczema	Bathe less; mild soap; if persists, see MD for ointment or change in diet	8
Itchy, yellow, flaky skin on scalp and brows	Seborrhea	If severe, see MD for ointment, shampoo, or change in diet	8
Red spots becoming blisters and then scabs	Chicken pox	Call MD for itch relief; keep clean; watch for complications	18
Tiny red dots in "warm" areas of skin	Heat rash	Lighter clothing	8
Coffee-colored flat marks at birth or later	Café au laits	Nothing; will stay; point out to MD if several and large	8
Slapped-cheek face, pink lacy rash on arms and legs	Fifth disease	No treatment; contagious only before rash; inform pregnant moms	18
Purple "bruises" on back, butt	Mongol spots	Nothing; will fade before one year	8
Small dark "mole"	Nevus	Not to worry, but point out to MD at next checkup	8
Pale pink splotches, esp. on back of neck	Salmon patch (stork bite)	Nothing; will fade on own by one year	8
White coating on tongue and inside mouth	Thrush	See MD to confirm diagnosis and for yeast medication	8
Shiny bump inside navel	Umbilical granuloma	Point out to MD at next checkup so he can cauterize	8
Large, soft navel bulge; larger with crying	Umbilical hernia	Nothing; will almost always be gone in a few years	8
Cone-shaped head at birth	Caput	Nothing; will gradually smooth out	8
Lopsided, swollen head at birth	Cephalohematoma	Nothing; will gradually smooth out	8
Generalized red dots after a few days of fever	Roseola	Nothing to do; worst is over; see or speak to MD to confirm diagnosis	18
Viral rash		See MD to make diagnosis	18
Pimples on mouth, hands, feet, butt	Coxsackie virus	If doctor confirms diagnosis, Tylenol, soft cool foods	18
Pimples on mouth, lips, occasionally hands	Herpes	If doctor confirms diagnosis, Tylenol, soft cool foods	18

More Spots, Dots, and Bumps

If your baby has . . .	He may have	Try this . . .	See Chapter . . .
Sandpaper rash, fever, red throat	Scarlet fever	See MD for throat culture, antibiotics	18
	Staph scarlet fever	See MD for diagnosis and treatment	18
	Scalded skin syndrome	See MD for diagnosis and treatment	18
	Drug reaction	See MD for diagnosis and treatment	18
Red welts all over after contact with allergen	Hives	Antihistamine (Benadryl); see MD if severe or persists	8
Little red dots with any infection	Viral rash	See MD to rule out other causes	18
Bumps or blisters in streaks	Contact dermatitis	Antihistamine (Benadryl); ask MD for prescription ointment	8
Purple rash on butt, legs; belly and joint pain	HSP	See MD for diagnosis and treatment	18
Fever for several days, rash, red eyes and lips	Kawasaki disease	See MD for diagnosis and treatment	18
Yellow blisters/crusts	Impetigo	See MD for diagnosis and antibiotic (ointment or oral)	18
Red, warm, swollen skin after bite or scratch	Cellulitis	See MD for diagnosis and antibiotic	18
Bulge in groin	Inguinal hernia	See MD to make diagnosis and refer for surgery	8
	Hydrocele	See MD to make diagnosis (can be watched)	8
	Undescended teste	See MD to make diagnosis; surgery needed if doesn't descend	8
Penis opening off center	Hypospadius, epispadius	See MD to confirm diagnosis and to determine if surgery needed	8
"Bent" penis	Chordee	See MD to confirm diagnosis and to determine if surgery needed	8
Lips of vagina fused	Labial adhesions	See MD to determine if topical treatment or separation necessary	8
Dry, peeling hands, feet	Dyshidrosis	Expose hands and feet; no footsie pajamas; moisturizer	8
Cheesy rash in skin folds	Intertrigo	Clean well and apply zinc oxide	8

Tummy Troubles

If your baby has . . .	He may have	Try this . . .	See Chapter . . .
Hard, infrequent stools (constipation)	Functional constipation	Push fluids, fruits; speak to MD about stool softener	17
	Lack of fluids	Push fluids	17
	Formula intolerance	Speak to MD about possible formula change if persists	17
	Excess of binding foods	Eliminate rice, banana; give other fruits	17
	Rarer medical causes	See MD for diagnosis and treatment if constipation severe and persistent	17
Nursed baby with infrequent but soft stools	Normal for nursed babies	No treatment needed; if fussy, glycerine suppository	17
Frequent, looser stools (diarrhea)	Toddler's diarrhea	Decrease juice intake to not more than 6 oz. per day	17
	Formula intolerance	Speak to MD about possible formula change if persists	17
	Nursing diet	Watch out for milk and other problem foods	17
	Stomach virus	Push fluids to prevent dehydration; binding foods; see MD if persistent	17
	Rarer medical causes	See MD for diagnosis and treatment if diarrhea severe and persistent	17
Persistent vomiting	Reflux	Call MD for treatment (antacids, thickened feeds, other) if persistent	17
	Stomach virus	Electrolyte solution; bland foods; see MD if persists	17
	Formula intolerance	Speak to MD about possible formula change if persists	17
	Nursing diet	Watch out for milk and other problem foods	17
	Pyloric stenosis	See MD to feel for "olive" in belly; may need sonogram for diagnosis	17
	Infection elsewhere	See MD for diagnosis and treatment if vomiting severe and persistent	17
	Rarer medical causes	See MD for diagnosis and treatment if vomiting severe and persistent	17

Respiratory Problems

If your baby has . . .	He may have	Try this . . .	See Chapter . . .
Runny or stuffy nose, cough	Cold	Saline nose drops, vaporizer; call MD if persistent or severe	18
	Allergy	Unlikely in baby, but possible if persistent and clear; see MD if unsure	18
	Normal newborn stuffiness	Saline nose drops, vaporizer	18
	Foreign body in nose	If one-sided, bloody, foul, see MD	18
Wheeze, cough, labored rapid breathing	Cold	Saline nose drops, vaporizer; call MD if persistent or severe	18
	Bronchiolitis	See your MD for a listen to chest; may need treatment	18
	Pneumonia	Esp. if there's fever or the child "looks sick"; see MD for a listen and meds	18
	Asthma	See your MD for a listen to chest; may need bronchodilator or other Rx	18
	Flu	If family is sick, consider flu; see MD for diagnosis	18
Cold, fussiness, poor sleep	Ear infection	See your MD for a peek in the ears and Rx if needed	18
Red eyes and discharge	Conjunctivitis (pinkeye)	See your MD for drops or oral medication	18
	Blocked tear duct	See MD for tear duct massage instructions; may need Rx	8
Noisy inhale, barky cough, labored breath	Croup	Steam, "night ride," to MD or ER if severe	18
	Foreign body	If choked on food or object, to ER stat	18
	Epiglottitis	If severe croup, high fever, drooling—to ER stat	18
	Flu	If family is sick, consider flu; see MD for diagnosis	18

General Signs of Sickness

If your baby has . . .	He may have	Try this . . .	See Chapter . . .
Generalized "blueness" (cyanosis)	Heart disease	The baby with blue hands and feet is normal; if blue all over, see MD	19
	Respiratory disease	The baby with blue hands and feet is normal; if blue all over, see MD	18
Fever (over 100°)	Viral or bacterial infection	Tylenol; call MD if baby seems sick or fever persists; see MD if under 4 mo.	18
Convulsion with rise in temperature	Febrile seizure	Cool towel, Tylenol or ibuprofen; to MD—don't panic	18
	More serious infection	Esp. if baby has been looking "sick"; see MD	18
Fussiness, poor feeds and sleep; fever	Ear infection	To MD for this sick-appearing baby	18
	Throat infection	To MD for this sick-appearing baby	18
	Infection elsewhere	To MD for this sick-appearing baby	18
Fussiness a few hours every evening; but fine all day	Witching hour	Will be gone in 3–4 months; brief rock or soothing music worth a try	15
Fussiness all day	Colic	Any child who is fussy all day should see the MD	15
	Reflux	Any child who is fussy all day should see the MD	17
	Ear or other infection	Any child who is fussy all day should see the MD	18
	See emergencies	Any child who is fussy all day should see the MD	20
Strong-smelling urine	Urinary infection	See MD for urinalysis, culture, Rx	18
Fail. to thrive (persistent poor weight gain)	Congenital heart disease	Esp. if heart murmur or cyanosis; see MD	19
	Hypo-, hyperthyroidism	Often detected on newborn blood screen, but not always; see MD	19
	Malabsorption	Esp. if diarrhea; see MD	17
	Celiac disease	Often with loose stools (occasioanally hard); see MD	17
	Other medical causes	See MD	17, 19

Emergencies

If your baby has . . .	He may have	Try this . . .	See Chapter . . .
Passed out or is confused after head injury	Concussion	To MD or ER; may need X-ray, CAT scan; observation	20
Vomiting or changed behavior after head injury	Increased pressure in head	To ER	20
Head injury with none of above	Innocent head trauma	Observe for hour before sleep; awaken to check responses	20
"My baby won't stop crying!"	Ear infection	Especially if cold symptoms, to MD for diagnosis and Rx if needed	18
	Tourniquet injury	Check out fingers and toes for swelling; untwist if you can; to ER if not	20
	Incarcerated hernia	If bulge in groin, to MD stat	8
	Torsion of testicle	Baby boy with one swollen testicle, to MD stat	8
	Acid, alkali poisoning	A drooling baby who has gotten into cleaning supplies, to ER stat	20
	Scratched cornea	Especially if one eye red or tearing, to MD to diagnose and treat	20
	Nursemaid's elbow	Baby "tugged" and not moving one arm, to MD to pop back in	20
	Urinary infection	Fever or fussiness, sometimes urine odor, to MD for tests and Rx	18
	Bacteremia, viremia	Fever, fussy, no focus of infection, to MD for blood tests	18
	Intussusception	Intermittent crampy pain, eventually with "jelly" stools, to MD	17
	Thrush	White tongue and inside mouth, to MD for yeast Rx	8
	Reflux	Persistent vomiting and discomfort, to MD for diagnosis and treatment	17
	Colic	Fussy and gassy all day; to MD to rule out other causes and to treat	17
Burn with small area of redness	First-degree burn	Cover or rinse with cool water for 10 minutes; wash 2–3 times daily	20
Burn with blisters	Second-degree burn	If blisters break (don't break them), apply Bacitracin and cover after cleaning	20
Electrical burn or extensive, face, genital	Emergency burn	To MD or ER	20

More Emergencies

If your baby has . . .	He may have	Try this . . .	See Chapter . . .
Drooling, choking, inability to swallow	Foreign body in esophagus	To the ER for removal stat	20
	Epiglottitis	Esp. if fever, hoarseness, barky cough, to ER stat	18
	Acid, alkali ingestion	A drooling baby who has gotten into cleaning supplies, to ER stat	20
Choking, cough, pale or blue, difficulty breathing	Aspiration in windpipe	Back blows with baby facedown, then chest thrusts with baby face up, call 911	20
Puncture or cut after exposure to animal	Dog or cat bite	Wash 10 min., apply Bacitracin; to MD if on face, extremities, genitals, or if bite is from a stray	20
Tiny black, brown, or gray spot	Tick bite	Tweeze out; wash well; call MD if tick imbedded over a day or if fever, rash develop	20
Red mark with halo, then cramping	Black widow spider bite	To ER for treatment if spider has red hourglass under belly	20
Blister, then crater; rash and vomiting	Brown recluse spider bite	To ER for treatment if spider has violin shape on back	20
Snakebite red, bruised, swollen	Venomous snake bite	To ER for antivenin	20
Painful, rapidly swelling area	Bee sting	Ice, Benadryl; to ER if hives, severe swelling, or breathing difficulty	20
Persistent blood from nose	Bloody nose	Sit up straight, clamp soft part of nose with dry cloth for 15 minutes	20
¼" cut on face, ½" elsewhere, or deep	Laceration requiring repair	To ER for skin closure; ice, keep clean, tetanus if due	20
House plant in mouth	Toxic plant ingestion	Call poison control; different plants have different treatments	20
Ingested acetaminophen (Tylenol)	Acetaminophen toxicity	Call poison control to calculate amount taken and if treatment needed	20
Ingested caustic substance	Acid/alkali ingestion	Give water or milk right away and to ER stat	20
Ingested unknown amount vitamins	Vitamin overdose	Call poison control to calculate amount taken and if treatment needed	20
Ingested other drug	Overdose	Call poison control to calculate amount taken and if treatment needed	20

APPENDIX 2

INTERNET WEB SITES

These are just a few of the many good Web sites
of interest to parents:

Adoption
www.comeunity.com/adoption/health/clinics.html
www.kidshealth.org/teen/your_mind/families/adoption.html
www.kidshealth.org/parent/positive/family/medical_adopt.html

AIDS
www.aidsmap.com/web/pb2/eng/FC923847-FE61-4355-A035-CE8
    D98C862BD.htm

Breast-feeding
www.aap.org/family/brstguid.htm
www.4woman.gov/Breastfeeding/print-bf.cfm?page=228

Car Seats
www.aap.org/family/carseatguide.htm

Cerebral Palsy
www.childrensdisabilities.info/cerebral_palsy/resources.html
gait.aidi.udel.edu/res695/homepage/pd_ortho/clinics/c_palsy/cpweb.htm

Child Care
www.kidshealth.org/parent/positive/family/child_care.html
www.aupairsearch.com
www.aupairinamerica.com
www.4nanny.com/parentspage.htm

Congenital Heart Disease
www.nlm.nih.gov/medlineplus/congenitalheartdisease.html

Cribs
www.aap.org/family/inffurn.htm

Divorce
www.kidshealth.org/parent/positive/talk/divorce.html
www.kidshealth.org/parent/positive/family/help_child_divorce.html
www.ivillage.com/topics/relation/0,,166906,00.html
www.divorce.com

Emergencies
www.babycenter.com/general/pregnancy/newbornprep/9298.html

Gay Parents
archive.aclu.org/issues/gay/parent.html
www.proudparenting.com

Muscular Dystrophy
www.nlm.nih.gov/medlineplus/musculardystrophy.html#generaloverviews

Single/Working Parents
www.kidshealth.org/kid/feeling/home_family/single_parents.html
singleparentsnetwork.com
www.parentswithoutpartners.org
www.singleparentcentral.com
www.fathers.com
www.singlerose.com

Temper
www.aap.org/mrt/factsbc.htm

Thyroid Disease
www.mydr.com.au/default.asp?Article=3437

Travel and Immunizations
www.cdc.gov/travel

Twins
www.nomotc.org

APPENDIX 3
YOUR BABY'S IMMUNIZATION RECORD

Vaccine	*When vaccine doses are usually given*	1st	2nd	3rd	4th	5th
Hepatitis B	Three in 1st year					
DTaP	Three in 1st year; one in 2nd year; one age 4–6					
Polio	Three in first year to year and a half; one age 4–6					
HIB	Three in first year; one in second year					
Pneumococcal	Three in first year; one in second year					
MMR	One at 12–15 months; one age 4–6					
Varicella	One at 12–18 months					
Other						
Other						
Other						
Other						

Enter dates of vaccines as they are given

My child has the following allergies: _____, _____, _____.

REFERENCES

AIDSMAP. Diagnosing AIDS. 2003. In *Aidsmap.com Web site*. London: NAM publications [cited April, 2003]. Available from World Wide Web: <http://www.aidsmap.com/web/pb2/eng/FC923847-FE61-4355-A035-CE 8D98C862BD.htm>.

Alfred I. Dupont Institute. 2003. Cerebral Palsy: A Guide for Care. In *Alfred I. DuPont Hospital for Children Web site* (online). Wilmington, DE: Alfred I. Dupont Institute [cited April, 2003]. Available from World Wide Web: <http://gait.aidi.udel.edu/res695/homepage/pd_ortho/clinics/c_palsy/cp web.htm#RTFToC3>.

American Academy of Pediatrics. 1999. Policy Statement: Cord Blood Banking for Potential Future Transplantation. *Pediatrics*, July, 116–18.

American Academy of Pediatrics. 1999. Policy Statement: Calcium Requirements of Infants, Children, and Adolescents. *Pediatrics*, November, 1152–7.

American Academy of Pediatrics. 2001. *A Woman's Guide to Breastfeeding*. Elk Grove, IN: American Academy of Pediatrics.

American Academy of Pediatrics. 2001. Just the Facts: The Battered Child. In *American Academy of Pediatrics Web site* (online). Elk Grove, IN: American Academy of Pediatrics [cited 2003]. Available from World Wide Web: <http://www.aap.org/mrt/factsbc.htm>.

American Academy of Pediatrics Committee on Drugs. 1998. Neonatal Drug Withdrawal. *Pediatrics*, June, 1079–88.

American Academy of Pediatrics Committee on Drugs. 2001. The Transfer of Drugs and Other Chemicals Into Human Milk. *Pediatrics*, September, 776–89.

American Academy of Pediatrics Committee on Infectious Diseases. 2000. *Red Book*. Elk Grove Village, IL: American Academy of Pediatrics.

American Academy of Pediatrics Committee on Pediatric Emergency Medicine. 1993. First Aid for the Choking Child. *Pediatrics*, September, 477–9.

American Academy of Pediatrics Injury Prevention Program. 2003. Choosing a Crib. *American Academy of Pediatrics Web site* (online). Elk Grove, IN: American Academy of Pediatrics [cited 2003]. Available from World Wide Web: <http://www.aap.org/family/inffurn.htm>.

Amherst College Emergency Medical Services. 1998. How to Perform Infant CPR. In *Amherst College Emergency Medical Services Website* (online). Amherst, MA: Amherst College [cited 2003]. Available from World Wide Web: <http://www.amherst.edu/jaloduca/cprinfant.html>.

Anderson, Jane E., MD, and Bluestone, Daniel, MD. 2000. Breath-Holding Spells: Scary but Not Serious. *Contemporary Pediatrics.* January.

Arnsmeier, Sheryl L., and Paller, Amy S., MD. 1997. Getting to the Bottom of Diaper Dermatitis. *Contemporary Pediatrics.* November.

Baby Center. 2003. Infant First Aid for Choking and CPR: An Illustrated Guide. In *Baby Center Web site* (online) [cited 2003]. Available from World Wide Web: <http://www.babycenter.com/general/pregnancy/newborn prep/9298.html>.

Darnell, Shellee, M.F.C.C. 2003. How to Be the Best Single Parent You Can. In *Divorce Wizards Web site* (online) [cited September, 2003]. Available from World Wide Web: <http://www.divorcewizards.com/top10singlepar enting.html.

Barrett, Douglas J., MD, and Sleasman, John W., MD. 1997. Pediatric AIDS: So What Do We Do Now. *Contemporary Pediatrics.* June.

Bosch, Joni ARNP, PhD, et al. 2003. Promoting a Healthy Tomorrow Here for Children Adopted from Abroad. *Contemporary Pediatrics*, February.

King, Bryan H., MD, et al. 1997. Mental Retardation: A Review of the Past 10 Years. Part I. *American Academy of Child and Adolescent Psychiatry.* December.

Carder, K. Robin, MD, and Weston, William L., MD. 2002. Atypical Viral Exanthems: New Rashes and Variations on Old Themes. *Contemporary Pediatrics*, February.

CDC. 2003. CDC Toxoplasmosis Fact Sheet. In *CDC Web site* (online). Atlanta: CDC [cited April 2003]. Available from World Wide Web: <http://www.cdc.gov/ncidod/dpd/parasites/toxoplasmosis/factsht_toxo plasmosis.htm>.

Chalik, Debbie. 1997. Selecting a Nanny. In *Iowa Parent Baby Guide Web site* (online). Des Moines: Iowa Parent and Family [cited 2002]. Available from World Wide Web: <http://family.disney.com/Features/fam ily_1997_12/iowa/iowa127nanny>.

Cheung, Michele, MD, and Lieberman, Jay M., MD. 2002. Infuenza: Update on Strategies on Management. *Contemporary Pediatrics.* October.

Child Care Aware. 1998. Finding Good Child Care (online). Parent Soup [cited 2002]. Available from World Wide Web: <http://www.par entsoup.com/library/dsi024a.html>.

Churchill, Robin B., MD, and Pickering, Larry K., MD. 1998. The Pros (Many) and Cons (a Few) of Breastfeeding. *Contemporary Pediatrics*. December.

Consumer Reports. 2003. Child Car Seats. *Consumer Reports*, May.

Consumer Reports. 2003. Strollers. *Consumer Reports*, May.

Consumer Reports. 2003. Flying with a Baby. *Consumer Reports*, March.

Contemporary Pediatrics Parents Guide. 2002. The Right Way to Store Breast Milk. *Contemporary Pediatrics*, August.

Donohoue, Patricia A., MD. The Adrenal Cortex. 1999. In *Oski's Pediatrics*, edited by Julia A. McMillan. Philadelphia: Lippincott Williams & Wilkins.

Donowitz, Leigh G., MD. 1999. At-a-Glance Guide to Infection Control in Day Care. *Contemporary Pediatrics*. November.

Dowd, Nancy E. 1997. *In Defense of Single-Parent Families*. New York: New York University Press.

Ferber, Richard, MD. 1985. *Solve Your Child's Sleep Problems*. New York: Simon and Schuster.

Ferrer, Fernando, MD, and McKenna, Patrick H., MD. 2000. Current Approaches to the Undescended Testicle. *Contemporary Pediatrics*. January.

Flax, Judy F., PhD, and Rapin, Isabelle, MD. 1998. Evaluating Children with Delayed Speech and Language. *Contemporary Pediatrics*, October.

Fleisher, David R., MD. 1998. Coping with Colic. *Contemporary Pediatrics*, June.

Gill, Jaspreet K., MD, and Gieron-Korthals, Maria, MD. 2002. What Pediatricians—and Parents—Need to Know About Febrile Convulsions. *Contemporary Pediatrics*, May.

Herman, Bruce E., and Skokan, Elizabeth G. 1999. Bites That Poison: A Tale of Spiders, Snakes, and Scorpions. *Contemporary Pediatrics*, August.

Holmes, Lewis B., MD. 1999. Congenital Malformations. In *Oski's Pediatrics*, edited by Julia A. McMillan. Philadelphia: Lippincott Williams & Wilkins.

Hughes, Robert E. 2003. The Effects of Divorce on Children. In *Ohio State Web site* (online) [cited August, 2003]. Available from World Wide Web: <http://www.hec.ohio-state.edu/famlife/divorce/effects.htm#PARENTAL_ ADJUSTMENT>.

Hutton, Nancy, MD. 1999. Special Needs of Children with Chronic Illnesses. In *Oski's Pediatrics*, edited by Julia A. McMillan. Philadelphia: Lippincott Williams & Wilkins.

Jellinek, Michael S., and Slovik, Lois. 1981. Divorce: Impact on Children. *New England Journal of Medicine*, September.

Jerkins, Linda. 2002. Is an Au Pair Right for You? In *FamilyFun Web site* (online) [cited 2003]. Available from World Wide Web: <http://familyfun.go.com/raisingkids/child/skills/feature/atlp77aupair/>.

Kemper, Kathi J., MD, MPH. 1996. Seven Herbs Every Pediatrician Should Know. *Contemporary Pediatrics,* December.

Kids Health for Parents. 2003. In *KidsHealth Website* (online). Jacksonville, FL: The Nemours Foundation [cited April 28, 2003]. Available from World Wide Web: <http://kidshealth.org/parent/medical/bones/muscular_dystrophy.html>.

Kirkland, Rebecca T., MD. 1999. Failure to Thrive. In *Oski's Pediatrics,* edited by Julia A. McMillan. Philadelphia: Lippincott Williams & Wilkins.

Koumourou, Robyn. 2002. Thyroid Disease in Children. In *Mydr.com Web site* (online). Australia: MIMS Consumer Health Group [cited April 2003]. Available from World Wide Web: <http://www.mydr.com.au/default.asp?Article=3437>.

Liacouras, Chris A., MD, and Baldassano, Robert N., MD. 1998. Is It Toddler's Diarrhea? *Contemporary Pediatrics,* September.

Lifton, Betty Jean. 1998. *Lost & Found: The Adoption Experience.* New York: Harper and Row.

Medela Corporation. 2002. *Breast Feeding Information Guide.* McHenry, IL: The Medela Corporation.

Medline Plus. April, 2003. Muscular Dystrophy. In *Medline Plus Web site* (online). Washington: National Institutes of Health [cited April 2003]. Available from World Wide Web: <http://www.nlm.nih.gov/medlineplus/musculardystrophy.html#generaloverviews>.

Medline Plus. March, 2003. Congenital Heart Disease. In *Medline Plus Web site* (online). Washington: National Institutes of Health [cited April 2003]. Available from World Wide Web: <http://www.nlm.nih.gov/medlineplus/congenitalheartdisease.html>.

Morelli, Joseph G., MD, and Weston, William L., MD. 1999. Sun, Kids, Moles and Melanoma. *Contemporary Pediatrics.* June.

Muñiz, Antonio E., MD, and Joffe, Mark D., MD. 1997. Foreign Bodies: Ingested and Inhaled. *Contemporary Pediatrics,* December.

National Women's Health Information Center. 2003. Breastfeeding Know How. In *4Woman.Gov Web site* (online). Washington: U.S. Department of Health and Human Services [cited 2003]. Available from World Wide Web: <http://www.4woman.gov/Breastfeeding/print-bf.cfm?page=228>.

Noel, Brook, and Klein, Art. 1998. *The Single Parent Resource.* Beverly Hills: Champion Press.

Novotny, Pamela 1988. *The Joy of Twins*. New York: Crown Publishing.

NIH. 2003. Facts About Dietary Supplements. In *NIH Clinical Center Web site* (online). Bethesda, MD [cited April 2003]. Available from World Wide Web: <http://www.cc.nih.gov/ccc/supplements/iron.html#provide>.

Nurko, Samuel, MD, et al. 2001. Managing Constipation: Evidence Put to Practice. *Contemporary Pediatrics*, December.

Olsen, Richard D., MD, Barbaresi, William J., MD, and Olsen, Gayle P., RN, MS, CRNP. 1998. Development in the First Year of Life. *Contemporary Pediatrics*, July.

Pearlman, Eileen M., and Ganon, Jill Alison. 2000. *Raising Twins*. New York: HarperResource.

Perrin, Ellen C., MD. 2002. Children Whose Parents Are Lesbian or Gay. *Contemporary Pediatrics*, October.

Rau, John D., MD. 2003. Is It Autism? *Contemporary Pediatrics*, April.

Scott, David T., MD, and Tyson, Jon E., MD. Follow-up of Infants Discharged from Newborn Intensive Care. In *Oski's Pediatrics*, edited by Julia A. McMillan. Philadelphia: Lippincott Williams & Wilkins.

Schmitt, Barton D., MD. 1996. How to Treat and Prevent Sunburn. *Contemporary Pediatrics*. May.

Shelov, Steven P., MD. 1991. *Caring for Your Baby and Child: Birth to Age Five*. New York: Bantam Books.

Steuber, C. Philip, MD. General Considerations of Neoplastic Diseases. In *Oski's Pediatrics*, edited by Julia A. McMillan. Philadelphia: Lippincott Williams & Wilkins.

St. James-Roberts, I., et al. 2003. Individual Differences in Responsivity to a Neurobehavioral Examination Predict Crying Patterns of One-Week-Old Infants at Home. *Developmental Medicine and Child Neurology*, June.

Teitel, Maurice, et al. 1988. *Breast-feeding: The Art of Mothering*. Port Washington, NY: Alive Productions.

Tyler, Anne. 1994. *Breathing Lessons*. Berkeley: Berkeley Publishing Group.

University of Michigan Health System. 2003. Burns. In *University of Michigan Health System Web site* (online). Ann Arbor, MI [cited 2003]. Available from World Wide Web: <http://www.med.umich.edu/1libr/pa/pa_burn ther_hhg.htm>.

U.S. Consumer Product Safety Commission. 2003. Choosing a Safe Playpen — and Using It Safely. *Discovery Health*, April.

Wagner, Mary H., MD, and Sherman, James M., MD. 1997. Cystic Fibrosis and the General Pediatrician. *Contemporary Pediatrics*, February.

Wisner, Catherine, et al. 2002. Postpartum Depression. *New Englad Journal of Medicine*, 18 July: 194–9.

ACKNOWLEDGMENTS

I am deeply indebted to a number of people whose support and guidance have helped me make a career from a calling and a book from a career.

Much love and gratitude go to my parents, Helen Altman and the late Irving Altman. Thanks, Mom, for giving me the freedom to be anything I wanted to be—as long as there was an "M.D." after my name. Thanks and love also to my in-laws, Lennie and Elaine Miller and Linda and Joel Scheer, for years of support and affection. Thanks to my "extended family": Jennie, Rachel, and Zack Scheer; Randa, Jason, Jenna, and Joelle Kronberg; and the very talented Monica Abend. Many thanks to dear old friends, the Tarshises, Weisses, Freemans, and Diamonds, and to dear older friends, Bruce and Babs Klein. To my wonderful lawyer and dear friend Stuart Tarshis, thank you for years of kindness and sage advice.

Heartfelt thanks to the Kidfixer family: my incredible partners, gifted pediatricians all: Bill Mesibov, M.D., Linda Jacobs, M.D., and Marcia Rubinos, M.D.; and our amazing staff: Sherrill, Sondra, Nora, Patty, Donna, Nina, John, Carmen, Dianne, Chrissy, Johanna, Marirose, Arlene, Susan, Theresa, and Stacy. You make each day a party. My sincere thanks also to the king of high-risk pregnancies, Victor Klein, M.D., for all his wonderful healthy twins, trips, and other "multiple blessings."

To Robin Rolewicz, my incredibly talented Random House editor, thank you for your hard work, skill, and for the very great role you played in making this book exactly what I had envisioned. Many thanks also to a great artist, Zachary Judd Scheer, for his fine illustrations. Thank you, also, Jake Greenberg, for all your help.

To all my wonderful patients and their parents, thank you for continuing my education every day and for providing me with a profession that does not require that I grow up—ever.

Finally, thank you, Sherrill, for thirty years (and counting) of love and support. It seems that I was always on-call when emergencies arose, and you handled each one perfectly—without the benefit of a user's guide. Our terrific sons are a tribute to your abilities as a parent. My love for you is a testament to your success as a wife. And thank you, Sam and Josh, for your unquestioning affection and tolerance, which have led me to believe that, with a little luck and a lot of love, most people can raise terrific kids.

vomiting, 81, 193, 219, 220, 233–7,
239–41, 259, 270–75, 278, 288,
289, 309, 318, 320, 323, 329,
330, 336; formula intolerance
causing, 236; infection causing,
236; intestinal obstruction causing, 236; projectile, 233; reflux
causing, 235

water heater settings, 314
weaning, 61
webbed toes, 293
witching hour, 217, 218, 219,
221
working mothers, 342

Zantac, 220

Stuart Altman was born and raised in New York. After graduating magna cum laude from Franklin and Marshall College in Pennsylvania, he studied medicine at Downstate Medical Center in Brooklyn, where he also graduated with honors. He is a fellow of the American Academy of Pediatrics.

After serving as chief resident in pediatrics at Long Island Jewish Medical Center, he joined a private pediatric group, called Kidfixers, on the North Shore of Long Island, where he has practiced for the past twenty-five years. With a uniquely personal approach to pediatric medicine, Dr. Altman and his associates spend a great deal of time and effort educating parents and providing continuous support.

This is Dr. Altman's first book. He is currently at work on a sequel, which will cover ages 1 through 13, entitled *The Kidfixer Kid Book*.